Power Beyond Scrutiny

POWER BEYOND SCRUTINY

Media, Justice and Accountability

Justin Schlosberg

PlutoPress
www.plutobooks.com

First published 2013 by Pluto Press
345 Archway Road, London N6 5AA

www.plutobooks.com

Distributed in the United States of America exclusively by
Palgrave Macmillan, a division of St. Martin's Press LLC,
175 Fifth Avenue, New York, NY 10010

British Library Cataloguing in Publication Data
A catalogue record for this book is available from the British Library

ISBN 978 0 7453 3292 5 Hardback
ISBN 978 0 7453 3291 8 Paperback
ISBN 978 1 8496 4870 7 PDF eBook
ISBN 978 1 8496 4872 1 Kindle eBook
ISBN 978 1 8496 4871 4 EPUB eBook

Library of Congress Cataloging in Publication Data applied for

Typeset from disk by Stanford DTP Services, Northampton, England
Simultaneously printed digitally by CPI Antony Rowe, Chippenham, UK and
Edwards Bros in the United States of America

For Chloe

Contents

Figures and Tables

Acknowledgements

I am indebted to the advice and guidance of Professor James Curran who supervised the doctoral research underpinning this book. I am also extremely grateful to Des Freedman and Natalie Fenton at Goldsmiths who provided support and encouragement throughout, and I received invaluable comments and feedback from Richard Keeble, Aeron Davis and Julian Petley.

This book would not have been possible without the time and insights offered by the 50 interview respondents from the world of journalism and the case studies examined. Many of them did so on condition of anonymity. Many of them have struggled tirelessly for justice and some have risked their jobs and professional reputations in the process. This book is dedicated to them. Of those that can be named, special thanks go to Campaign Against the Arms Trade, Iain Overton, Kaye Stearman, Dr Margaret Bloom, Martyn Day, Dr Michael Powers QC, Miles Goslett, Norman Baker MP, Phillip Knightley and Symon Hill.

Finally, my parents, brothers and wife – to whom I owe everything and always will.

Preface

In his revisionist account of British imperial history, John Newsinger vividly showed how dominant narratives have served to legitimise colonial power. In particular, they succeeded in disassociating the British empire from the brutality and oppression on which it was founded (Newsinger 2006:551). By such means as covertly employing local forces to quash rebellion through mass torture and killing, the legacy of a 'kinder, gentler' empire was sustained and persists in contemporary history books.

But in today's media-saturated environment, it is clearly harder to make crimes of the powerful so invisible. Ours is a reality in which we know of systemic abuse of power by corporations, military and governments – to some extent – by virtue of a growing transparency culture. That culture owes much to advancements in communications technology but also something to 'the collapse of social deference toward elites in every walk of life' (McNair 2003).

The public inquiry – in all its varying forms – is perhaps one of the defining features of the contemporary media age. The subjection of powerful people to intense questioning on our TV screens has become an almost ritualistic affair. Virtually no individual or institution seems beyond its reach and we have become accustomed to seeing prime ministers, bankers, media moguls, heads of police and even spies publicly 'humbled' in the face of aggressive questioning and seemingly relentless scrutiny. At the same time, digital communications have dismantled information monopolies pouring light into the informal networks of power that have long been accustomed to operating in the shadows. Such is the promise of information societies that no institution – public or private – is wholly immune to the surveying eyes of digitally-enabled publics.

In conducting research for this book, I wanted to find out what all this means for the capacity of traditional media – still the dominant news providers – to hold authority to account; what it means for the endurance of capitalist societies through foundation-rattling crises; and above all, what it means for democracy in the twenty-first century. Though scandal is by no means a new phenomenon in capitalist democracies, the present rate of public inquiries would suggest that it reaches beyond the mere salacious, or a narrow consensus of acceptable controversy. It is, on the surface at least, reflective of a growing resistance of concentrated power through the news media.

But in the midst of unprecedented exposure of institutional corruption, there is a nagging sense in which the promise of accountability remains unfulfilled. Inquiries come and go, often ending in farce or delayed far beyond the ever shortening attention span of the rolling news media; rank and file personnel are fired or prosecuted whilst their bosses are absolved of responsibility; scandals become submerged by other scandals; and with each new government comes the promise of a new era of openness and sincerity, only to descend into apparent sleaze and spin anew.

Contemporary democratic discourse places emphasis on accountability as the basis of power legitimacy and the scholarly literature across disciplines has reserved a special space for the media in that process, for better or for worse. But exactly who is held to account, when, how and by whom, remain troubling questions in the study of media, politics and power. Amidst displays of adversarial journalism without fear or favour, how far are powerful interests still able to control the agenda and manipulate outcomes? To what extent do notions like the 'great British democracy' and the 'end of secrecy' play a functional role in the legitimation of power in a similar way to which constructions like a 'force for good' have long justified imperial advance and conquest?

This book also interrogates the notion of media spectacle in a different way to that in which it has been commonly applied in critical media theory. In particular, its intimate association with sensationalism and tabloidisation threatens to obscure the role of spectacle in what are considered the mainstays of 'serious' or responsible news. The *Sun* might still be the most popular newspaper in Britain, and online news the fastest growing platform, but it is the serious news outlets of traditional media – public service broadcasting, broadsheets, weeklies etc. – which remain by far the most *credible* sources of news and information. And it is credibility which holds the key to ideological power.

The book marks the culmination of three years of research involving extensive analysis of archived television news programmes, as well as more than 50 interviews with a cross section of news producers and actors including journalists, news executives, politicians, campaigners, press officers, lawyers and civil servants. The core subject is terrestrial television news in the UK – a public service regulated platform with a longstanding reputation for high quality journalism.

My overall concern is not so much with scandal involving official misconduct or misdemeanour, but rather controversies that point to systemic institutional corruption of the kind that transcends individuals and party politics. These controversies are no longer rare exceptions in the contemporary newscape and their existence raises profound questions about the scope of accountability through the media. There has, however, been surprisingly little critical assessment of such coverage. This provided the overarching motivation for the research which led to this book; a core premise being that only by examining those instances where mechanisms of accountability appear most far reaching, can we gain a new understanding of ideological power in the age of transparency.

1
Introduction

ACCOUNTABILITY AND LEGITIMATION OF POWER

Starting from the notion that authority is legitimised power, Max Weber articulated three bases of legitimation: the personality of leaders, traditional deference and rational-legal bureaucracy (Weber 1993). Although legitimation historically consisted in some combination of these, it is rational-legal authority which is the primary source of legitimation in modern western states. Popular allegiance is not to individuals who hold power, but to the procedural framework and rules which both structure and contain it.

When we consider what makes power and authority legitimate today, it is usually reducible to various formal or informal accountability institutions including government, regulatory authorities, legislative assemblies, civil society groups, the media, and so on. In short, accountability is the means by which power is restrained and publicly monitored. It ensures that abuses of power are checked and its scope limited to the pursuit of collective goals based on some measure of public consent or democratic mandate. So pervasive is the term in contemporary democratic discourse that, in the words of Ben Pimlott: 'We live in a culture of accountability, in which everybody is accountable to someone else, and those who declare themselves not to be accountable are condemned out of their own mouths' (Pimlott 2004:103).

But if accountability is the contemporary buzz-word for democratic legitimacy, it is also an ambiguous and fuzzy term lacking in clear semantic boundaries. Schedler (1999) helps clarify the picture somewhat by presenting the concept as exhibiting two faces: answerability and enforcement. The former requires the exercisers of authority to provide adequate information and justification for their actions on demand by citizens or those agencies mandated with oversight authority. Such agencies may include state bodies, civil society groups or the media. Their demands for information and justification are what *calls* authority to account:

[Answerability] continues the Enlightenment's project of subjecting power not only to the rule of law but also the rule of reason. Power should be bound by legal constraints but also by the logic of public reasoning. Accountability is antithetical to monologic power. It establishes a dialogic relationship between accountable and accounting actors. (Schedler 1999:15)

Central to this relationship is the force of transparency which also underpins contemporary democratic discourse. But transparency alone does not capture the full legitimising force of accountability which requires public oversight to be in some sense *consequential* in controlling power and deterring abuses. For that Schedler invokes the notion of enforcement, which empowers citizens via representative agencies to apply sanctions when power is abused or not exercised in accordance with democratic mandates. Such sanctions may be administered as a result of prosecution in the case of criminal action or negligence, but can also take the form of embarrassment through public disclosure of unethical behaviour or electoral defeat if policies fail to live up to citizens' expectations. The important point is that whilst answerability demands that the actions of the powerful are properly *justified*, enforcement ensures that the powerful have sufficient incentive to act in a *justifiable* way. Clearly, elections are a key mechanism of accountability that under ideal conditions can satisfy both the criteria outlined above. Challenging candidates, along with the media, induce incumbents to explain decisions taken in office (answerability), under the threat of being voted out if they fail to convince the electorate (enforcement). But whilst it is fairly clear how answerability and enforcement is formally applied to elected public officials, the picture becomes decidedly messier when we consider how private power is held to account, or those elements of state power that may be beyond the oversight reach of elected officials.

Since not all actions of the powerful are publicly visible, liberal democracies depend on a chain of accountability mechanisms with deferred responsibility, ultimately linking back to the will of the electorate. In the UK for instance, private corporations are accountable to regulating authorities; regulating authorities, police, security services and various public bodies are accountable to the government; the government is accountable to Parliament; Members of Parliament are said to be accountable to their local constituents via elections; and all authority publicly accountable via civil society and a free and independent media.

But in this layered model of deferred accountability, responsible institutions become vulnerable to capture by the groups and interests they regulate. This calls our attention to the purported role of journalism as a last line of public interest defence. Through investigative reporting in particular, journalists can institute a form of answerability and enforcement across the board, calling not only public officials to account, but also corporations, the security services, religious institutions, NGOs and even the media themselves. Answerability consists in the information that journalists source from centres of power, either by authorised or unauthorised means, and the justifications elicited through the 'right of reply'. Enforcement may consist in the public embarrassment that investigative exposure can bring, and/or in the triggering of more formal mechanisms of enforcement via prosecutions, regulatory sanctions etc.

Of course, individual journalists and media outlets are themselves vulnerable to influence 'capture' by their sources, employers or owners. But in theory at least, a sufficiently plural and diverse media system should be able to hold itself to account. Competition between media players ensures that each is effectively monitored by the others and that the sector as a whole is resistant to broad or endemic corruption.

CONTEST AS A FOUNDATION OF ACCOUNTABILITY

Indeed, it is this element of contest which proves essential to effective accountability and the legitimation of power in capitalist democracies. But legitimate contest necessitates some degree of a level playing field. The problem was alluded to by Robert Dahl who asked, in the preface to his seminal inquiry into the political system of New Haven, 'how does a "democratic" system work amid inequality of resources?' (Dahl 1961:3). At root here is a recognition that power is not limited to the domain of transparent political institutions replete with formalised checks and balances, but is to some degree constitutive of social relations (Mouffe 1999). Consequently, political *influence* is not limited to that exercised via the ballot box. At the heart of Dahl's question is a concern that unequal distribution of resources (an inevitable outcome of the capitalist mode of production) can lead to unequal distribution of power; unequal distribution of power can lead to *concentration* of power; and concentrated power can undermine democracy by creating conditions of oligarchy (rule by a few).

Liberal revisionists in the first half of the twentieth century (Lippmann 1925; Schumpeter 1987 [1942]) contended that some degree of oligarchy was both necessary and desirable: elite power and a largely apathetic citizenry were seen as functional necessities of stable and cohesive industrial societies. More recently, liberal media theorists such as Michael Schudson have argued that the public should not be apathetic but rather *inactive*. In other words, it should be left to the media to go on alert and only then should citizens spring into action (Schudson 1995).

But the notion of a largely apathetic citizenry has never sat comfortably with liberal pluralists. They have long sought to reconcile unequal distribution of power with what Dahl called America's 'universal creed of democracy and equality' (Dahl 1961:3). Fortunately, in spite of his initial concerns, Dahl went on to find that the system is to some extent self-correcting; that inequalities are in fact 'non-cumulative' and hence 'dispersed'. If one person is better off in one resource, such as wealth or knowledge, it does not necessarily mean they are better off in other or *all* resources. This notion of 'dispersed' power or influence is synonymous with a degree of openness and contestability in the political system. For some early pluralists, notably Truman (1951), it was not just that the system was open to contest; it also provided somewhat of a level playing field through the 'multiple memberships in potential groups based on widely held and accepted interests that serve as a balance wheel in a going political system like that of the United States' (Truman 1951:514). Others placed emphasis on the increasing disconnect between those who *own* the means of production in late capitalist societies, and those who *control* them (Parsons 1986 [1960]).

This is not to say that Dahl, or liberal pluralists generally, celebrate the status quo of power distribution in advanced capitalist democracies. Later accounts in particular painted a much more uneven picture and acknowledged the dominance of certain groups, albeit still within an overall system characterised by polyarchy. According to Lindblom (1977) for instance, this boiled down to just two rival sources of control over political authority: elections and big business. More recently, some pluralist accounts have taken a turn towards more normative rather than descriptive arguments. Mouffe (1999) for instance, argues for a conception of democratic politics that admits a place for the role of passion rather than just rational deliberation. It is a position that helps to explain why certain acts – such as throwing a shoe at the President – can be imbued with such politically powerful symbolism. For Jeffrey Alexander (2006), conflict in pluralistic societies is tempered by the glue of social solidarity. It is a force which can and *must* bind society's increasingly fragmented and disparate groups within a 'civil sphere'.

On closer analysis, it is not just the more recent accounts which invoked normative aspirations. Critical pluralism has long conceived of power in capitalist democracies as legitimate because it is *contested* within a relatively *open* (if not entirely balanced) political system. In heterogeneous societies, interest conflict is perceived as not only a necessary but also a desirable outcome; the lifeblood of democracy. It is desirable because it is the hallmark of a free society and consistent with a 'marketplace of ideas'. This competitive interaction and resultant compromise, according to classical liberalism, provides the most efficient and effective means of maximising the common good. The ultimate outcome is an *aggregation* of diverse interests in a pluralised society.

The important point for the purposes here is that dispersed power supports accountability via the invisible hand of polyarchy. It ensures, for instance, that although elections are not the exclusive channel of political influence, they are nevertheless a significant one which helps to detach political power from economic power. In this sense, polyarchy does not institute accountability in and of itself, but it creates conditions in which accountability mechanisms can function *legitimately*.

But the work of early liberal pluralists provoked a much stronger normative response from deliberative democracy theorists which posited that power can and should be detached from social relations (Rawls 1972; Habermas 1989 [1962]). These accounts focused on consensus rather than compromise – the kind that is said to emerge from ideal conditions of public speech and debate. It was no longer enough for legitimacy to consist in a mere aggregation of interests. The power structure of society must reflect what is both morally and rationally the most justifiable outcome. The key to legitimacy here lies in the force of deliberation manifest through a public sphere devoid of barriers to participation. This produces a genuinely *public* opinion which in turn regulates and holds authoritative power to account.

But my primary interest is in how power *is* legitimised, rather than in how it could or should be. To that end, the liberal pluralist notion of polyarchy provides a useful tool with which to conceptualise how accountability mechanisms are assumed to work. My central argument is that the contemporary discourse of accountability rests implicitly on a notion of contest and dispersed power, such that its mechanisms are *ultimately* beyond capture by powerful interests. This is at least partly because the higher the degree of contest and dispersal, the greater is the relative power of accountability institutions *vis-à-vis* the entities which they hold to account. This does not mean that all accountability institutions must be permanently and completely corruption free. Rather, the legitimation force of accountability requires that its institutions must not be endemically and *irrevocably* corrupted. To this end, we need a second order of accountability such that institutions which apply it are themselves subject to some kind of public oversight.

As already suggested, it is journalists who carry this final burden in liberal democracies, exposing the failures and limitations of accountability, and triggering appropriate reform and redress. But before examining how journalism has been conceived as an accountability force, it is worth noting a problem with liberal pluralist accounts which foreshadowed contemporary media power debates. Critics pointed out that liberal pluralists tended to describe a particular variant of power; and one which did not seem to capture a reality of growing corporate concentration and US military expansion after the Second World War. This meant that elite decision-making and the exercise of 'real' power was increasingly a closed door exercise and distinguishable from the lower level day-to-day politics of state government (Mills 1959). According to Steven Lukes (Lukes 2005 [1974]), what Dahl and his colleagues had described was a one-dimensional view of power based on instrumental action and observable conflict between its holders and subjects. They had overlooked more nuanced forms of power based on non-decision making and covert conflict (Bachrach and Baratz 1970), as well as inaction/latent conflict – what Lukes called the 'third dimension' of power.

The latter is not, according to Lukes, beyond empirical scrutiny and examples can be found in studies which demonstrate the agenda setting power of elites. In a comparative case examining the issue of air pollution in US cities, Crenson (1971) demonstrated that particular corporate interests could be a key factor in keeping the issue off the public agenda – not so much through active lobbying as through their mere presence. The public reputation of US Steel in Gary, Indiana for instance, meant that the corporation 'influenced the content of the pollution ordinance without taking any action on it, and thus defied the pluralist dictum that political powers belongs to political actors' (Crenson 1971:69–70).

But in focusing on covert or latent conflict, Crenson's analysis does not tell us anything about controversies which *do* hinge on overt conflict. What's more, such conflicts are not – in the contemporary landscape at least – in any sense limited to a 'middle layer' of politics as Mills suggested. Perhaps the most vivid example in recent times is the controversy that continues to surround the decision (and alleged conspiracy) by US and UK governments to invade Iraq in 2003. But we do not have to look hard for other examples of media-led controversies that strike at the heart of government-corporate-military power. They include all three cases covered in this book.

The attributed origins of such contestability in the media have been widespread. These include resistance to dominant cultural messages by a growing populist culture, as well as sub cultures (Hebdige 1979; Fiske 1989); increased sociocultural heterogeneity and emergent issue conflicts (Blumler and Gurevitch 1995); a widening of educational opportunities (McQuail 1986); interest group proliferation (Berry 1984; Meyer and Tarrow 1998); market-generated populism (Willis 1990); and proliferation and divergence of media outlets (Norris 2000).

But media contestability as a line of thinking found its voice most explicitly in studies of journalist-source relations during the 1980s and 1990s. Broadly, three interrelated origins of contestability have been identified: journalistic agency, alternative source strategies and elite source conflict. It is worth stressing however that liberal pluralism is not a clearly delineated field within media studies and many of the authors and works referenced in the following discussion would not sit comfortably under such a label. The focus is rather on the ideas and thinking behind notions of contestability and openness in media systems, which are traceable in some way to the literature outlined above.

JOURNALIST AUTONOMY

Pluralist positions are united in their conception of a much greater degree of journalist autonomy than critical theory allows (Tunstall 1971; Gitlin 1980; Ericson, Baranek et al. 1989; Hallin 1994; Schudson 1995; Althaus 2003; McNair 2006). They tend to stress the symbiotic, co-operative and mutually dependent nature of that relationship (Tunstall 1971; Blumler and Gurevitch 1995). Autonomy is thus imbedded in the structural position that journalists occupy with respect to elite sources, enabling them to offer much needed publicity in exchange for the information and content that elite sources provide (Schlesinger and Tumber 1994; Blumler and Gurevitch 1995). But autonomy also owes something to the growing *visibility* of elites as a result of the development of mass communication technologies (Thompson 1990; Schlesinger and Tumber 1994). According to this view, transparency is tantamount to scrutiny: the more we see of the powerful, the more vulnerable they are to our judgements and the less opportunity they have to abuse their power.

It is often asserted that autonomy is upheld by professional values that endow 'watchdog' journalism with the highest credibility and celebrate the reporter's fearlessness in the face of power (Ericson et al. 1989; Schudson 1995). The most celebrated modern historical example is the Watergate scandal of 1972 that eventually forced Richard Nixon out of the US presidency. But it was not the initial sin of burglary and political espionage which brought Nixon down. Rather, it was the act of 'cover up' – that is, subversion of accountability institutions through suppression of evidence and a disinformation campaign targeting legal authorities and journalists alike. According to orthodox views, it was a fearless press which eventually exposed this cover up by gaining access to crucial insider accounts. So pervasive was the culture of press antagonism towards elites in the aftermath of Watergate, it has been accused of fostering widespread public cynicism and apathy (Graber, McQuail et al. 1998).

If professional values have any positive influence on journalist autonomy, then Public Sector Broadcasting (PSB) can provide a particularly powerful counter weight to dominance, not least because such values find their clearest and most explicit expression in PSB discourse. The point is not lost on radical thinkers who, for instance, have cited the role of the UK's publicly owned Channel 4 in widening opportunities for the expression of minority and marginalised views (Hall 1986) and emphasised the *potential* for PSB to offer a 'third way' between Marxist and market liberal prescriptions (Garnham 1986; Curran 1991).

In its more modest formulations, watchdog antagonism ensures that the interests of journalists and their sources remain distinct and at times conflicting (Blumler and Gurevitch 1995). The symbiotic nature of journalist-elite source relations is not therefore always harmonious according to pluralist accounts. Rather, they are best viewed as a site of perpetual co-operation and competitive struggle with the barometer of relative advantage swinging according to different contexts, periods and societies (Ericson et al. 1989). It is this fluidity and dynamism which characterises much of liberal pluralist accounts of the media and contrasts sharply with the more static and structuralist models associated with radical functionalism:

> The credibility of given political actors may vary over time, as indeed may the scope for oppositional and alternative views to force their way onto the political agenda. The scope of the public sphere is not fixed for all time, and its relative openness or closure is an outcome of political struggle. Consensual times may give way to those of extreme crisis, and vice versa. (Schlesinger and Tumber 1994:23)

The key point about dynamic models of news output is that the professional culture of journalists prescribes different modes of practice according to different political contexts. Thus, when liberal democratic norms are transgressed by political actors, journalists are more likely to adopt attacking rather than balancing positions (Gans 2004).

Beyond this, more static models posit that the structural position journalists occupy in relation to elites tip the balance of power permanently and completely in their favour. At its logical extreme, political elites are portrayed as effectively captured by journalists, whose logic of stage management and narrative selection dictate the nature of news output (Meyer and Hinchman 2002). According to this thesis,

> The leitmotif of effective spin-control is that you can only control the media by submitting to them. To these elites, submission appears to be the key to securing the primary resource of their political lives: the legitimation of power by consent. (Meyer and Hinchman 2002:52)

Civil Society institutions and parliamentary democracy are progressively undermined by the 'systems world' of the media in its perpetual drive to maximise audiences at whatever cost to the public interest. Whilst such arguments suffer from an implicit appeal to a golden age of liberal democracy or the public sphere, there is a related and more convincing current in the literature that posits journalism as an integral and indistinguishable element of the political system (Blumler and Gurevitch 1995, Schlesinger and Tumber 1994).

Perhaps the strongest indicator of journalist autonomy is the power to select stories and speakers, even if from a limited horizon of elite sources (Gans 1979; Ericson, Baranek et al. 1989; 1991). This ensures that journalist accounts 'are hardly limited to hand-outs from the powerful' (Gans 1979:182) and that official definitions can be routinely contested by journalists themselves, if not by competing sources. One key aspect of the power of selection identified by Deacon and Golding (1994) is the propensity of journalists to distinguish between 'advocates' and 'arbiters' amongst sources. The former are perceived as tailoring and manipulating their messages in order to gain maximum currency in news coverage and are thus treated with a greater degree of suspicion and attack by journalists. Arbiters, by contrast, are seen as more 'neutral' voices and afforded relative deference accordingly.

But journalistic agency extends beyond mere selection of sources, stories and frames. It enables instances whereby journalists themselves 'take the initiative in the definitional process' (Schlesinger and Tumber 1994:19) by, for instance, investigative exclusives or an active and direct challenging of elite sources. This kind of autonomy is often accentuated by particular circumstances. Thus for Gitlin (1980), changes in coverage of the Vietnam War stemmed from a widening gap between official claims and facts on the ground as observed by journalists. At the same time, coverage was influenced by journalists' own personal connections to the war – whether as concerned parents of sons who might be drafted, or as younger journalists aligned with the counter-culture movement. Autonomy is not therefore an exclusively structural condition but contingent on a host of external influences, not least the degree of what has been termed 'cultural congruence' between a particular controversy and 'the dominant schemas' of common culture (Entman 2004).

The important corollary between these various arguments is that journalists are not, as many radical accounts would have it, the unwitting servants of their elite source masters. Consequently, elite influence over the news is always 'equivocal, transitory and unresolved' (Ericson, Baranek et al. 1989:2). Even if elite sources do attain relative power over journalists and alternative sources, this advantage is not a structural given but has to be 'won' and moreover, 'sustained interpretatively and evaluatively through a series of battles' (Deacon and Golding 1994:202).

INTER-ELITE CONFLICT

Broad and frequent conflict between elites is another crucial factor in contestability and in leveraging journalist autonomy (Deacon and Golding 1994, Gitlin 1980, Schudson 1995). Consequently there is, according to Schudson, 'a vital arena of acceptable controversy' in which disconnects between dominant political and economic groups inhibit the ability of any one group to set or control the media agenda (1995:43). Indeed the very distinction between official and non-official sources, along with its associated delineation between elite and alternative opinion, has been called into question. As Schlesinger and Tumber point out, many organisations carry quasi-official status and even some pressure groups are state-funded and only relatively autonomous. What's more the boundaries shift over time:

> Writing in the 1970s, it may have been obvious to talk of the CBI [Confederation of British Industry] and TUC [Trades Union Congress] as major institutional voices. But with the disappearance of corporatism in Britain under successive Conservative governments, such interests have lost their one-time prominence. (Schlesinger and Tumber 1994:19)

The key point from a pluralist perspective is that elite sources do not speak with one voice and are not clearly distinguishable from non-elite sources, resulting in the variety of contesting views that appear regularly in the news (Hartley 1982). What seems certain is that many of the most infamous investigative scoops from Watergate to the 'sexed up' Iraq War dossier owed much, if not all, to sources of elite dissent. It also seems reasonable to assume that journalistic agency can to some extent foster and encourage elite conflict which resonates with core news values both on the level of democratic idealism and dramatic narrative construction (Schudson 1995; Davis 2003). The important question for the purposes here is what happens when elites *do* close ranks in a controversy and how far are they able to control the nature, extent and consequences of coverage?

ALTERNATIVE SOURCE STRATEGIES

The source relations literature during the 1990s went beyond elite conflict and uncovered evidence of a widening playing field of source competition involving pressure groups, NGOs and trade unions (Ericson, Baranek et al. 1989; Deacon and Golding 1994). Source competition derives from the fact that the level of media resources available to a given institution is not static but varies over time (Miller 1994; Rucht 2004), rendering source strategies significant. Crucially, source competition has both fuelled and been fuelled by the rapid expansion of the public relations industry in recent decades (Blumler and Gurevitch 1995; Davis 2002). This has engendered what Schlesinger and Tumber call 'an inescapable promotional dynamic that lies at the heart of contemporary political culture' (1994:271). Much like the force of journalist autonomy, public relations competition ensures that elite influence over news is far from effortless or guaranteed.

More crucially, elite influence – as well as the capacity of alternative sources to interrupt the flow of official stories – is contingent on a variety of factors that are not limited to relative resource capacity. These include the permeability of organisations to information leaks and their ability to control the timing of information release to maximum effect (Ericson et al. 1989), their ability to develop sympathetic journalist contacts (Schlesinger and Tumber 1994) and encourage identification as offering independent rather than partisan opinions (Deacon and Golding 1994). Underpinning these strategies must be an awareness of a competitor's moves whether to gain support through coalition-building or mount effective opposition by for instance, 'astute timing or discrediting its credibility' (Schesinger and Tumber 1994:39).

Consequently, whilst competition may be on unequal terms given the relative resource advantage of state and corporate institutions, alternative sources can employ a variety of successful strategies to get their voices heard. Evidence of such successes has been well documented in arenas such as law and order (Ericson et al. 1989, Schlesinger and Tumber 1994) and taxation (Deacon and Golding 1994), among others. The cumulative effect of these processes is that the extent, duration and audibility of non-official voices in any news controversy are much less predictable than radical models suggest.

What we are left with is a picture of contestability that both extends and blurs the borders of inter-elite conflict so as to include a melting pot of different groups, all engaged in a perpetual struggle for media attention. Whilst it should be emphasised that none of these accounts envisage source competition on equal terms, the fact that some groups in society are vastly more powerful than others does not detract from the *opportunities* for influence often afforded to the less resourced. It is this relative openness that legitimises power and ensures that the flow of information and ideas is beyond absolute elite control.

THE MEDIA AS INSTRUMENTS OF ACCOUNTABILITY

All this served to reinvigorate the literature on media accountability which has been explicit in delineating two levels: accountability 'through' and 'of' the media. The significance of the former, as mentioned earlier, is that journalists are seen as endowed with the potential and responsibility to institute accountability across the board of power (rather than just public officials). But there are two further characteristics of the media which endow them with a special role among accountability institutions. First, the media are in a unique position to apply multiple orders of accountability, applying it to concentrated centres of power as well as the more formal monitoring and regulatory institutions which oversee them. Second, they have a much wider array of information tools available compared to other accountability institutions. Off-the-record briefings by officials, Freedom of Information requests, hacking and leaks are all part of the armoury by which journalists can institute answerability and enforcement. Third, the media can give voice to less-resourced sources and consequently play an 'equilibrating' role in the field of interest conflict. This can enhance dispersed and redistributive power, reducing vulnerability to capture in the first instance. Consequently, journalism can play both an ex-ante as well as an ex-post role in regulating accountability institutions.

Finally, as already mentioned, the media are unique in their capacity to be self-correcting, delivering accountability 'of' themselves. In theory at least, this stems from the capacity of journalists in a pluralised mediascape to perform an oversight role on each other. The widespread phone hacking by journalists at the former *News of the World*, which hit headlines across the news media in 2011, was exposed not by the Press Complaints Commission or the police, but by rival journalists at the *Guardian*. In this light, it seems reasonable to assume that media pluralism and polyarchy within the political system are to some extent mutually enhancing. Dispersal and contest in society at large will likely engender pluralist contest within and between sections of the media, and vice versa.

In this way, contestability ensures that instances of corruption are just that: instances. Corruption is not *synonymous* with establishment interests as it is in autocratic regimes. Within liberal democracies, allowing for a given passage of time, the balancing forces of power will ultimately root out its abuses because governments come and go, corporations are monitored by NGOs, not all journalists are the mouthpieces of their sources, and so on.

The extent to which these balancing forces pertain in reality remained, however, an unresolved question at the turn of the millennium. Furthermore, just as the liberal pluralist take on power legitimacy began to establish itself firmly within media sociology, it had to contend with an enveloping *crisis* of legitimacy in western political systems. With the growth of the public relations industry, contest had become increasingly between competing propaganda rather than genuine ideas (Davis 2002, Miller 1994). This is said to have engendered widespread popular cynicism manifest in declining voter turn-outs and a growth in extra-parliamentary politics (Blumler and Gurevitch 1995).

NEW PLURALISMS AND ARENAS OF CONTEST

Partly as a response to these developments, pluralism post-2000 has evolved beyond interest group conflict and models which emphasise the ultimate aggregation of interests as the basis of power legitimation. For Chantal Mouffe (1999), a reconstituted pluralism must be based on the ineradicable dimension of contest, whilst ensuring that 'us and them' becomes an opposition between adversaries rather than enemies, with each conceding the other's right to defend their position.

Such attempts to bridge a gap between aggregative and rationalist or moral conceptions of democratic legitimacy did not mean that liberal pluralism was on the back foot. Indeed, many of the currents associated with the age of crisis have been linked to the destabilisation of political communication (Dahlgren 2005). Moreover, for every crack in the system that appeared to be sealing, pluralists have found a new one in the emergent globalised and digital mediascape. In an age of decentralised, de-territorialised, multi-way and micro media platforms, the control paradigm in radical critiques began to seem ever more quaint (McNair 2006). For some optimists, it no longer makes much sense to even talk of mass-media power, or indeed mass audiences. Rather, new technologies enable media users who, through peer to peer networks of communication and collaborative knowledge tools, are usurping power away from media professionals, owners and elites in general (Negroponte 1995; Poster 2001). This shift in the distribution of media power is said to be manifest in global 'publics' and a global politics based on diverse and horizontal networks, transnational social movements, permanent campaigns and various forms of digital activism (van de Donk, Loader et al. 2004).

Though the unbridled optimism expressed in regards to new media empowerment reached its zenith in the late 1990s, more tempered accounts (following the market crash of internet stocks in 2000) continued to endow digital technologies with a deterministic empowerment potential. Of most significance for the purposes here is the ways in which new technologies of news production and distribution have been said to advance journalist autonomy, with particular reference to liberating time and space constraints. In terms of time, new technologies mean journalists can access and communicate data with increasing speed (Livingston and Bennett 2003), often pre-empting intervention from official sources. This renders access to the 'field' as well as non-elite sources more efficient and cost-effective. In terms of space, the web greatly enhances the plurality of news providers, and the quantity of content that can be published. Though this is not necessarily correlated with an increase in 'quality' or diversity in any sense, it has undoubtedly given voice to amateur journalists and 'writer gatherers' unshackled by the editorial constraints on their professional counterparts (Couldry 2010).

The development of so-called 'web 2.0' technologies post-2000 seemed to deliver on the promise of early digital idealists, with special significance for news production, distribution and consumption. In particular, the inexorable rise of social media sites like Facebook and Twitter has not only opened up new spaces of information diversity online, but also proved to have a growing influence over the mainstream news agenda. The engagement of professional journalists with social media has underlined their significance to 'old media' as a newsgathering tool (Chadwick 2011). But they are equally implicated in contributing to, or constructing anew the public sphere. Nic Newman assessed the impact of social media on the UK 2010 general election and found that, for young voters in particular, social networking sites played a very important role in facilitating discussion, with one quarter of 18- to 24-year-olds posting election-related comments on Twitter and Facebook (Newman 2010). He also found that newspapers and broadcasters were turning to social media as valuable sources of news. In the midst of widespread uprisings across North Africa and the Arabian peninsula during 2011 (the so-called 'Arab Spring'), reference to the politically disruptive potential of social media reached new heights. Commentators spoke of a 'leaderless digital watchdog, an unwavering force that ensured the international eye would not stray far' (McCarthy 2011).

Alongside social media, new sources of pluralism have been observed in the development of global news networks. In particular, the longstanding Anglo-American hegemony established through CNN and BBC World has been challenged by the rise of Qatar-based network Al Jazeera (El-Nawawy and Farag 2002). The channel has been particularly cited as the source of alternative frames for the US-led War on Terror following the Al Qaeda attacks in New York and Washington in 2011; and the responses of US political elites seemed to underline its disruptive potential (Fordham 2011). But Al Jazeera has also been cited as playing a key role in both mobilising, and drawing attention to the Arab Spring movements of 2011. Significantly, these events procured unprecedented collaboration and cross-influence between mainstream and social media platforms (Pintak 2011).

One key effect of all this is that abuses of power are both detected and circulated at a rate and on a scale unseen in the analogue era. The capture and exposure of the Abu Ghraib prisoner abuse scandal in 2004, for instance, was a function of 'digital cameras and the rapid global dissemination of the photographs made possible by new media technologies' (McNair 2006:158). But it was one particular news story dominating global news headlines in November 2010 which was to prove pivotal in sparking a renewed digital utopianism. This was the unprecedented leak of confidential US diplomatic cables facilitated by the enigmatic and controversial website *Wikileaks*. The resultant 'end of secrecy' polemic found its voice in reference to a new 'information war' between state-corporate power on the one hand, and hackers and cyber democracy activists on the other (Brooke 2011). Whilst acknowledging new opportunities for information control by incumbent elites, Brooke's account is nevertheless an extreme invocation of digital contest:

> We are at an extraordinary moment in human history: never before has the possibility of true democracy been so close to realisation. As the cost of publishing and duplication has dropped to near zero, a truly free press, and a truly informed public, becomes a reality. A new information Enlightenment is dawning where knowledge flows freely, beyond national boundaries. Technology is breaking down traditional social barriers of status,

class, power, wealth and geography, replacing them with an ethos of collaboration and transparency. In this new Enlightenment it isn't just scientific truths that are the goal, but discovering truths about the way we live, about politics and power. (Brook 2011:58)

THE NEW MEDIA HANGOVER

Such exuberance flows from a discursive focus on the opportunities of resistance afforded by digital technologies. Despite vehement opposition from those who take new opportunities for surveillance and control as their starting point (Morozov 2011), both sides of the polemic employ a narrative emphasis on conflict, change and opportunity.

What the utopian/dystopian discourse overlooks are patterns of continuation and reinforcement of power relations in the new information environment. Hindman (2009), for instance, demonstrates that in spite of the 'blogosphere' explosion, blogs about politics attract only a tiny fraction of web traffic, the majority of which is concentrated on those run by mainstream elite professionals. In spite of the 'long tail' thesis which predicts the flourishing of niche and alternative products and information sources on the web, online news audiences are increasingly concentrated around the top 20 outlets. These in turn have emerged as the domain not of 'pureplay' original news websites, but of major corporate news organisations and dominant online aggregators. A major study by Pew Research in 2011 found that of the top 25 most visited news websites in the US, 17 were those of so-called 'legacy' media organisations (Pew Research Center 2012).

New media mythologising also mistakes the spread of digital communications networks with the *displacement* of conventional media platforms. As far as news goes, broadcasting remains overwhelmingly the most consumed and credible platform (Ofcom 2011; 2012). Despite online growth, television viewing in the UK increased in 2010 and the audience for television news remained unchanged. And contrary to the digital democracy promise, the uses of online news have been found to be increasingly entertainment rather than information oriented (Boczkowski and de Santos 2007).

Even if online news does become the dominant news medium there is no guarantee that this will enhance the contestability of elite power which is said to be evolving in various forms including expansion of copyrights (Lessig 2004); concentration of ownership among and between internet service and content providers (Mansell and Jarvery 2004); commodification and packaging of information products (Mosco 2004); and their distribution according to a 'Daily Me' diet of personally targeted news (Sunstein 2001). What's more, processes of control are going unchecked due to the difficulties in regulating a globalised network as well as a neoliberal policy paradigm that, despite political rhetoric, conceives of internet users as exclusively consumers rather than citizens (Dahlgren 2005).

With regard to specific technologies of news production and delivery, these have unleashed new pressures in respect of journalist autonomy at least as much as they have relinquished old ones. Indeed, rather than enhancing access to the field, the cost efficiencies yielded by new technologies are said to increasingly confine journalists to the newsroom, spurring a growth in recycled reports and '2nd hand' stories in which news outlets themselves become sources for other providers (Davies 2008). At the same time, new technologies have fostered a 'culture of immediacy' in newsrooms and an increasing-focus on 'event-driven' news that, if anything, has elevated the structural advantage of official sources (Livingston and Bennett 2003; Lewis, Cushion et al. 2005). Growing competitive pressures, fostered in part by the explosion of online outlets, has also heralded a crisis in professional journalism as reporters face increasing insecurities, pay cuts and budget constraints, all of which play to elite advantage (Barnett and Gaber 2001). These processes have fed into a triumph of soft over hard news, homogenisation over diversity, and popular over quality outlets (Schudson 1995; Franklin 1997; Bagdikian 2004; Born 2005; Davies 2008). This in turn is said to have narrowed contestability by ring fencing the space for genuine dissent within the ever shrinking 'quality' news sector (Gans 2004).

The structural advantage of official sources has been further enhanced by the growth of state secrecy under the banner of the War on Terror (Lashmar 2008). In spite of the apparent openness promoted by new media technologies and Freedom of Information legislation, state secrecy has increased in both budget and legislative remit in tandem with the expansion of government bureaucracies and asymmetrical warfare (Keeble 2004).

Journalist autonomy has also been eroded by the exponential growth of corporate power in media markets, fuelled by mutually enhancing processes of conglomeration, concentration and market liberalisation (Garnham 2000; Doyle 2002; Bagdikian 2004; Curran and Seaton 2009). As a result, media corporations themselves increasingly share the interests and ideas they have traditionally served in acquiescence to advertisers. In short, 'the issue is no longer simply that the media are compromised by their links to big business: the media are big business' (Curran 2002:220).

RADICAL RESPONSES

The professional values that are said to ensure that the interests of journalists and their elite sources remain distinct have also been called into question. On the surface, these values would appear to undermine elite dominance in their emphasis on balance, impartiality, and most acutely, holding power to account. Yet these very ideals may themselves be viewed as tools of dominance leading to 'a subtle long term mobilisation of bias' (Davis 2007:101). This is primarily because notions of balance and impartiality do not account for the fact that the odds are pre-emptively stacked in favour of elites. In practice then, journalistic balance may merely reinforce the power of elite sources (Curran 2010).

The pluralist spotlight on inter-elite conflict has also been turned on its head by a developing current in the literature that focuses on the news media as an exclusive intermediated space for the negotiation of power amongst elites (Mancini 1991; Davis 2003; Kepplinger 2007). Far from exposing the real business of political and policy decision-making, which continues to be largely a closed door exercise (Freedman 2008), the media are exploited by elites to gain institutional and individual advantage in securing popular support. This amounts to a 'refeudalisation' of the public sphere whereby power is presented to the public but beyond effective scrutiny (Habermas 1989 [1962]). The fact that elites compete on a surface level through the media, does not mean that power relations are dissolved: 'Inter-elite contestation does not, as political pluralists suggest, merely result in polyarchy and dispersed power. It also leads to public exclusion as the parameters for debate and negotiation become narrower' (Davis 2003:55).

In response to the pluralist spotlight on the role of source strategies in widening the field of news contestability, radicals have highlighted counter trends stemming from commercial pressures. With the growth of corporate media power, information is becoming increasingly privatised resulting in cost barriers to access for more in-depth and reliable sources (Schiller 1996; Bagdikian 2004). Moreover, industry consolidation has resulted in a rationalisation of resources that has hindered the contestability of official stories, most notably through the decline of investigative reporting (Tunstall 1993; Born 2005).

And in response to the endurance of public service news as a refuge for 'balanced' and contesting perspectives, radicals have emphasised the degree to which its output is indirectly but no less effectively conditioned by market forces (Sparks 1995; Franklin 1997). The BBC requires a substantial audience share in order to maintain its legitimacy and justify its guaranteed funding via the license fee. But the terms of competition for audiences are set by the corporate media who, for instance, determine production costs through their role as equipment suppliers and fix the market price for creative labour (Murdock 1982). What's more, new technologies have prompted a crisis of legitimacy for public service broadcasting by undermining defences based on spectrum scarcity (McChesney 1999). Far from acting as a countervailing force to corporate conglomeration, it is argued that the BBC has been 'captured' by it, mimicking resource cuts, centralisation of production and news commodification.

But the crucial deficit of pluralist accounts for the purposes here concerns an inattention to aspects of *containment,* as opposed to contestability within news discourses. These aspects are often apparent in the very instances where the media are held to be most resistant to elite dominance. Thus, whilst Al Jazeera may have played a mobilising role in respect of the Arab Spring in North Africa, it was conspicuously quiet over unrest closer to its headquarters in Doha. And although the news media were instrumental in bringing the prisoner abuse scandal at Abu Ghraib to the attention of mass global audiences, they played an equally pivotal role in ensuring the story was largely confined to the actions of a few low-ranking soldiers (Bennett, Lawrence et al. 2006). This was contrary to hard evidence available to journalists at the time of a top-down directed policy of torture. More broadly, critical analyses of controversy in the media have long been an influential current in the literature, unveiling clear instances of ideological bias in issue representation and construction (Glasgow University Media and Beharrell 1976; Schlesinger, Murdock et al. 1983; Miller 1994).

Radical critiques of liberal pluralism trace their roots to Marxist analyses of power and the reproduction of social and economic relations. These assert that the 'function' of the mass media is to propagate the legitimating ideology of the ruling class. As such, the 'agenda' is functionally limited to a consensus framework that excludes questioning of the established social or economic order. Whilst for some, this consensus revolves around a moderate centre ground within the spectrum of established political parties (Chibnall 1980), others maintained that it disproportionately favours conservative or right-wing parties (Miliband 1973). The common thread is an underlying claim that the media do not make power legitimate, they make power *appear* to be legitimate.

It is one thing to say that control of the ideological apparatus of the state enables the spread of dominant ideas. But Marx was very unclear as to what that apparatus consists in and much less how it actually functions. Agents of social hegemony evolved in the development of Marxist theory from labels such as 'intellectuals' (Gramsci, Hoare et al. 1971), 'teachers' (Althusser 2008) and 'the school' (Poulantzas 1978) to frameworks that gave primacy to the mass media in the dominant ideology equation (Miliband 1973). But these accounts merely asserted that ownership and control of the mass media, or the means of 'mental production', are determining factors in the representation of reality. They still did not explain *how*.

INDEXING

One such explanation that has been advanced in various guises has centred on the notion of 'indexing'. According to this theory, dissent in the media is triggered all but exclusively in response to a split in elite ranks (Hallin 1994; Livingston and Bennett 2003). For Hallin (1994), indexing provides the bench mark according to which journalists will respond – and crucially legitimate – any given controversy. It traces its roots to the structural model of Primary Definition that emerged in the 1970s which posited that the perceived reliability and authority of officials provided them with a default advantage over alternative sources. There are at least two conditions that determine this privilege. First, the activities of leading political figures and other elites are intrinsically newsworthy in virtue of their widespread consequences and hence their suitability to dramatic narrative constructions (Galtung and Ruge 1965; Sigal 1973; Tuchman 1978), and they are also often the 'key holders' to public information (Golding and Elliott 1979, Miller 1994). But perhaps most significantly, officials are able to provide a regular diet of cost effective news content via routine press releases and pre-scheduled events (Davis 2007; Fishman 1980; Gans 1979, 2004; Sigal 1973). Such practices reduce the uncertainty endemic in the search for 'novelty' in news and symbolic production more generally

(Garnham 2000). They also help to overcome time and resource constraints under which journalists operate.

The important distinction of the indexing model was its conception of a relatively dynamic process, with the degree of consensus among elites liable to shifts over time and subject to a range of variables and influences. For radical functionalists, indexing merely amounts to an ideological constraint on the breadth and depth of contestability in news: 'The media do contest and raise questions about government policy, but they do so almost exclusively within the framework determined by the essentially shared interests of state-corporate power. Divisions among elites are reflected in media debate, but departure from their narrow consensus is rare' (Chomsky 1989:75).

A more nuanced version of this thesis admits a wider arena of contestability, with indexing forming the basis of a 'cascading activation' model of news framing (Entman 2004). According to this model, whilst elite conflict may trigger public debate through the media, the content of that debate is further modified by interventions at various stages in the news filtering process. Such interventions may stem from journalistic agency or public opinion and were given considerably greater force by the decline of the Cold War ideological paradigm. This was said to have rendered public responses to foreign affairs less predictable, heightening the media's role in 'representation' and bounding public opinion indicators to media frames. According to Entman, the Cascading Activation model moves beyond indexing in highlighting the fact that journalists may sometimes take a stronger dissenting line than that of either elite detractors or public opinion, though this is regulated to some extent by the force of professional values and motivations.

THE PROPAGANDA MODEL

A common theme among radical accounts is attention to the ways in which media elites are immersed within the power structure of society, sometimes obscuring the very distinction between journalists and their sources. For one thing, there is an element of disjuncture between the professional 'disclosure' ideology associated with resistance and opposition to elite sources, and the reality of day to day working conditions in which journalists often share in the material lifestyles of their sources (Tunstall 1971). But there is also significant overlap in the socio-economic backgrounds of media and political elites (Ericson, Baranek et al. 1989; Gitlin 1980; Sparks 1986) who together 'take all the important decisions about what is going to happen, how it is going to be reported and what will be done with anyone who objects. They are the ruling class' (Sparks 1986:84). A corporate worldview is said to then filter down to media managers via a process of socialisation. This leaves them 'committed to the maintenance of the going system in its main outlines' by virtue of their bonds of experience and relationships with corporate elites (Gitlin 1980:258).

One explicit articulation of this view is the Propaganda Model (Herman and Chomsky 2002 [1988]) which emphasises the holistic nature of state-corporate power and dismisses notions of journalistic agency altogether. The model incorporates elements of primary definition – insofar as officials are afforded a dominant role as news sources – as well as indexing (contestability in the media is pegged to dissenting elite sources which are nonetheless rare and limited in scope). But the pillars of official source dominance are not professional ideology as much as the structural foundations derived from the media's entrenchment within the market system, and the state's role as both market regulator and protector. Thus, in addition to their ability to offer the carrot of subsidised news, official sources can wield the stick of 'flak', including the threat of license withdrawal or libel suits. Alongside these, the model cites the political economic 'filters' of ownership and advertising, as well as (in its original formulation) anti-communist ideology. Here, ideology is conceived not as a broad blanket of ideas and beliefs but as a doctrine with specific propaganda purposes.

In keeping with other models of dominance, the Propaganda Model does not have much to say about the effects of ideological bias. Whilst this has been the central charge of many of its critics, the model itself is divorced from notions of mass indoctrination. Rather, it is chiefly about 'media performance and behaviour with uncertain and variable effects' (Herman 2000:103). It is, however, inextricably linked to agenda setting which unites it with all theories of dominance as outlined here. In short, the underlying claim is that the mass media, on behalf of elites, effectively set the terms and limits of public debate.

Dissent in the mainstream media, according to this model, is limited to questions over strategy and tactics rather than overall policy goals and justifications, and public debate is grounded on assumptions that do not challenge the existing social and political structure. Whilst these notions are shared by more hegemonic conceptions as outlined above, it is the depiction of elite fractures as rare and superficial which sets the Propaganda Model apart. Much like the articulations of earlier cultural theorists, in particular the Frankfurt School, the model allows little if any room for genuine contestability in news media, or for that matter journalist autonomy and agency.

It is perhaps in view of this feature that the Propaganda Model has inspired vociferous critique from both liberal pluralists and radicals alike. Some of these have been made with explicit reference to the model's overly deterministic and functionalist conception of ideology (Eldridge 1993; Hallin 1994; Schudson 1995). Some dismiss the equation between structures and functionalism altogether arguing that ownership or organisational factors, such as time and budget constraints, or indeed market fundamentals, are not synonymous with ideological influence, even if they result in media portrayals that favour elite interests on balance (Schudson 1995; Bennett 2009). And even those who sympathise with the model's broad prescriptions have criticised its limited applicability outside of the commercially dominated US media system (Freedman 2009; Sparks 2009).

The key limitation for the purposes here is that the Propaganda Model – and dominant ideology models more broadly – do not account for the increasingly routine cases of 'exposure' through the mass media of corruption at the heart of the military industrial complex. These controversies clearly extend beyond questions of tactics or strategic goals, or any conception of a mainstream political consensus (as evidenced by scandals which elicit bi-partisan defences). Just as liberal pluralist accounts have tended to shy away from aspects of framing and agenda containment within the news, their radical counterparts have avoided close analysis of stories which smack of genuine contestability.

CONTAINING THE AGENDA

In 1963, Bernard Cohen famously remarked that 'the media may not be successful much of the time in telling people what to think, but is stunningly successful in telling its readers what to think about' (Cohen 1965 [1963]:13). This statement served to reinvigorate the study of media audiences after persistent findings that pointed to 'minimal' effects (Scheufele and Tewksbury 2007). In essence, agenda setting refers to a correlation between issues that receive prominence in the media and issues that are considered important by mass audiences. Thus, agenda setting models attempt to track the extent and ways in which the media agenda sets the terms of public debate (McCombs 2004). In this sense, they bridge the gap between media production and effects studies focusing on two key spheres of reception: policymakers and publics.

Framing has been linked to agenda setting insofar as it influences not what people think about, but *how* they think about them. To this extent, framing has been characterised as 'attributed' or second level agenda setting – the transfer of issue salience from within the context of a given news story or event to the cognitive understanding of news audiences (McCombs 2004). For others, the key influence of framing on interpretive frameworks consists in its capacity to construct meaning. In other words, 'framing focuses not on which topics or issues are selected for coverage by the news media, but instead on the particular ways those issues are presented' (Price, Tewsbury et al. 1997).

But the significance of framing and agenda setting for the purposes here lies on the production rather than effects end of the equation. In this context, both agenda setting and framing have roots in gatekeeper theories which posit that journalists and editors control information flows, consciously or otherwise, through the processes of story and issue selection (Tunstall 1971; White 1997 [1957]). For radicals, these processes provided a conception of media power which pre-figured Lukes' third dimension: significance was held to lie not in what was reported so much as in what was left *off* the news agenda. In opposition to effects-based models which focused on influence over audiences, the starting point of gatekeeping models is on prior influences over media agendas and frames. Such influences include news values, ideological predisposi-tions and media management strategies by sources, which laid the foundation for later structural accounts of ideological dominance (Hall, Critcher et al. 1978; Herman and Chomsky 2002 [1988]; Entman 2004).

But agenda setting and framing models are not necessarily invoked by those who wish to advocate a theory of dominance. The key ideologically-driven question is not whether but in what *form* discursive framing takes place. The role of journalists in filtering vast informational 'noise' into a concise and coherent news format is considered a necessary, desirable, and essential aspect of the media's democratic function (Gans 1979; Dahlgren 1991). This is especially the case in a post-digitisation mediascape, where the explosion of information sources has rendered reliable and coherent news an increasingly elusive good. Filtering is not therefore intrinsically incompatible with pluralist notions of contestability and dispersed power. The key question turns on whether story and issue selection are ideologically driven.

It is worth emphasising that agenda setting and framing models are concerned with the relative *prominence* of particular issues and events in the news, rather than simply with which are included or excluded. This question has become all the more pertinent amidst the digital explosion of news outlets and platforms. The boundary between what is in or out of the news is becoming increasingly blurred and at the same time, individual news outlets are becoming increasingly conscious of, and focused on their particular audiences. Prominence must therefore be considered not just in terms of headline billing or time allocation, but in terms of audience reach.

But there has been a tendency within the radical literature to eschew such differences in favour of a focus on homogenising and tabloidising trends in news output (Franklin 1997; Thussu 2007), just as there has been a tendency in the pluralist literature not to consider prominence in terms of audience reach (e.g. Norris 2000). What seems certain is that the exponential expansion of outlets and formats over recent decades has fostered some kind of diversity in news. Beginning with the birth of commercial television in 1955, the UK has seen the emergence of a range of formats at various points in the schedule from 'light news' characteristic of breakfast TV and daytime discussion programmes, to late-evening analysis and current affairs editions. The 1980s also saw a marked increase in the regularity of news 'bulletins', as well as the rise of documentary and factual programming. In addition to all this, by the early 2000s, digital TV subscribers had the choice of at least three 24-hour news channels. Clearly, the extent of proliferation in television news is difficult to ignore but the critical question remains not whether, but what kind of diversity is on offer.

The problem with totalising views of diversification or homogenisation is that they circumvent the stratified nature of access to differentiated news programmes, as well as the marketing values that underpin audience segmentation. Access stratification in news is intensified because specialist formats require, rather than promote prior understanding, manifest in a failure to provide 'the kind of analysis or context that might explain the meaning and significance of a story' (Lewis, Cushion et al. 2005:443).

A tiered conception of news provision, in which diverse and critical views are concentrated in an elite tier of outlets, seems more convincing (Bourdieu 1998). But this presents a critical problem for the democratic legitimacy of news as articulated by Downing:

The petit bourgeoisie are communicated with in different ways to those generally used to the working class. Far more is explained to them, they are much more likely to be invited to think and reason for themselves (though always within the bounds of bourgeois ideology). The petit bourgeoisie are not fed sex, sensationalism, soap operas, sport detail, the *Sun*, but current affairs programmes, documentaries, serious plays, international news, art programmes, book reviews, *The Times*, the *Economist*. Journalists are in their class, and what is more, if they switch on radio or TV they are quite likely to find other members of their class talking about some issue or another. This fosters a feeling of belonging to the circles whose opinion counts; it is nutritive of the class alliance between them and the bourgeoisie. (Downing 1980:159)

An ironic consequence then, is that divisions within and between dominant groups in society owe much to the relative diversity of information to which they are exposed, a factor which engenders both division, but ultimately class alliance.

Clearly, however, the class dividing line between media output implicit in the above statement does not account for the range of news services and formats on offer today. A news programme targeted primarily at women, for instance, would be unlikely to fit comfortably in either a 'petit bourgeois' or working-class category. This raises a conceptual problem: how to understand substantial differences in the content of news programmes as apart from mere presentational differences associated with branding.

By examining coverage of a particular type of controversy – one which threatens to undermine dominant narratives around accountability – we can gain insights into the ideological character of news discourse. It follows that by comparing such presentation and frames between programmes and outlets, we can get a clue as to the extent of differentiation (and by default, audience discrimination) which reaches beyond mere differences in style and format, and does not rely on dubious notions of news quality. This is the basis for the comparative context adopted throughout this book.

SUMMARY AND BOOK OUTLINE

I have argued that the concept of accountability rests implicitly on a degree of openness and contestability within the political system, and that the media – in liberal pluralist terms – play a crucial role in facilitating it. This is achieved by providing a platform for source competition (both inter-elite and elite-alternative), and by the professional values of watchdog journalism which ensure that journalists themselves – with or without the support of alternative sources – are capable of fearless scrutiny of power. In this way, journalism, from a liberal pluralist perspective, can go some way to delivering on the accountability promises of answerability and enforcement. More crucially, it can deliver on a second order of accountability which ensures that formal institutions of oversight – as well as the media themselves – are subject to public monitoring and control.

On the surface, controversies involving misuse or abuse of power are ubiquitous in the contemporary newscape. But the liberal pluralist case necessitates a degree of journalist autonomy that extends beyond a capacity to merely expose wrongdoing. It requires firstly that the controversy is ultimately not contained in favour of those under scrutiny. By containment I refer to the means by which a news controversy may ultimately fail to deliver on the accountability promises of answerability (sourcing all relevant information pertaining to a misuse or abuse of power) and enforcement (ensuring that the powerful in question are deterred from future abuses or misuses).

This is an empirically answerable question but one which requires attention to a much more diverse array of variables than either liberal pluralists or their radical critics have tended to focus on. For instance, the degree of issue prominence within a frame or agenda – a potentially potent force of containment – must be investigated through comparative analysis of outlets which target different audience types and sizes. In terms of framing *scope*, attention must be paid to how far journalistic scrutiny extends beyond the activities of the powerful to include the functioning of institutions that are charged with monitoring and policing them. The timing of news exposés is equally significant, as is the duration of coverage, since accountability holds less meaning if coverage is retrospective or conversely, if it ends prematurely.

All these questions warrant a 'why?' addendum. What seems clear from the outset is that the constraints impacting on journalists – be they external or self-imposed, conscious or unconscious – are neither as static and structurally determined as radical models suggest, nor as dynamic and fluid as liberal pluralists contend. This suggests the need to inquire not just when and where media systems are relatively open or contained in their scrutiny of power, but why they are open at certain points and contained at others within the time and space of news output.

It is hoped that this kind of inquiry will provide an insight into whether aspects of containment are merely inevitable anomalies or serve an ideological function. If the latter, this is likely to consist not in the promotion of a particular set of ideas, but rather in a particular *ideal*; one which is encapsulated by a view of corruption as always marginal, isolated, inevitable, detectable and fixable, and never endemic, systemic and beyond control. The legacy of Watergate still resonates amongst journalists today. According to one interviewed for this study: 'It's the ultimate in journalism to be able to bring down a Prime Minister and most leaders are threatened not by something they did wrong but by the cover-up. Almost always it's the cover-up. That's what got Nixon.'

But even liberal reflections on this iconic controversy have questioned the apparent triumph of watchdog journalism widely depicted in popular discourse. It was after all not the media, but the FBI, federal prosecutions and Grand Jury which led the case against Nixon with the mainstream media entering relatively late in the game (Schudson 1995). More crucially perhaps, the coverage itself left deeper questions of institutional power untouched such as the involvement of the CIA (Bennett 2009). This led to a 'system works' conclusion with the media hailed as accountability champions.

The book proceeds with detailed discussion of three case studies involving news stories that threaten to prise open the arena of 'acceptable' controversy and interrogate the shadowy heart of state-corporate power. Chapters 2 and 3 examine coverage of corruption in the British arms trade and in particular, the notorious and long-running 'Al Yamamah' scandal. Chapters 4 and 5 focus on the media furore – as well as silence – triggered by the Hutton Report in 2004 which poured scorn on the BBC and all but absolved the government in connection with the death of outed BBC source, David Kelly. Finally, chapters 6 and 7 probe the coverage in relation to the unprecedented leak of US diplomatic cables in 2010. In doing so, the case study offers potential insights into the nature and scope of information control in the digital age. In the concluding chapter, we will return to some of the themes outlined above and in particular, the case will be made for a new way of understanding ideological functionalism in the media.

Part I

Covering Corruption

2
High Crimes

THE AL YAMAMAH DEAL

The Al Yamamah controversy has been a recurring news story in the UK for the best part of 25 years. Ever since the British and Saudi governments first signed a memorandum of understanding for the sale of UK fighter jets in 1985, allegations began to surface in the press of secret 'kick back' commissions to key agents and negotiators. However, the story acquired cross-media attention in December 2006. This followed a decision taken by the Serious Fraud Office (SFO) to terminate an investigation into British Aerospace Systems (BAe) with respect to the Al Yamamah deal. It was from then a recurring feature on mainstream television news until February 2010.

The decision to halt the investigation pointed to apparent government interference with due process. It was said that the decision was timely to the extent that investigators were on the verge of a breakthrough and 'about to be granted access to key Saudi bank accounts'.[1] It is significant that it was this decision which elevated the long-running story on to prime-time television news. What made the controversy sufficiently newsworthy for television was not so much the original sin (bribery/corruption), but what looked like determined attempts to suppress it. It was this aspect of the story that seemed to call up the media's cadre of outraged journalists. In simple terms, if the state institutions of law and order could not secure justice of their own accord, it was up to the media to force their hand.

The key background context to the story as analysed here concerns the impending renewal of the Al Yamamah arms deal, specifically with reference to the exclusive sale of Euro fighter 'Typhoon' jets, formally agreed in July 2007. The aircraft were developed in partnership with other European countries which led to fierce competition for sales as contractors and governments battled for a return on their investment in an increasingly austere economic climate. With the UK's fledgling manufacturing sector on the ropes, the largest single export deal of the century so far would inevitably be a matter of public policy priority. But BAe had long been at the centre of successive government initiatives in securing international arms deals.

Clearly then, the story cast its spotlight on the heart of state-corporate power. The scope was systemic in the sense that it did not centre on the actions of specific parties or individuals. In essence, it was a story about a foreign policy continuum that survived successive governments and prime ministers and attracted bi-partisan endorsement, at least from the front benches of Parliament.

The story was also ideologically sensitive to the extent that it conflicted sharply with dominant narratives around bribery and corruption in international trade. In November 2006, coinciding with the termination of the SFO investigation, the government released a DVD entitled 'Crimes of the Establishment', detailing its anti-corruption strategies on a global scale.[2] Distributed to diplomatic posts, governments and media around the world, this initiative was perhaps exemplary of an attempt to square a round public relations hole. The UK is a signatory to the OECD Convention on Bribery and Corruption which states that investigation and prosecution 'shall not be influenced by considerations of national economic interest, the potential effect upon relations with another State or the identity of the natural or legal persons involved'.[3] Consequently the Prime Minister, along with the Attorney General and other government spokespersons, were at pains to stress the national security implications of the SFO investigation, though no evidence was provided for this. It was in any case rejected by both the High Court and OECD as inadequate grounds for halting the inquiry.

In summary, there are at least three distinct but related ways in which this controversy implicitly challenged the legitimacy of the established order. First, as alluded to in the introduction, at the heart of the controversy were allegations of ministerial interference with due process. This prompts questions over the efficacy not just of individuals and groups who wield power, but of the very institutions and procedures that legitimate their power. Second, the controversy targets a pillar of the 'military industry complex' – namely the relationship between successive governments and Britain's largest weapons manufacturer. Third, it exposes inconsistencies between policy substance and rhetoric, challenging a dominant narrative that the British government works to combat rather than engage in bribery and corruption in international trade.

COVERAGE OVERVIEW

Our analysis is focused on terrestrial television news output between 2006 (following termination of the official investigation) to the announcement of plea bargain settlements in 2010. On the surface, the controversy was in many ways exemplary of the news media's potential to effectively scrutinise and hold power to account. It gave considerable voice to alternative and non-official sources including Campaign Against the Arms Trade (CAAT), Corner House Research, individual whistleblowers and experts critical of the government and BAe. Dissent also stemmed from within elite ranks – notably Liberal Democrat MPs and business leaders from other leading sectors of the economy, but also lawyers, High Court judges, the OECD and the US Department of Justice. By providing a platform for these contesting views, the media fulfilled its liberal pluralist function by ensuring that all stakeholders had a voice.

Secondly, and more crucially, the media did more than just provide a level platform for official and contesting views alike. They played an equilibrating role – attempting to redress any structural advantage afforded to official sources by actively challenging and attacking their positions whilst allowing contesting sources to present their views largely without scrutiny. In this sense the media acted *on behalf* of what was perceived as the public interest and in many ways the controversy developed as a battle not so much between competing sources, as between official sources and the journalists themselves.

Journalist autonomy was alive and well across a relatively broad spectrum of news outlets. The very emergence of the story owed much to the work of investigative reporters who co-operated closely with both investigators and campaigners. In this sense, coverage of the controversy lived up to liberal pluralist visions. The opening of the SFO inquiry followed a build-up of primary source documents and whistleblower accounts sourced by the burgeoning efforts of two investigative journalists at the *Guardian* newspaper.[4] The intense media scrutiny over the decision to halt the inquiry arguably paved the way for campaigning groups to pursue a judicial review case that initially ruled in their favour.

But whilst the coverage demonstrated considerable expressions of journalist autonomy and even outrage, this was limited to particular contexts and particular outlets. Of crucial significance for the purposes here is the complicity of the media in bringing the story to an apparent close. In spite of intense cross-media scrutiny over a prolonged period, the government was left off the hook and BAe managed to escape prosecution altogether. The controversy culminated in an apparent resolution with the announcement of a package of out-of-court penalties producing a headline figure of £280 million. But the settlement made no mention of corruption (let alone alleged government sanction of corruption); incurred fines worth only 1 per cent of BAe's annual turnover; and denied the public an opportunity 'to discover the truth about bribery claims' through legally imposed disclosure.[5]

Even at the various peaks of the controversy, coverage on terrestrial television news was marginalised in key respects. The BBC and ITN devoted over three hours of television coverage between November 2004 and March 2010, but it was only once featured as a lead headline,[6] appearing most often towards the end of a programme and billed as 'other news' or 'other headlines'. Within this output there were clear discrepancies in the nature and scope of coverage. For one thing, the distribution of coverage on mainstream channels heavily favoured the late evening broadcasts (see Table 2.1). On one occasion a report was advertised at the end of an early evening ITV edition as featuring on *News at Ten*. This demonstrates that the relative prevalence of coverage on late evening broadcasts was not just a function of the news cycle but on occasion at least, an editorial decision as to when and to which slice of the audience it was most appropriate.

Table 2.1   Distribution of coverage within mainstream audience channels

	Lunch time	Early Evening	Late evening
BBC 1	17%	30%	53%
ITV 1	8%	20%	73%
Total	13%	26%	61%

Sources: National Film Archives, BBC Online

But by far the most widespread divergence in coverage was between minority and mainstream audience serving channels (BBC Two/Channel 4 and BBC One/ITV1 respectively). The former were responsible for 75 per cent of the total news reportage dedicated to the controversy across all four channels. *Channel 4 News* had the broadest coverage, with by far the greatest number of reports and total length of airtime allocated of any news programme across the four channels (see Table 2.2). BBC Two's *Newsnight* on the other

Table 2.2 Analysis of coverage breadth and depth

	BBC1 Lunchtime News	BBC1 Six O'clock News	BBC1 Ten O'clock News	BBC2 Newsnight	ITV Lunchtime News	ITV Early Evening News	ITV Late Evening News*	Channel 4 News
Number of reports	4	5	10	6	1	2	5	16
Total length of reports	6 mins	11 mins	19 mins	44 mins	2 mins	5 mins	18 mins	58 mins
Average length of reports	93 secs	127 secs	113 secs	439 secs	114 secs	147 secs	128 secs	219 secs
Proportion of air time	5%	7%	6%	15%	6%	8%	7%	7%

Sources: National Film Archives, BBC Online
* also includes figures for *News at Ten* which replaced the *Late Evening News* in 2008

hand, despite featuring far fewer reports than *Channel 4 News*, had the most in-depth coverage with the story occupying the greatest average length and proportion of airtime by a significant margin. The latter figure is proportionally adjusted to account for the longer duration of analysis news programmes. It is therefore significant insofar as it demonstrates that differences in the extent of coverage between bulletins and analysis programmes cannot be attributed to their relative programme duration alone.

Another figure that transcends the limitations of relative programme durations was the marked contrast in the propensity of different outlets to feature pro-government versus dissenting sources in their reports. Table 2.3 compares the time allocated in reports to such opposing voices across the sample. These figures should be treated with a degree of caution since within any given report the balance did not necessarily reflect the critical slant of the piece as a whole. Nevertheless, they do suggest that analysis programmes did not merely cover the controversy in greater breadth and depth, but were actively more critical of the government and BAe compared to their mainstream counterparts.

Table 2.3   Balance of pro-government (protagonist) and dissenting (antagonist) voices in news reports

	Analysis programmes	*Main bulletins*
Protagonists	258 seconds	204 seconds
Antagonists	362 seconds	168 seconds

Sources: National Film Archives, BBC Online

NB Figures on reports broadcast between November 2004 and February 2010. 'Protagonist' sources were taken to denote those who spoke on behalf of or in support of the government and BAe. 'Antagonist' sources were all those who were explicitly critical of the government and/ or BAe. Equivocal or ambiguous voices were discounted from the analysis, as were statements during interview exchanges in which sources were challenged by reporters. This was to ensure that the sample included only those excerpts of reports that gave a favourable presentation to the speakers in each case.

Clearly, the relative time allocation in the schedule of analysis programmes compared to mainstream programmes was instrumental in enabling them to probe deeper into the context and analysis of key issues, a point that has been well made in the literature (e.g. Hetherington 1985). A typical midweek evening edition (Monday to Thursday) lasts 50 minutes, compared with 30 minutes for early- and late-evening programmes on BBC One and ITV. In the Al Yamamah controversy, reports on analysis programmes were typically three to four times longer than their bulletin counterparts. Crucially, extended reports featured more background, context and analysis, as well as being more favourable to antagonist sources. Time limitations restrict mainstream news reports by requiring them to focus attention on the core parameters of a story. This limits their capacity to go beyond event-driven reporting which tends to favour the pronouncements and sound bites offered by official sources (Hall et al. 1978).

But by far the greatest indication of differentiation between analysis and bulletin coverage was the propensity of the former to adopt more critical discursive frames (as opposed to voices), as will be discussed further below. But it should be borne in mind that whilst such differences are to some extent reflective of containment, they may also be viewed as tantamount to at least a limited degree of openness. The fact that journalist autonomy was demonstrated most convincingly in a particular tier of news outlets does not detract from the fact that it did exist. Perhaps more enlightening are the *similarities* between analysis and bulletin coverage in respect of particular frames. Here we see occasional instances of openness but starker evidence of outright containment, notably in the coverage of the joint settlements announced in February 2010.

THE BIG PICTURE

Central to the controversy narrative were allegations of high level corruption between BAe, the UK government and Saudi Arabia. How this corruption was framed revealed important distinctions in the nature of coverage, in particular, whether it was framed as systemic or limited to the actions of specific parties and individuals. Overwhelmingly, television news reports focused on the individual placed at the centre of bribery allegations: Prince Bandar of Sultan. But in doing so, they did not shy away from the broader context of the corruption allegations. References to Prince Bandar were almost always contextualised by citing his connections to global centres of power. He was at turns described as the 'world's most significant diplomat';[7] 'the darling of the West';[8] a 'middle man' with access to the 'corridors of power' on both sides of the Atlantic[9] and whose 'personal airbus even has landing rights at RAF Brize Norton'.[10]

Special reports, notably on a *Newsnight* edition in February 2008, went further than merely citing the extent of his influence, analysing instead the nature and source of that influence: 'Two things strike you [about Prince Bandar] – his phenomenal wealth and his enormous international influence. And they're indivisible'.[11]

In describing wealth and power as 'indivisible', the reporter is making an implicit, generalisable reference to the cycle of corruption in international arms deals. The wealthier Prince Bandar becomes off the back of illegal commission payments, the greater his access and influence. As his access and influence is enhanced, so in turn is his role in brokering agreements.

Analysis in special reports also provided contextual insight into the *flow* of influence from corporate lobbyists to government, and from the government to investigative branches of the state. This put the complex nature of systemic corruption in the spotlight:

> In a case where a head of state may be involved, a geopolitical ally that's important to the US may be involved, then we detect aberrant procedures within the Department of Justice [...] It's clear that the higher up the bribe goes, the larger the bribe, the more important a transaction, the more likely it is that politics will become involved.[12]

Thus, whilst all programmes tended to frame corruption around the central figure of Prince Bandar, this did not necessarily restrict the context. Crucially, Prince Bandar was frequently and broadly portrayed as the connecting node in a network of interdependent centres of power. This imbued the controversy with a sense of ultimate scandal, transcending the indiscretions or misdemeanours of individual characters.

DAVID AND GOLIATH

In addition to the pull of the ultimate scandal, alternative sources gained traction through the media's penchant for David and Goliath discursive frames. Explicit in some treatments and implicit in most was a narrative of the weak taking on the powerful and winning. The 'unlawful' High Court ruling in April 2008 concerning the decision to halt the SFO enquiry was described by BBC One's *News at Ten* as 'scathing', accusing the SFO of 'abject surrender'.[13] ITV was also the only channel to broadcast a report on alleged 'dirty tricks' by BAe in the run up to the High Court ruling: 'This tiny peace group [CAAT] says it was infiltrated by a spy working for Britain's biggest arms company BAe. Someone somehow managed to steal dozens of confidential emails and pass them on to BAe.'[14]

The language here, pitting the 'tiny peace group' against 'Britain's biggest arms company', is illustrative of the willingness of journalists even on the main bulletins to go beyond impartiality codes in adopting the David and Goliath narrative. The very announcement that campaigners had won the right to challenge the decision was celebrated as a triumph of the weak – 'today they won victory' – and although it was 'unlikely that the investigation will be reopened', an unlawful ruling would nonetheless 'send a clear message about how the government should act in the future'.[15]

Campaigners were acutely conscious of this framing as a competitive advantage. According to Symon Hill, radical peace activist and former press officer for CAAT, the narrative of the weak taking on the strong was critical to the publicity that campaigners achieved: 'Had the judgement gone against us I don't think that would have got so much coverage. Government not defeated in court isn't so much of a news story in a sense. Powerful people not defeated by people less powerful than them isn't anything new.'

If campaigning groups provided the David figure against the government and BAe's Goliath, the court room provided the arena of battle. The dramatic significance of the legal proceedings is in one sense self-evident, according to Hill: 'people like the idea of somebody taking the government to court'. But there was a complex array of interrelated forces that made judicial involvement a particular media spectacle. Indeed the media played a key part in driving the proceedings. Hill reflected on both the expectation and encouragement that the media provided for legal action right from the start of the campaign:

It was dropped on – this is ingrained in my memory – it was dropped on a Thursday evening and on the Friday afternoon when we said we were considering legal action – we only had to say we were considering it – and then the media just – I think I probably had more media calls that one day than I'd had in the six months I'd been working there.

According to his account, CAAT hadn't planned or decided on legal action in the immediate aftermath of the decision. But the fever of interest from both journalists and prospective law firms prompted the announcement of legal action within two days of the SFO decision. As much as anything else, this provided CAAT with a relieving sense of 'leading the media agenda rather than being pulled along by it'.

Aside from the obvious narrative appeal of court room drama and the David and Goliath discourse, judicial proceedings and the

High Court victory for campaigners provided journalists themselves with a sense of vindication. The *Guardian* in particular had been campaigning for several years on the Al Yamamah controversy – long before it was picked up by other outlets or by television news. According to Kaye Stearman, press officer for CAAT, 'a lot of the evidence that the SFO was looking at in investigating BAe had been produced by the *Guardian* investigations'. Victory in the High Court therefore provided both a sense of restorative justice as well as a justification and effective return for a significant investment of newspaper resources. This return was manifest not just financially but through industry recognition and credibility. In 2010, Rob Evans and David Leigh of the *Guardian* jointly received prestigious press awards for their work on the Al Yamamah controversy.

The existence of a legal case also provided a degree of official sanction for widespread coverage of the story. It certainly added credibility and weight to the voice of campaigners. But there was, above all, a sense in which the process itself became the story with all its twists and turns and stamp of judicial authority. According to Symon Hill: 'There wouldn't have been so much of a story without a legal case. Yeah we would have still kicked up a fuss but the legal case made it a bigger story and I have to admit at the time I probably underestimated – I did underestimate – how big a difference it would make.'

Disclosure of documents during the court proceedings proved central to the media momentum that was sustained. This had two significant effects in terms of retaining the media spotlight. First, the emergence of paper documents themselves provided a bank of tangible 'evidence' that amplified both the official sanction and vindication elements of the narrative. Second and equally significant, the documents provided a rare insight into the machinations of power behind closed doors and behind the wall of press officers and special advisors that political reporters face on a day to day basis. As one solicitor involved in the case observed:

> During the course of the proceedings we obviously got – heavily redacted – but we got a lot of disclosure of internal government documents and minutes, letters from the Prime Minister and so on, about effectively what was happening behind the scenes in the run up to the decision being taken and that obviously got a lot of media attention because they love it – seeing the inner workings of what's going on in government.

But the flow of influence was not unidirectional and the media spotlight provided fertile ground on which to launch and successfully prosecute the case. Lawyers exploited media attention in a variety of ways, at times seeking to maximise coverage and at other times seeking to contain it. This was done not only through the control of information releases, but also through active engagement with the media:

> We do spend a lot of time speaking with the media because the nature of the cases we do which tend to get coverage and media coverage can be used as a tool. It can help a case [...] it can certainly bring the prospect of something winning – that sense of right and wrong that ultimately underpins whatever the law says. You can get a long way with a sense of real injustice and media coverage really does assist that.

Ultimately of course, media strategies on the part of lawyers were aimed at positively influencing the decisions of judges who were seen as far from beyond the media's reach. The appointment of Justice Moses to the High Court case was viewed by campaigners and their solicitors as particularly helpful given his media savvy reputation. This was underpinned by the uncommon decision to release a media summary of his judgement.

ACCOUNTABILITY FRAMING

Analysis programmes exhibited some tendency to question the effectiveness of the judicial process. In 2007, anchor introductions to reports on *Channel 4 News* were set against a backdrop of the BAe logo and Saudi flag with the by-line 'law flawed'. This is in some sense an inversion of the more commonly used tag 'unlawful'. It suggests that the problem is not so much the actions of the government or BAe, but the law or legal system itself – it's incapacity to provide appropriate sanction against crimes of the powerful.

Even when confining the story to the case at hand, coverage on analysis programmes adopted a notably less impartial approach than the main bulletins. Emphasis was placed on the decision to halt the investigation as being one effectively 'made by politicians',[16] contrary to legal convention that requires the SFO to act independently of government: 'We can see from documents and letters released to the High Court how far Tony Blair and his ministers were willing to go to get the investigation stopped, how they increased the pressure month by month.'[17]

Analysis programmes also stressed that it was the gathering momentum, rather than stalling of the investigation that acted as a catalyst to its closure, with investigators 'about to be granted access to key Saudi bank accounts when the investigation was pulled'.[18] This was in direct opposition to the Prime Minister's view that the inquiry would not have 'gotten anywhere' even if it had been allowed to continue.

In the aftermath of the decision, *Channel 4 News* reports brazenly focused on government interference into investigative proceedings and allegations of cover-up. In June 2007 the programme ran a report on revelations that the Attorney General had ordered the SFO to 'hide' details of BAe payments from the OECD.[19] Three months earlier, one journalist offered frank testimony as to the behaviour of UK officials at an OECD meeting in Paris:

> [There was] a strange and testy atmosphere in the air. The British government really was out to put its case very strongly and brought out the big guns, really trying to water down the wording [of the OECD report], cross out reference to a potential investigation, suggestions even that they tried to resist media appearances by [OECD Chair] Mark Peith, even trying to wind up the press conference.[20]

Analysis programmes also questioned the meaning of apparent accountability outcomes, as epitomised by one news anchor's challenge to a campaigner following victory in the High Court: 'what happens now – you've won but have you won?'[21] The implication of this question is that even an unlawful ruling is not sufficient to bring the government or BAe to account – that they may be, in essence, above the law. It is a sentiment equally captured in a statement by Mark Peith, Chair of the OECD Working Group on Bribery and Corruption, in which he highlights the difference between accountability procedures and accountability outcomes: 'in the UK there is quite an impressive amount of investigations but very few of these move on to prosecution or even to the courts'.[22]

BLOOD ON OUR STREETS

Official source frames were predominantly concerned with threats associated with the SFO inquiry. At its most extreme, this involved warnings of impending 'blood on our streets' – the primary justification for terminating the SFO inquiry, and couched more broadly as a threat to national security and strategic relations with Saudi Arabia. Alongside this, there was a secondary frame that centred on threats to UK jobs and industry, and how these two were related to each other revealed subtle but important qualifications in the coverage.

Virtually all reports throughout the life of the story made some reference to the economic context of the controversy, often in emphatic terms: 'At stake are thousands of jobs and contracts worth billions of pounds'.[23] Most carried footage of Typhoon jets, which were the subject of £40 billion of export revenue according to the terms of the Al Yamamah contract renewal. The BBC's first full length report on this renewal was a business piece broadcast on the lunchtime bulletin.[24] Not surprisingly, it constructed the economic context in a positive light, celebrating the boost to British business and making only passing reference to the controversial circumstances surrounding the original deal. Sources described the renewal as 'good news for all'[25] and pointed out its potential to serve as a catalyst for UK arms export growth: '[The Saudis] trust the Brits and that's good for us in selling to other people'.[26]

Given the scale of the commercial stakes, later news reports generally highlighted the threat that the SFO investigation had posed to UK economic interests. But this was not necessarily an endorsement of the government or BAe's case: both the Prime Minister and Attorney General repeatedly placed emphasis on national security considerations over commercial factors as the basis for terminating the enquiry, in line with OECD regulations. Both the main bulletins and analysis programmes alike implicitly questioned this rationale by emphasising the commercial context. Reporters cited the commercial threat in connection with the halting of the inquiry more frequently and explicitly than the threat of 'blood on our streets' espoused by the Attorney General. However, the government did not abandon the commercial threat as justification. It was merely relegated in an attempt to comply with OECD regulations. According to Tony Blair,

> I don't believe the investigation incidentally would have led anywhere except to the complete wreckage of a vital strategic relationship for our country in terms of fighting terrorism, in terms of the Middle East, in terms of British interests there, quite

apart from the fact that we would have lost thousands, thousands of British jobs.[27]

The threat to jobs and industry remained a 'vote winning' frame for official sources, in spite of the OECD pressure. Accordingly, the commercial threat angle in television news reports could be constructed in such a way as to either endorse or undermine official sources. An important distinctive quality of the latter approach was attention to the government's media strategy. Not surprisingly, this occurred predominantly in the analysis programmes where journalists tended to qualify official statements on national security with reference to OECD regulations: 'The Attorney General conducted a Whitehall-wide exercise to see if the SFO case might be called off on the basis of jobs and the economy...that would have been illegal under the terms of the OECD anti-bribery convention.'[28]

Analysis programmes also implicitly challenged the assumption that the investigation would have harmed the UK economy in two ways. First, reports generally placed relatively greater emphasis on the threat to BAe as a company rather than the UK economy as a whole. This was particularly evident in coverage of the US government's decision to investigate BAe in 2007. *Channel 4 News* highlighted the centrality of the US military market for BAe's growth strategy and the significance of the investigation's timing. One headline stated that 'fresh from the Saudi bribery rumpus, BAe gobbles up American defence manufacturers but Congress is on their tails'.[29] The following week another report highlighted the commercial impact on BAe of the US decision, pointing out that 40 per cent of their existing business was already tied up with the US military and the decision to open a new investigation had wiped £1.6 billion off the company's value.[30] Crucially, at no point did the reporting draw parallels between what's bad for BAe and what's bad for the UK economy as a whole.

Both *Channel 4 News* and BBC Two's *Newsnight* also provided a more nuanced insight into the role of competitive market forces compared to the bulletins. In particular, they pointed to the impact of commercial lobbying in spurring the *continuation* of investigations as well as putting the lid on them: 'From the start competitors suspected Britain was illicitly greasing the wheels.'[31] 'I guarantee you all [BAe's US] competitors will be urging their bought Congressmen to be screaming about foreign corruption.'[32]

The discursive effect here is to highlight the role of commercial lobbying in influencing policy outcomes and to frame the commercial threat as being directed chiefly at the interests of companies, not necessarily countries. *Newsnight* also paid close attention to BAe's lobbying efforts with one report quoting former Foreign Secretary Robin Cook's assessment that 'BAe appears to have the key to the garden gate of Number 10 – what BAe wants is never denied.'[33]

Another way in which analysis programmes challenged the commercial threat angle was by turning it on its head. In effect, the threat was reframed as being potentially heightened rather than averted by the decision to terminate the investigation. On 1 February and 6 February 2007, *Channel 4 News* ran two reports that cast the threat to UK economic interests as a bi-product of a more general threat to the UK's international reputation. This was largely in response to condemnation of the SFO decision from business leaders such as Mark Moody-Stewart (head of Anglo American). As one MP remarked during a studio interview:

> I'm not pretending it's easy. There've been outspoken statements by some of the leading institutional investors in the UK. They have said they think that this investigation being stopped in this way will do huge damage to the City of London [...] The City of London is now fighting a battle with New York and other centres of finance throughout the world. Integrity, honesty is absolutely essential to winning that battle [...] We are an economy heavily dependent on finance more than ever before.[34]

More broadly, journalists on all programmes emphasised the damage to the UK's diplomatic standing with several references to the 'embarrassment' caused by the fallout from the controversy. But here again the threat to the UK's international reputation was framed in a relatively more critical fashion by analysis programmes. This was done by drawing attention to notions of double standards in government policy and rhetoric: 'Remember this John – "we have done more than any other country in the world to push anti-corruption efforts" – the words of the PM to you no less in January. Well he can't say that anymore'.[35]

The same journalist made repeated reference to the promotional anti-corruption DVD that the government had released around the same time that the decision was taken to stop the SFO investigation.[36] Whilst the UK government was accused of corruption by the OECD, 'diplomats travel the world with a tax payer funded DVD designed to persuade developing country leaders to crack down on bribery.'[37]

The wider consequences of the apparent double standards were implicit in reports that spoke of the 'snowball effect' on other countries and investigations around the world. In breaking with both OECD convention and its own stated ideals, it was suggested that the UK government had opened the Pandora's box of corruption. In one *Newsnight* interview, South African president Jacob Zuma – himself the subject of corruption allegations involving BAe arms sales – posed the question: 'Why should rulers be allowed to pick and choose on matters that relate to the application of the rule of law?'[38]

The official response to that question was that the decision to halt the SFO enquiry was taken in view of the unique nature of Saudi–UK relations. The threat posed by the on-going enquiry to those relations would impact not only on national security, but also regional security in the Middle East and by implication, the wider world. But again, this frame was constructed in various and contrasting ways. Reports on all programmes tended to highlight the 'special' nature of Saudi–UK relations and the significance of Saudi Arabia as 'an important ally in the fight against terrorism, a dominant oil producer and the biggest customer of the British defence industry.'[39] Reports on mainstream programmes tended to accept such maxims uncritically, and in particular, the official contention that Saudi Arabia had threatened to withdraw intelligence: 'If [the SFO] does re-open this case, Gordon Brown will have to weigh up whether the Saudis will see through their threat to stop sharing intelligence.'[40]

Newsnight, in particular, however, questioned the evidence behind the national security justification. The contrast between mainstream and analysis programmes on this point is exemplified in the following statements made by reporters for BBC's *Ten O'Clock News* and *Newsnight* editions: '[The threats] were explicit – stop the probe or trade will suffer and we'll stop co-operating on counter-terrorism.'[41] 'The intelligence services in the UK never had any intelligence that the Saudis were going to withdraw co-operation. Others are very sceptical about this.'[42]

However, on the previous night a different reporter on the *Ten O'Clock News* was more circumspect about the government's attempt to regain the media initiative: 'Dropping the investigation is an embarrassing climb down for the PM, also announced today coincidentally ahead of his trip to the Middle East – coincidence.'[43]

Even on the issue of national security then, mainstream television news scrutinised official positions, albeit marginally. That the framing gap here between bulletin and analysis programmes was at its widest nevertheless served to highlight the relative autonomy and antagonistic approach of *Channel 4 News* and *Newsnight* journalists. As well as questioning the basis of official proclamations on the threat to national security, these programmes went further and in effect inverted the national security threat angle. As one alternative source remarked: 'Of course national security is an issue but what could damage national security more than the message that Britain will give in to foreign threats?'[44]

In summary, the discursive frame of 'threats' was constructed around the sub themes of economy, reputation and national security. Each of these in turn was constructed in contrasting ways, at times lending weight to official definitions and at other times questioning and critiquing them. In each case analysis programmes exhibited a stronger adherence to the latter set of constructions as compared with the main bulletins. This gap was most acute when covering the issue of national security where prime time news journalists were more likely to accept this justification at face value. Nevertheless, even here question marks were raised in mainstream coverage and the failure to scrutinise official definitions of the threat did not amount to an active endorsement of government policy as legally or ethically justified.

MISSING DIMENSIONS

The Al Yamamah controversy was, in essence, a story that targeted the top of the British state-corporate establishment. Not only was it focused on alleged crimes of one of the UK's largest exporters, but it was equally if not more concerned with government collusion in those crimes. The very fact that the controversy recurred repeatedly on terrestrial television news provides base line evidence of pluralist openness. We have seen how top-level narratives were constructed around the background context of the story, the battle between campaigners and the government, and on occasion, even the apparent failure of accountability processes. But alternative frames in these contexts were overwhelmingly the preserve of *Newsnight* and *Channel 4 News*.

Coverage in the main bulletins on the other hand, exhibited a marked tendency to repeat official assertions without question and to construct reporting frames around them as implicit assumptions. The government's overt justification for terminating the SFO inquiry – the national security threat – leant itself to headline-friendly slogans such as 'blood on our streets' which were repeated largely without challenge. And with regard to the threat to jobs, reports in the main bulletins took for granted the equation between what's good for BAe and what's good for the UK economy.

Perhaps more seriously, accountability appraisals were notably absent from the main bulletins. This is not to suggest that reports were uncritical of government interference in investigative proceedings – far from it. But they were set against a discursive framework in which justice ultimately prevails. Crucially, such frames were adopted primarily in response to the High Court ruling in favour of campaigners, thus implicitly championing due process. The government and BAe had acted illegally but the judicial system had worked successfully to uncover it and uphold the charge of the relatively resource-poor plaintiff.

However, despite the distinction of analysis programmes in this framing, there was another aspect of accountability framing in which they were equally complicit in containment. This is evident when we consider the discrepancy in coverage levels between two key events: the High Court's initial unlawful ruling in favour of CAAT, and the subsequent House of Lords quashing of that verdict on appeal. The former coincided with a peak in coverage across all four channels analysed during research for this book. The quashing of the appeal, in contrast, did not make any of the news broadcasts.[45] Yet this event entirely absolved the government of any wrongdoing and left the spotlight of the story exclusively on BAe, paving the way for the plea bargain settlements. The focus of television news coverage up to this point had been almost exclusively on the government's role in suppressing the investigation into BAe, rather than the alleged crime itself. In view of this, we might have expected the Law Lords ruling to spark outrage that the government had not only behaved 'unlawfully', but that they had *gotten away with it*. Instead, the silence of television news seemed to suggest that the Law Lords ruling was treated as authoritative and definitive; that the government had not erred after all.

Another aspect of convergence between analysis and bulletin programmes was in the focus on background contexts in reports. Whilst this superficially appeared to promote understanding of the controversy's depth and complexity, it drew attention to the historical rather than *on-going* contexts. For instance, whilst *News at Ten* went as far as highlighting a 1989 National Audit Office report into allegations of 'slush funds' that was never published, it neglected to report the fact that Mensdorf de Peuilly was arrested in connection with BAe slush funds as recently as 2009.[46]

What was missing from the coverage as a whole was discussion of broader contexts beyond the framework of the Al Yamamah controversy itself. In-depth reports in particular could have drawn closer attention to the impact of UK–Saudi relations on the Israel–Palestine conflict, or the growth of religious extremism in the region and globally. Reports also neglected broader ethical concerns in relation to state sanctioned trade exports – in particular whether the sale of arms to regimes with extremely poor human rights records is consistent with espoused foreign policy values. And all but one edition of *Channel 4 News* failed to examine the links between Al Yamamah and the Export Credit Guarantee controversy, according to which the UK tax payer effectively insures arms manufacturers against non-payment by their international clients.

GOLIATH VICTORIOUS

When it came to reporting on BAe's eventual settlements with both the SFO and the US Department of Justice, there were a variety of ways in which television news across the board was complicit in the official strategy to bring closure to the story. For one thing, reporting on the settlements was relatively limited in terms of quantity. *Newsnight*'s report lasted 3.2 minutes in contrast to an average of 8.1 minutes for the five other reports it ran during the life of the story. Qualitatively speaking, there was a tendency to obscure the extent of the SFO's capitulation in the plea bargaining process. This was strikingly evident in light of a *Channel 4 News* edition in October 2009 which reported that 'attempts to strike a bargain between [SFO and BAe] broke down last night as the SFO asked the company to accept a fine of over a billion pounds'.[47] In exchange, BAe was offered a reduced charge, crucially avoiding acknowledgement of corruption or bribery. But by the time the parties had reached their settlement four months later, there was no mention of the fact that BAe had successfully bargained more than 97 per cent off the initial offer and still only accepted the reduced charge of 'accounting irregularities'. What's more, this settlement brought to a close all the remaining investigations that the SFO was conducting into BAe activities around the world, including the sale of a military air traffic control system to Tanzania, a country that does not have an air force.

Another way in which television news effectively endorsed closure was evident in their failure to scrutinise the US portion of the settlement. Although considerably larger than the SFO settlement, it was relatively small when judged against outcomes in comparable cases. As one edition of *Newsnight* noted in 2008: 'The German engineering giant Siemens was fined 800 million dollars in the US after admitting to its financial scandal. If BAe is found guilty the penalty is likely to be far higher. It's seen as a critical case for cleaning up international trade.'[48]

In the event, BAe was forced to admit to charges of deliberately obstructing the Department's investigations. Although considerably short of a corruption charge, it is nevertheless more serious than the SFO charge of accounting regularities. But whilst the latter charge was mentioned repeatedly in television news reports, the more serious plea was relatively absent.

Analysis news reports did highlight the strategic implications of the reduced charge for BAe's expansion in the US, noting that the avoidance of 'the c-word' meant that they could continue to bid for lucrative contracts stateside. But in tandem with main bulletins, analysis programmes were on the whole equivocal as to whether the actual settlement was good or bad for the company. Typical of the response was a description of the outcome by one correspondent as 'an expensive way to wipe the slate clean'.[49]

Framing the outcome as a defeat for BAe – or at least a partial one – implicitly suggested that both the SFO and Department of Justice deliberations were not compromised by improper influence or interference. This to some extent pre-empted the need to probe the deeper and more difficult questions that were very much the focus of earlier coverage. Documents disclosed during the High Court proceedings had already raised question marks over the SFO's independence. But news programmes had also featured testimonies that suggested the US Department of Justice might equally be vulnerable to executive pressure. For instance, as well as drawing attention to the threatening influence of BAe's US competitors, earlier reports also highlighted the strategic importance of BAe to the US military: 'If BAe Systems North America was in some way excluded from federal contracting it would immediately create problems for the US military and the intelligence community. [BAe] is engaged in some of the most secret programmes of the intelligence community, programmes the government doesn't even acknowledge exist.'[50]

The US justice department was also constrained by the reluctance of the White House 'to antagonise their friends the Saudis'.[51] As one source put it: 'The Department of Justice now has to investigate a deal between a company that makes equipment crucial to American troop safety in Iraq and one of the President's best friends.'[52]

Indeed, throughout the coverage, improper influence had been framed in relation to the apparent capture of the government by BAe lobbyists, and the subsequent influence of government over the legal and investigative branches of state. So long as these questions were raised, they served to demonstrate the media's own independence from that flow of influence. Their neglect in the final analysis forces us therefore to consider the alternative: that the news media ultimately failed in their fourth estate obligations. Part of the problem was that journalists did not adequately drill down in to the details of the deals which were announced simultaneously late on a Friday afternoon. By the return of regular scheduled news programmes on the following Monday the announcement was already old news and the media momentum had been largely lost.

A final way in which reports on the settlements did little to expose accountability limitations was evident in their tendency to adopt the narrative of 'change'. This was achieved by giving near exclusive voice to the view that BAe is, today, 'a very different beast', with sources reiterating the dictum: 'You can be really confident we're a changed company. We've changed our board. We've changed all of the policies of the company.'[53]

It is perhaps significant that the only appearance of a BAe representative throughout the life of the controversy occurred at this point with the company's chairman granting the BBC an extended interview. But in contrast to previous recorded interviews with elite sources, this statement was neither probed nor challenged in the report. We were left wondering what the assumed change amounted to, especially in respect of policy. Had BAe stopped making payments to third parties? Were they still selling military systems to countries that didn't need them 'at a price they couldn't afford'?[54] Such changes appeared to be some way off the company's stated 'responsible trading principles':

- We understand and support our customers' national security and other requirements;
- We assess carefully our products and services with the objective that neither BAe Systems nor our customers are exposed to significant reputational risk;
- We work to BAe Systems' values in all that we do; and
- We are as open as practicable about the nature of our business.[55]

As well as neglecting to scrutinise the outcome of the case, there was little questioning of the plea bargaining process that led up to the settlements. With the exception of one *Channel 4 News* report,[56] the legitimacy and transparency of that process went unchallenged, despite the criminal nature of the charges. Nor did any programme point out that the government was not subject to accountability proceedings. This was in marked contrast to earlier reports, which affirmed that the alleged illegal payments were made in the full knowledge of the Ministry of Defence,[57] that BAe was a mere contractor to an agreement between the Saudi and UK governments,[58] and in essence no more than 'alleged co-conspirators'.[59] One earlier report had gone as far as to suggest that from a policy perspective, BAe and the government were virtually indivisible:

> Any prosecution would also likely have failed once it became clear the government was part of any financial arrangement. The British government knew all the time what was going on. They were complicit. Indeed in this whole affair it's hard to see the difference between BAe and Downing Street.[60]

The same journalists that had amplified the concerns and outrage of campaigners over the decision to halt the inquiry, offered a much more muted account of their views in relation to the settlements. The difference between the media's response to the two events was as stark as that between journalist and campaigner rhetoric regarding the settlements. For the latter, there was no doubt as to who had ultimately won the legal battle. According to Paul Ingram, consultant at the strategic think tank Basic, 'there was no damage. I mean those fines were paltry to be frank'.

Despite expectations of considerably higher fines espoused in earlier news reports, broadcast journalists reflected on the outcome in much more qualified overtones, as illustrated in the comments of one BBC news reporter:

> I think it was probably better for BAe than having to go through criminal prosecution – it was certainly better for them than that, because that would have been appalling in publicity terms to be in the dock and they avoided being in the dock. But they didn't get a clean bill of health and there were probably question marks as well about what really happened.

Regardless of whether the fines represented by themselves a substantial sum, they were by any standard a small price when measured against the rewards of the settlements. BAe had succeeded in getting multiple investigations quashed on both sides of the Atlantic; avoided resignations and the central charge of bribery and corruption; secured the renewal of the Al Yamamah contract; and perhaps most significantly, the company was freed to expand and bid for lucrative new contracts in the US.

In summary, we have seen that coverage of the Al Yamamah controversy, despite the overall appearance of contestability, was limited in three key respects. Firstly, although it surfaced periodically across television news over the course of five years, the extent of coverage is best described as partial. This was reflected in the tendency of all news programmes to bill the story as 'other news' rather than as a main headline, and the tendency for coverage to be concentrated on the late evening and news analysis broadcasts. Secondly, critical analysis on key issues such as the threat to national security and accountability measures were largely the preserve of outlets on the minority audience channels, and on the whole, these programmes covered the controversy in considerably greater depth and breadth than their mainstream counterparts. Finally, there was wholesale failure to adequately scrutinise official source definitions relating to the closure of all investigations in 2010, the legitimacy or effectiveness of the plea bargaining process, and the stark lack of government accountability.

3
Framing Foundations

NEWS VALUES

Having examined the scope and limits of the coverage, we now turn our attention to the forces which shaped and determined them. A starting point in respect of the scope is to focus on news values. In particular, there were several aspects of the story which struck a chord with journalists and editors alike. First, the story inherently lent itself to multiple framing angles as already observed. This enabled different journalists with various persuasions, and different editors with distinct perspectives of their audience interests, to cover the story in a variety of ways. Kaye Stearman, press officer for CAAT, summarised the story's adaptability to different news frames: 'You've got the British political angle, you've got the Saudi angle, you've got the geopolitical angle, you've got the financial angle [...] it's a subject of continuing fascination.'

As well as enabling different treatments of the story, multiple angles also added up to a powerful element of mystique and gravitas. As a senior BBC news reporter reflected: 'You had government, you had big business and big bucks, and you had judicial involvement too. And you also had a certain level of glamour and intrigue to do with the countries that were involved which created an element of spice.'

The same respondent suggested that this element of spice was compounded by the dramatic qualities of the narrative subjects. Journalists talked of the 'colourful' language used by sources on all sides of the debate, but particularly those attacking the government and BAe:

I remember the Lib Dems in particular, no surprise, but their criticism was very colourful. They may sort of say 'this was nothing short of a scandalous outrage'. The language was very, very strong [...] there were essentially a lot of people who were very, very vociferous in their criticism.

The core thrust of the story as it evolved also appealed strongly to post-Watergate news values. This is because it was chiefly concerned not with the original sin (BAe making corrupt payments to secure arms deals) but with the decision to terminate the SFO inquiry and the Prime Minister's alleged involvement with that decision. David Cohen, feature writer for the *London Evening Standard,* explained why a controversy surrounding the Prime Minister is the ultimate scandal: 'It's the ultimate in journalism to be able to bring down a Prime Minister and most leaders are threatened not by something they did wrong but by the cover-up. Almost always it's the cover-up. That's what got Nixon.'

But journalists did not just have eyes on the prize as far as their professional credibility was concerned. At least as much of a genuine concern were the public interest implications of the story. In particular, the controversy prompted key questions concerning the health of the economy, national security and democracy, as summarised by one senior BBC reporter:

> It was an issue of importance for all sorts of different reasons because of our national security given our relationship with Saudi Arabia, huge cash interests for a very large British business [...] It also related back to an issue that comes up time and again in Westminster which is the role of the government's law officers and whether they can be a judge and advisor at the same time and you see again and again that comes up as a story whether over this or whether over the legal advice for the war in Iraq – the position of the Attorney General and the foreign office to be an independent legal voice but yet part of the government machinery is an interesting clash.

But above all, the story provoked genuine journalist outrage due to the sheer boldness of the government's apparent obstruction of due process on behalf of suspect interests. It was the decision to terminate the inquiry that 'got a lot of people's backs up' and transformed the story from a *Guardian* newspaper exclusive, to a headline that spanned across the political spectrum of the broadsheet press. As Symon Hill, a radical peace activist and former press officer for CAAT, observed:

> It just had dodgyness written all over it. It was the government intervening in a criminal investigation for what looks like a political or commercial reason so even media that was sympathetic

to the government or media that thought that was justified can still see it was a big news story in itself.

The political climate at the time of the SFO decision was not an insignificant backdrop to the outrage it provoked. Tony Blair was nearing the end of his premiership and the Labour government was in the twilight of a decade in office. 'Dodgy dossiers' and 'New Labour spin' were media catchphrases closely associated with Blair's style of leadership and fresh from the failure to uncover weapons of mass destruction in Iraq, the mainstream media were on the front foot in their scrutiny of government decisions. According to another respondent active in the campaign against BAe: 'The media don't necessarily like being taken for granted by the powerful. Tony Blair was just so blasé with what he did it was stupid.'

Campaigners at the time were also well placed to exploit this mood in the mainstream media. As well as having a body of media contacts built up over 30 years of direct action against the arms trade, CAAT had developed a strong reputation for authenticity and expertise despite being a small and under resourced NGO. As Kaye Stearman remarked: 'BAe has been a focus for a long time for us so we are not seen as people who are jumping on a bandwagon to be fashionable. Even if people think we might be misguided they see us as being sincere and well researched.'

All campaigners interviewed for this book reflected on the controversy as being exemplary of the cracks in the system that enable radical activists to exploit the mainstream media for resistance effects. What seems certain is that the Al Yamamah controversy – at least in the period between the decision to halt the SFO inquiry and the High Court ruling against it – was ripe for mainstream media attention in its possession of a rich tableaux of newsworthy criteria. These appealed equally to both commercial and public service concerns, to self-identified 'campaigning' journalists as well as reporters who consider themselves 'detached impartial observers'. As well as raising serious political issues seen as tantamount to public sphere concerns, the controversy embodied the drama, intrigue and gravitas seen as necessary to engage audiences in that debate. Notably, it conformed to a narrative of challenging the powerful that resonated strongly with the values of adversarial journalism. For investigative reporters and their editors, the story's promotion to mainstream status provided a much needed return on a long running investment. The suspicion and cynicism with which journalists commonly viewed Tony Blair's style of leadership at the time further opened the arms of the mainstream media to the cause and concerns of alternative sources.

JOURNALIST AUTONOMY

Before going on to assess the role of elite dissent in generating and sustaining media interest, it is worth considering some of the underlying factors that enabled what looked like a healthy degree of journalist autonomy. For one thing, in spite of a long term decline in investigative reporting, key vehicles for it remain within 'serious' news outlets, for whom industry recognition and perceived credibility are intrinsically valued assets. This is particularly the case within public service broadcasting as a senior BBC news executive indicated:

> These things are about the vehicles quite often. So there is still a *Panorama* which is a vehicle for investigative reporting, *Newsnight* is a vehicle for investigative reporting, the *Today* programme is a vehicle for investigative reporting. There's a lot of radio current affairs – *The Report*, *Five on Four* – all vehicles for investigative reporting and I don't think there's been any diminution of the vehicles – certainly not on the BBC for investigative reporting [...] and that journalism that they do is leveraged out across all outlets.

The important point here is that so long as these vehicles are retained, their output can be 'leveraged' into more mainstream outlets both within the BBC's stable of programmes and more widely across the news media. Indeed, the Al Yamamah case was arguably demonstrative of how investigative journalism in one outlet can fuel media interest more broadly in spite of restrictions associated with exclusivity (as will be discussed further in Chapter 7). The *Guardian*'s repository of investigative scoops also provided an easy databank for mainstream outlets to draw on once the confluence of major story criteria began to surface. Television news outlets at times made explicit reference to revelations in the *Guardian* and virtually always relied on information that was unearthed through the work of their investigative reporters. In addition, Symon Hill pointed out that the story's spread owed at least something to the particular structural dynamics of the UK's broadsheet market:

> Because the *Telegraph*, despite being a right-wing paper, gives its journalists relative freedom about what to report on and how

to report on it [...] it meant we got quite a lot of favourable coverage from them. Had a *Guardian* journalist been in favour of the arms trade, the *Guardian* would never have given them as much freedom to write like that [...] Also people like me who are on the radical left would tend to slag off the *Telegraph* or *The Times* and the *FT* and so on and that's understandable. But actually yes they're interested in pushing an agenda but they're also interested in selling papers.

The suggestion here is that although the majority of broadsheets are aligned with conservative values and Conservative politicians, they are sensitive to a liberal-minded readership. Equally, and in contrast to the tabloid market, broad representation is seen as essential to maximising both readership and credibility. Commentaries and editorials often espouse a variety of positions and there may be a marked distinction between the political leaning of the front and middle pages.

Journalist autonomy therefore varies not just between, but also within, particular outlets. Within any given paper, feature writers, columnists and specialist correspondents are paid more, tied less to the rubric of the daily news cycle and afforded significantly greater editorial freedom than reporters. Within broadcasting, it is current affairs journalists that receive the bulk of news resources in terms of time and investment in investigative reporting. Even in the midst of a 'climate of caution' within BBC journalism, of which more will be discussed below, both journalists and executives emphasised autonomy in story selection. According to a senior BBC news reporter: 'I've never been in the situation ever and I don't think I know any colleagues – I'm sure I don't know any colleagues – who have been told, asked or advised not to do a story because an issue is hot.'

What seems clear is that without significant journalist autonomy and the remnants of an investigative journalism sector, however diminished in size and scope, the Al Yamamah controversy would not have gained the media traction it did regardless of its newsworthy credentials.

INDEXING

If a degree of journalist autonomy was essential to the duration and scope of coverage, so were the various splits within establishment ranks most notably within Westminster, big business and the legal profession. The breadth and significance of elite dissent were readily acknowledged by campaigners, as one campaigner observed:

> I think in terms of our general campaign it was very helpful that we could publicise businesses that have said this harms British business, that we could publicise the number of MPs that signed our early day motion including six Tories – Tories don't sign Campaign Against the Arms Trade motions – that the Foreign Affairs Select Committee had said it had harmed Britain's image abroad, that we had people opposing it who were not the usual peace activists, who were not the usual lefties [...] That really helped.

The decision to halt the SFO inquiry clearly sparked outrage amongst various groups and individuals that can by any measure be characterised as elite. Within Westminster, dissent emanated from a range of outspoken backbench MPs but also the Liberal Democrat party as a whole. Key figures from the party both capitalised on and fanned the flames of media interest by making regular television appearances when their political rivals from both sides were noticeably absent. As one BBC reporter put it, 'of course the Lib Dems being behind it made a big difference [...] they made it into a political story.'

Outside of Westminster, business leaders – notably Sir Mark Moody-Stewart (Chairman of Anglo American) – publicly expressed their opposition to the SFO decision citing the purported threat it posed to the UK's international trade reputation. On the face of it, such signs of a fractured establishment would appear to support a case for indexing theory which posits that levels of contestability in the media are by and large set by those of elite dissent (see Chapter 1). However, such a finding should be treated with caution since much of the elite dissent could be characterised as relatively marginal and there remained, to some degree, a unified 'club at the top'. Certainly the existence of an effective bi-partisan consensus on the issue between the two major parties reflected the centralised power which the Al Yamamah controversy exposed. More than simply implicating successive Conservative and Labour governments in alleged collusion with BAe's corrupt practices, the controversy pivoted around a super tier of elite influence occupied by the Prime Minister, Defence ministers and the board of BAe. For a long time BAe staff held a permanent and official presence within the Ministry of Defence (MOD) through the Defence Export Services

Organisation – a unit within the MOD lobbying on behalf of British arms manufacturers. The department was a relic of BAe's former status as a state owned company and officially transferred to the UK Trade and Industry department in 2008. But there remains a stark level of overlap between BAe and MOD officials, as indicated by a senior government press officer: 'If you go to the Ministry of Defence you will see so many people who work for BAe – they have passes for the Ministry of Defence. They're almost interchangeable.'

Campaigners maintained that BAe's influence was one way: 'It's not that BAe is a department of the Ministry of Defence, it's that the Ministry of Defence is a department of BAe.' This was attributed partly to a prevailing culture within the MOD, and partly to a special relationship between Tony Blair and the BAe board, as Kaye Stearman observed:

> There was far more closeness between BAe and Number 10 then there was between Number 10 and the SFO [...] There was a club at the top – Mike Turner, Dick Olver, Tony Blair, the other ministers who took that sort of approach – Jack Straw and so on. Robert Wardle [SFO director] was certainly not in that club [...] I think he made the wrong decision but he resisted it for as long as he could.

The important point about a 'club at the top' is that it does not need to encompass a unified conspiratorial group of elites. All it needs to be effective in exercising its will is the membership of key decision makers. According to Symon Hill: 'The SFO may have been unhappy with it but like most people when push comes to shove they shrug their shoulders and accept what the powerful decide. It sort of falls into place quite easily.'

From this perspective, political dissent within Westminster may be considered marginal to the locus of decision-making power. This is not to dismiss the significance that it had in generating and sustaining media interest in the story. But it does expose a weakness in the theory of indexing which is that few if any elite decisions fail to attract dissent from other elites, particularly if the frame of reference is set broadly enough to include backbench MPs, professionals, experts, Trade Union leaders, or even NGO activists. The list is inexhaustible and any circle around an elite stratum is almost certainly arbitrary. What matters most in any given context is not so much elite status as decision making power. In this case power was concentrated in the hands of a super elite that excluded even key members of the cabinet. It's perhaps little wonder that the SFO decision was announced when Hilary Benn was on official business in Southeast Asia. According to sources, he heard about it for the first time 'on the news'.

Another factor that would appear to undermine indexing theory was the delayed reaction of elite dissenters who surfaced predominantly in response to burgeoning media interest, rather than the other way round. This pattern is less clear, however, when we consider the role of lawyers who were instrumental in providing journalists with the courtroom drama they needed. Had it not been for the offer of *pro bono* legal work, campaigners would never have been able to launch their case against the government and the story would plainly have 'lost its legs'. As it happened, campaigners received a clamour of offers from law firms immediately following the SFO announcement. According to Symon Hill, 'that's partly how we knew how big it was'.

This statement is revealing. It suggests that it was lawyers, at least in tandem with the media, who determined the 'size' of the issue in publicity terms. But even if lawyers were as quick on the case as journalists, they were conscious from the outset of the advantages presented by a high profile case. A solicitor acting on behalf of campaigners highlighted the importance of a broad spectrum of media interest:

> I think it helps firstly that it was such a high profile case – I think the *Guardian* had been campaigning on the BAe corruption stuff for years but it wasn't confined to the left-wing media it was right across the media and there was a fairly shared – animosity is the wrong word – but a fairly shared sense that what BAe had generally been doing over the years was wrong from all angles of the media and that sort of cross – not party political – but political spectrum of media always helps a case. It makes the judges feel I think on much firmer ground where there's general outrage about something as opposed to outrage from one quarter, be it the right or left of the media. So I think as a starting point that put us in pretty good stead in running the case.

As well as being good for the case, media profile was beneficial to individual lawyers, as Symon Hill observed:

> For particularly the more junior lawyers involved it was good for their careers. It was a more high profile case than they'd usually be

involved in. It was good for their reputations and for their image and so on. They were seen as lawyers standing up for human rights, siding with the underdog and I didn't realise straight away how interested the legal profession generally were in our case [...] for young left-wing lawyers it was clearly one of the main cases they'd been following and they were really impressed by it. I was quite taken aback – I wasn't used to impressing lawyers.

This is not to suggest that lawyers weren't motivated in the main by what they perceived, according to Kaye Stearman, 'as an interference with the due process of law'. But it does indicate the difficulties in disentangling media action and reaction, which is essential to the indexing thesis. Even if the response of lawyers preceded that of journalists, it clearly rested in part on a foreshadowing of intense and broad media coverage. In other words, journalists did not simply provide a mouthpiece for dissenting lawyers and their campaigning clients. The potential scope of their interest itself provided an important vehicle for the legal campaign. In this case the relationship between the two – and between journalists and elite dissenters across the board – may be best described as mutually supportive.

There is one last consideration to address in determining how far the case study supports or undermines indexing theory. A difficulty arises when we distinguish between elite dissent on and off the record. As illustrated above, the former might be characterised as predominantly reactive, surfacing in response to journalist outrage, or at least in conjunction with it. Off record dissent, however, may have played a more proactive role in generating media interest. Whilst dissent within parliament was vociferous, there were significant splits behind the scenes within the executive, perhaps most notably within the cabinet itself. As Kaye Stearman observed: 'One thing I would say about the December 2006 announcement is that of course not all ministers were happy with that. It was pretty much an open secret that Hilary Benn wasn't happy with it and he was supposed to be the government's anti-corruption champion.'

Beyond the cabinet, disclosure documents that emerged during the High Court proceedings detailed key communiqués in the run up to the inquiry termination and suggested that the Prime Minister, Attorney General and SFO director were by no means singing from the same hymn sheet. Arguably the strongest and most threatening dissent within the state stemmed from the SFO itself. According to campaigners their press office, following the announcement of termination, was left with one representative whilst the remaining staff went to the pub 'in disgust'. One leading SFO investigator was even spotted at a benefit event organised by campaigners to help raise funds for the legal challenge.

Whilst it seems probable that such murmurings played a part in fuelling journalist interest in the case, it is difficult to substantiate. More convincing evidence points to the role of BAe's competitors in stoking the fires of journalist outrage. Indeed, the original impetus for the first investigations into BAe's arms dealings with Saudi Arabia, likely stemmed not from campaigners but from the company's competitors. Paul Lashmar was an investigative journalist working at the *Observer* newspaper and was one of the first journalists to look into the case, along with David Leigh. But their curiosity was prompted from above rather than below:

> Essentially Leigh and I were asked by senior management to investigate Al Yamamah but the request had come through the channels of Tiny Rowland who had an interest in Dassault. Dassault was a rival to BAe and David and I decided this would put us in an impossible position – a clear conflict of interests. So we refused and it was part of a huge internal battle over Tiny. David and then I walked. Both of us then took up Al Yamamah related investigations in different ways. David Leigh has persisted over 20 years and really made more contribution to what was going on than any other journalist or arguably person.

Indeed, BAe's foreign competitors were believed by some to have continued to fan the flames of the controversy, even after the SFO termination. Their lobbying efforts might have played a part in bringing the case to the attention of the OECD and the US Department of Justice. Certainly interventions and announcements by those institutions coincided with spikes in media coverage and added further weight to the cause of campaigners. However, experts interviewed for this book expressed some doubt over whether BAe's competitors would ultimately want to draw too much attention to corrupt practices which were considered to be endemic to the international arms trade as a whole. As one senior UK civil servant put it: 'A lot of people say, well everyone does it – we have to do it in order to get contracts. It's very messy.'

HAPPY ACCIDENTS

Other factors extraneous to journalist autonomy, news values and elite dissent also helped ripen the ground for contestability in the coverage. These included apparent blunders in the government and BAe's media strategies. Ironically, much of the build-up to the peak of media interest may have been stirred by BAe themselves. In an attempt to aid their lobbying efforts at getting the investigation quashed in 2006, the company released press notices warning that the investigation had put the Al Yamamah deal in jeopardy. These followed and drew on a study jointly commissioned with the Saudi government into the deal's economic impact.

As well as actively seeking media interest in the case prior to the termination decision, BAe may have also alienated sympathetic voices in outlets such as the *Daily Telegraph* and the *Financial Times* through exaggeration of the threat posed to British jobs. As Symon Hill observed: 'The *FT* is not the sort of paper that somebody with my political opinions might necessarily identify with, but they do pride themselves on the accuracy of their reporting and if fifty thousand jobs are not dependent on it they won't say that they are.'

Mistakes were also made by the government in respect of timing. The announcement of the termination was made late afternoon on the day Parliament went in to recess. Whether or not this was intended to prevent Parliamentary debate over the issue is a moot point. It certainly looked that way to the media. According to one government press officer, late afternoon announcements are always foolhardy: 'If you put anything out after lunchtime on any day you might as well just put something on your website saying we're trying to hide this. Because there's no point. People are not stupid.'

Another aspect of the timing was that it was announced during the pre-Christmas period, a notorious 'dry' patch in the news diary. It was not, to adapt a well-worn phrase, a good time to bury bad news. More significantly perhaps, the government and the Prime Minister were simply unprepared for the extent of backlash. As one press strategist put it,

> To be honest if I was advising Tony Blair I wouldn't say 'get the Attorney General to stand up in the Commons and just announce it's being dropped because of national security'. I'd try and get the SFO to say they had investigated and there wasn't enough evidence; I'd do another announcement about something big on the same day to try and cover it up and all the rest of it. I just think

Tony Blair was by that point too blasé to do a decent cover-up if I can put it as crudely as that.

Whether the result of mistakes, misfortune or over confidence, these factors were undoubtedly important in amplifying the media's response to the termination of the inquiry. In any case, the media's response to a given event may be attributable in part to entirely random factors. In the words of one respondent, 'sometimes it's just a bit unpredictable'. But when we turn our attention to the forces that shaped containment in the coverage, official and BAe source strategies look rather more effective. Whatever damage may have been done by media blunders they did not eclipse what proved to be, in the end, a successful management of the scandal.

MAGIC NUMBERS

Perhaps most significantly, official and BAe sources succeeded in amplifying the 'threat' in the various discursive contexts that it was framed. Much of this success seemed to come down to playing with numbers, particularly with regard to the jobs threat, as Symon Hill explained:

[The Saudis and BAe] jointly commissioned a report which said that the Saudi's latest order might create eleven thousand jobs across the whole of Europe. BAe then took the line officially – when they were lobbying for the investigation to be dropped – of saying that it would create sixteen thousand jobs in Britain which was ludicrous [...] Then the *Daily Mail* starting saying fifty thousand [...] and then you were wondering – are they just increasing it themselves, are they actually believing this and getting it wrong or is BAe being very clever? You don't really know. And then there was one claim of a hundred thousand in the *Independent*, of all things, which surprised me. But there's only sixty-five thousand people working in arms trade dependent jobs in the whole of the UK. These were the jobs that would supposedly be created by the deal but then Simon Heffer in the *Telegraph* said that fifty thousand jobs would be lost if the deal didn't go ahead. And of course once the investigation was dropped and the deal was signed then BAe admitted most of the jobs the deal created wouldn't even be based in the UK anyway and it's doubtful if it's creating as many as a thousand jobs in Britain.

With regard to the plea bargain settlements, the official announcement was clearly designed to amplify the extent of the penalty imposed, packaged as it was to include both the SFO and Department of Justice fines. As another campaigner explained:

> The fact that they managed to announce it together and that the SFO and [US Department of Justice] agreed to that and that was no doubt part of the agreement – I mean that just showed how much BAe got their own way really, because it allowed them to present it as one big thing. Even now I'll say to people 'BAe paid 30 million to the SFO' and they say 'oh no wasn't it 280 million? Oh no that's the American bit as well'. People misremember it. They think they paid more than they did. Yes BAe held up its hands and said it had done wrong. But it did it all in one day, in one press release, one Friday afternoon.

The packaging of numbers is a common strategic media response to bad stories. According to a senior government press officer:

> When you've got a really big problem and you're throwing a few bits and pieces at it that don't really amount to much the classic thing is to put it up together as this big package and unveil a package of measures and try and make it seem a lot more substantial and you know, six million funding for this when really it's not really going into anything. Yes that happens an awful lot.

In the jobs threat context, the playing up of numbers was not always a formal or overt strategy on the part of BAe or the government which made it harder to combat from an alternative source perspective. According to Kaye Stearman:

> This strategy of concentrating on jobs – because that's what people are worried about, that's what matters to people – was a difficult one and what made it mostly difficult was this distinction between what the BAe press office officially said and what a lot of their friends in the media were saying [...] There's what they'd say and then there's what they'd be happy for other people to say which was very difficult because it was hard to point the finger at BAe for being untruthful because it wasn't them – it was Simon Heffer or it was Richard Littlejohn, or whoever. You didn't know where things were coming from. It was a sort of defence against the dark arts.

From the government's perspective, the jobs threat was a difficult but important horn to blow: important because it was perceived to be 'what people are worried about'; difficult because it was unlawful as a justification for terminating the inquiry. Tony Blair's handling of this conflict was seen by one BBC reporter as exemplary of his media management skill:

> There was a classic Tony Blair quote which stuck with me. He said 'this decision is nothing whatsoever to do with the thousands upon thousands of jobs at risk' in a classic Blairite 'I'll remind you exactly what this is about whilst saying something else entirely different' [...] It's always been in my head when people say 'why was Blair good at what he did?' – I often use that as an example.

As already demonstrated, the jobs frame did not succeed in quelling the tide of questions in the media concerning the legality and ethics of the government's actions. It may however have played a part in softening the ground for acceptance of the plea bargain settlements. The strategy certainly ensured that the threat to British jobs posed by the SFO investigation was accepted by most television journalists as a given. Even if it was not the primary focus of reports, its basis was rarely if ever questioned.

SILENCE

As well as amplifying the threat in the context of jobs, official sources appeared to be employing a media strategy of silence. This was perhaps most notable in the absence of official representatives from live television interviews. Edited clips of official sources in news reports taken from public appearances or pre-recorded interviews often provide an opportunity for officials to state their case unchallenged, even if it is questioned subsequently by the reporter. A live studio interview, however, enables the news anchor to probe and challenge the official script so as to expose weaknesses or contradictions in the arguments presented. Lead presenters on both *Channel 4 News* and *Newsnight* have developed a notorious reputation for aggressive questioning of elites along these lines and they persistently remarked on the unwillingness of the Attorney General or other senior sources to appear. This is indicative of an official media strategy aimed at containment and it may well have been crucial in keeping the story away from lead headlines.

Complementary to this approach was an attempt to frame the controversy as relating primarily to events in the past, absolving the need for officials to comment on or accept liability for the actions of their predecessors. In the words of a senior political reporter at BBC's Millbank: 'One kind of big line of defence was to say "well look it was absolutely nothing to do with us, we weren't here, not us Guv, leave it, none of our business, we don't know anything".'

This response seemed to be supported by a covert campaign to amplify the historical context of the story, similar to that employed in the jobs threat strategy. According to Symon Hill,

> Mensdorf de Peuilly was charged in December 2009 and yet Dick Olver [Chairman of BAe] even now will talk about things in the past. You had columnists saying 'oh, why should we worry about what happened 30 years ago?' or whatever. And again it wasn't that BAe were claiming that it was all in the 80s but they talked about it in the past, the columnists said it was all in the 80s and it was about creating this general atmosphere.

As in the case of jobs, it is not clear whether or not BAe actively engaged in a misinformation campaign or whether factual errors in the media were primarily the work of sympathetic journalists, mistakes, exaggerations or the news rumour mill. This particular case does however highlight that broader contexts and background do not always work in favour of presenting a more balanced, accurate or contestable picture of events. Even within two-minute reports on mainstream bulletins, reporters regularly paid attention to the historical background of the case. The above quotation suggests that this may have hindered rather than aided the voice of campaigners.

The strategy of silence was also manifest in 'passing the buck' responses, as one BBC reporter described: 'They would say and they did say at the time this is the SFO's decision, nothing to do with us. We've been quite clear all along, it's their call.'

The SFO for their part insisted that the decision was made solely on the basis of advice from the security services concerning the alleged Saudi threat to withdraw intelligence co-operation. No evidence was, or perhaps could have been, provided for this. True or not though, the security services represented a last line of defence for official sources. Unlike the Prime Minister, Attorney General or SFO Director, they could not be questioned as to the basis of their allegations.

As media coverage intensified, official sources increasingly adopted the national security threat angle over that of jobs. This was partly because of the legal implications as already mentioned. But also partly, no doubt, because recourse to national security considerations absolves the need for officials to evidentially justify decisions. It equally resonated with the wider terrorism discourse in the media. Not surprisingly, the language intensified as the controversy deepened, from 'strategic threat' to 'blood on our streets'.

CLOSURE

Again, however, it is difficult to ascertain what if any beneficial impact this had on the government and BAe's case given the scrutiny it gave rise to, at least in the analysis programmes. Much clearer in this respect was a fourth and final apparent strategy employed by official sources – that of accepting a measure of culpability. In the event, this amounted in practice to BAe's admission to 'corporate misdemeanours' in relation to the SFO inquiry, and 'obstructing investigation' by the US Department of Justice. But as already mentioned, official sources clearly sought to amplify the penalties imposed on BAe as a means of avoiding accusations of a whitewash and deterring on-going scrutiny. As Kaye Stearman observed:

> I think BAe would have liked it to be presented as a defeat for BAe in some ways in that they had held up their hands and could now be seen as progressive [...] I think it would have made a big difference if the media had presented it as a success for BAe – that they'd got away with it.

The framing of the settlements also demonstrated the apparent efficacy of due process and enabled a line to be drawn between BAe's past and present. Crucially, it suggested the system *en masse* had worked: BAe had done wrong, the media had exposed it, the judicial system imposed an appropriate penalty and the company had reformed its practices as a result.

This 'hands up' approach represents a culmination of an official source strategy that evolved in response to fluctuating and on-going scrutiny in the media and law and order institutions. Figure 3.1 depicts this progression which begins with suppression of information, represented by the decision to terminate the original SFO investigation. This was followed by a strategy of silence – avoiding live television appearances, framing the problem as historical, and passing the buck of decision responsibility. As the controversy wore on, officials increasingly adopted a counter information campaign, here represented by the threat amplification in respect of first jobs, and then national security. Finally, the strategy focused on a 'hands up' approach in which emphasis was placed on wiping the slate clean following a just and substantial penalty.

Figure 3.1   A progression of official source response to media 'crisis'

In practice, media management strategies did not perfectly obey such a linear function. For instance, the counter information campaign arguably began with BAe's lobbying activities prior to the decision to terminate the inquiry. Whether or not this was a strategic error as discussed earlier, the model is instructive in depicting the changing nature of official source responses to an on-going and developing scandal.

NEWS VALUES REVISITED

To understand why official sources ultimately succeeded in drawing a line on the controversy, it is necessary to examine what happened to media coverage in the aftermath of its zenith. This occurred around the High Court's ruling against the government in April 2007. Coverage resurfaced intermittently in the ensuing 18 months, primarily in response to moves by the OECD, Department of Justice and the SFO. But it never regained the momentum it had during the build-up to the High Court's decision. Crucially, the Law Lords repeal of that decision in the summer of 2007 attracted no coverage at all from any of ITN or BBC's television outlets. Respondents were unanimous in their assessment of the un-newsworthiness of this event. Not only did it fail to conform to the David and Goliath narrative that spurred coverage before and around the High Court judgement, but it actively contradicted that narrative. Furthermore, as a solicitor involved in the case pointed out, the media fuel of disclosure documents had largely run dry by the time the case reached the Law Lords:

I think it was just a sublimely good judgement – the High Court one – and there was so much interesting information that came out that when it came to the much drier legal arguments in the House of Lords [...] people lost interest. All the juicy bits had come out.

Journalists may also have lacked the motivation to cover an event that cast doubt on their own earlier aspersions and predictions. With regard to the muted coverage of the plea bargain settlements, the level of fines announced was considerably below forecasts made by some journalists during the build-up to the announcement. According to Symon Hill: 'The journalists who six months before were saying "oh, BAe will have to pay out 700 million pounds or a billion pounds" were wrong and there's an element to which they don't want to necessarily draw attention to their inaccurate predictions.'

By emphasising BAe's culpability and punishment, the news coverage suggested that along with lawyers, investigators, and campaigners, journalists had at least played their part in 'putting things right'.

ALL IN A HEADLINE

The combined package of fines provided headline material that inflated their measure of justice, playing into the hands of official source strategies. According to a senior BBC reporter:

Journalists are instinctively quite gung-ho and the traditional measure of a good story is how you write the top line. If your top line is 'the government is today consulting on a new way of ...' that is less interesting in a traditional journalistic sense than, say, 'council tenants could lose their houses'.

Others argued that the event did not lend itself to any dramatic top line and that this played a part in subduing the coverage. As Hill observed:

If BAe had to pay out more it would have been a bigger storm and something where nobody clearly wins or it's not clear who wins or nobody claims to have won or nobody admits to having lost – something without a clear result one way or the other is just less newsworthy.

But we should be careful not to attach too much significance to the headline suitability of the event. There was certainly a range of plausible dramatic headlines that could have questioned the effectiveness or legitimacy of the accountability process. Consider these hypothetical examples:

BAe ESCAPES BRIBERY AND CORRUPTION CHARGES
BAe LET OFF THE HOOK AGAIN BY THE SFO
BAe TRIUMPH IN SETTLEMENTS: NO RESIGNATIONS,
NO MORE INVESTIGATIONS

Instead, the mainstream media ran a series of headlines implicitly endorsing the plea bargain settlements as a suitable and proportionate outcome. The sombre tone of serious justice was encapsulated by the four headlines run by BBC News Online on the day the settlements were announced:

BAe SYSTEMS HANDED £286M CRIMINAL FINES IN UK AND US
SERIOUS FRAUD OFFICE: BAe FINES A WARNING TO
COMPANIES
BAe CRIMINAL FINES 'A SERIOUS EMBARASSMENT'
BAe HOPES ITS SFO SETTLEMENT MARKS A NEW CHAPTER

END OF THE ROAD

Perhaps the most significant factor prompting the alignment of news values with official source strategies was 'story fatigue'. By the time the settlements were announced the story had been recurring as a regular television feature for over three years, and for considerably longer in the press. The need for editors to 'move on' from a story was another point of consensus among key figures interviewed for this book. It was most emphatically put forward by a government press officer:

> The thing about the dynamics of the media – it can't maintain that level of hype. Everyone almost wants the break clause for them to move on to something else and the media are quite happy if you say 'right I think let's have an inquiry' and they'll say 'ok you know what, we can move on to something else now'. The editors are probably sitting there thinking 'that's quite good because I don't think we could have kept that going'

The announcement of the settlements clearly provided a much needed sense of closure to the story for news editors. But it would be foolhardy to assume that the issues which the controversy raised will not resurface. The point about story fatigue is that it is symptomatic of a news cycle that may repeat itself once the issue has been left long enough to become sufficiently new again. According to Symon Hill: 'One of the real scandals is how much influence [BAe] has in government and that will resurface again. It's gone up and it's gone down and it will go up again.'

In a sense though, the scandal's recurrence in different guises is itself indicative of the media's failure to induce meaningful accountability. Part of the problem was the media's attraction, if not dependence on the court room. This meant that once the settlements were announced and there appeared to be little chance of BAe facing prosecution, there was not much fuel left in the story. According to one campaigner: 'They're interested in legal processes and investigations because they're going on, more than necessarily the issue behind it [...] BAe continuing to be accused of something by campaigners is less of a story.'

There was a sense of resigned acceptance amongst journalists that little more could be done to shed light on the controversy. According to a senior BBC reporter: 'Well you kind of think once you get to a settlement actually what more can you do [...] The parties had agreed to come to the end of the road.'

In fact, legal proceedings continued with campaigners mounting a failed bid for a judicial review of the SFO settlement. But by then the story had lost its media momentum. This was at least partly attributable to herd behaviour amongst the news media that can contribute to an unspoken consensus of what is and is not a news story.

By contrast, the perception of exclusivity can also limit the breadth of coverage. In this case, the controversy was commonly viewed as a '*Guardian* story', particularly during its embryonic stages. Symon Hill remarked that this problem was confounded by the fact that the *Guardian* itself actively sought to perpetuate its exclusivity:

The *Guardian* saw it as their campaign and other media saw it as a *Guardian* story. So I think one of our successes over the year and a half of bringing the legal action was actually getting the *Independent* interested because they saw it as something the

Guardian had a monopoly on [...]. It got to a point actually where I felt we had a more positive relationship with the *Independent*.

This sentiment was reflective of a tension between campaigners and campaigner journalists, and the spread of the story was no doubt slower than it might have been, were it not for perceptions of exclusivity. But the impact of this perception should not be overstated. The important point is that the story did in the end *spread*, the main fuel for which was a combination of courtroom drama, and a David/Goliath narrative engendered by the legal case. It might not have attracted the kind of saturated mainstream coverage as other controversies but the media response was sufficiently broad and persistent to give weight to the legal campaign and induce the kind of official responses applicable to crisis media management.

What is clear, however, is that the closure framing owed much to the dynamics of the news cycle – in particular the need to move on from stories that were perceived to have run their course. Central to that perception was the declared end to investigations and judicial scrutiny. This deprived the news media of the controversy's primary raw material (disclosure documents) as well as the official sanction bestowed by the advancement of judicial process.

ALTERNATIVE SOURCE STRATEGIES

But the final act in the Al Yamamah story was not the work of journalists and official sources alone. In at least one respect, the emphasis on culpability and punishment chimed with the strategies of alternative sources as they sought to maximise publicity around the issues at the heart of their campaigns. Even a solicitor on the case conceded that there was much more to the goals of campaigners than just winning the legal battle: 'Although we ultimately lost [...] from the client's perspective it was all about bringing this into the public domain, making it embarrassing for the government and the SFO that this could have happened, and that was all achieved.'

According to Symon Hill: 'The case was part of the campaign. We were doing other things so that we would raise the issue politically, we would get a lot of coverage about arms company influence in government. It was part of a wider campaign.'

The point here is not that campaigners welcomed or even accepted ultimate defeat in the courts (or outside of them). But the central goal of their campaign was to draw attention to corrupt practices in the arms trade, rather than shortcomings in the legal system. This engendered a conflict that was reflected in CAAT's own press release headline on the day the settlements were announced:

BAe GUILTY BUT WILL NOT FACE COURT

To be clear, CAAT were outspoken against the failings of the plea bargaining system. But this criticism was implicitly subdued in highlighting that the settlements had delivered a guilty verdict, however limited. It should be remembered that official sources only tacitly endorsed a guilty verdict. The lack of definitive clarity made it incumbent on campaigners to place emphasis on it. Had they not, the ambiguity of the outcome meant there was at least a possibility that a different and much less welcome frame might have surfaced:

INVESTIGATIONS FIND BAe NOT GUILTY OF CORRUPTION
AFTER ALL

It is self-evident that this kind of response would have been the worst media outcome from a campaigner's perspective. But there is another more compelling force which led campaigners to offer partial endorsement of the settlements. This stemmed from a perceived need to be seen as welcoming, in the words of Paul Ingram, 'the principle of demonstrated guilt' and not to be seen as dismissing out of hand what was a long-awaited accountability resolution:

> Campaigners and organisations like our own have our reputations to consider too and we don't want to be seen as continually negative and harping away and never being satisfied which is a very real potential, very real issue. BAe admit to guilt and we criticise them – the story then becomes our unwillingness to be reasonable.

In this light, we can glimpse the impact of the closure strategy, exploiting both the limitations of the news cycle and strategic disadvantages of alternative sources to maximum effect. Whether intentional or not, the closure strategy succeeded in outmanoeuvring both campaigning journalists and campaigners themselves.

More broadly, the reluctance of campaigners to question the legitimacy of settlements was reflective of a strategic priority to maximise publicity around BAe's corrupt activities, rather than focus on the issue of accountability. For one thing, even if they were ultimately successful in the courts, it was doubtful whether the legal system could have delivered meaningful sanction anyway, as a solicitor working on the case attested:

> You've got to remember that had we won that wouldn't have meant that the investigation would be re-opened. That would have meant it would go back to the [SFO] Director who would have to retake the decision lawfully in accordance with the guidance of the courts [...] Even had we won in the House of Lords that wouldn't have actually produced necessarily the end result of a reopening of the investigation. It was probably highly unlikely to have produced that end result.

The centrality of exposing BAe's corruption to the CAAT media campaign meant that campaigners themselves were relatively silent in response to the Law Lords judgement. According to Symon Hill: 'People weren't generally reporting on the case when we lost it. If they were reporting on it I wanted to get our message across but if they weren't I wasn't pushing it out there.'

Rather than questioning the legitimacy of the decision therefore, both campaigners and journalists followed each other in opting to remain quiet.

Resource limitations were also a factor for campaigners who pointed out that BAe's press office employed several times more people than CAAT as a whole. This meant that drops in the intensity of coverage were actually a mixed blessing, as Kaye Stearman reflected:

> I have to say that if we did have *Today* or *Newsnight* ringing up every week I don't think we'd cope, quite frankly, because we're a small organisation and you get run ragged the times when you are in the news. So it's probably just as well that it's not a constant story because you just couldn't do it I think.

Resource issues did not of course dampen campaigners' expression of outrage or indeed inhibit their attempts to bring a judicial review of the settlements. In this respect there was a marked difference between them and the journalists who all but went silent on the issue. But they were nevertheless to some degree unwittingly complicit in the spectacle of accountability. The primary goal of seeking publicity for the core issues of their campaign meant that comparatively less attention was paid to the inadequacies of the justice system.

Like journalists, campaigners were in a sense concerned more with exposure than seeking justice, at least in the short term.

AUDIENCE BARRIERS

We have seen how an interaction between source strategies, news values and organisational factors manifest in containment within news reports, particularly in the closure framing that overwhelmingly favoured the government and BAe's case. It remains for us to consider the forces which led to the differentiation of coverage between different points in the schedule, ensuring that certain key frames never reached a critical mass audience.

The Al Yamamah controversy was rooted in investigative journalism both in the print and broadcasting sectors. As discussed earlier, the breadth of coverage that resulted from this suggests not only that a mainstay of investigative journalism persists (in spite of a long-term decline in allocated resources) but also that in the right circumstances, this can act as a vehicle for generating wider coverage of the controversy. On close analysis, however, key limitations were found in relation to where the controversy was covered. Most notably, coverage on television news was concentrated on late evening bulletins and news analysis programmes. This represents an important restriction in respect of audience access. Journalists and editors on these programmes perceive themselves as addressing an elite and opinion forming audience. They are a reflection, according to one senior BBC executive, of 'the British Establishment talking to itself'.

A key explanatory factor here is the different newsroom cultures of production (Born 2005). One BBC current affairs journalist highlighted the significance of juxtapositional cultural backgrounds within the *Newsnight* newsroom:

> It's a combination of intellect and conformity [...] We've got our degrees and we're good little children and we've kind of ticked all those boxes. But at the same time we have come to the media with some kind of dual or triple culture [...] We may be American, we may be Jewish, we may be Muslim, but it attracts people who have spent their entire lives negotiating a difference between home and the collective establishment of which they're a part [...] It helps them to see things from other people's points of view.

The suggestion here is that multiculturalism within specialist newsrooms results in an editorial stance that is relatively more sympathetic to alternative sources. Another distinctive cultural dimension of such newsrooms is a desire among journalists to emulate filmic formats – documentary or even drama – so as to distinguish themselves from mainstream news programmes: 'Most of the people that work on *Newsnight* are very clever and they've got some training and understanding of news. But they have a yearning to go for the longer form […] they have visions of being in the film industry.'

This is significant because, traditionally, documentary formats have not been subject to the same rigours of impartiality as more conventional news programmes. In their exclusive focus on a particular point of view, current affairs documentaries in the 1980s routinely scrutinised and attacked official scripts in relation to the Falklands War and sectarian violence in Northern Ireland, amongst other controversial topics (Holland 2006). In the 1990s, the BBC began to cut down on the current affair documentary format with the result that surviving editions faced greater pressure to attract commercial size audiences. This trend had a knock-on effect in re-allocating to *Newsnight* those investigative or in-depth reports increasingly rejected by Current Affairs. As one BBC insider put it:

> *This World* used to be 30–40 programmes a year […] BBC Two doesn't do that fixed slot thing anymore so there are only about 12. So they've chosen to do things that compete for audience because they've been told to do that by their commissioners who are the channel controllers. So they are reluctant for example to use reporters. They want celebrities to present their programme because it will bring [the audience] in […] So the drama is the protagonist […] even *Panorama* – for example they wanted to do something about petrol prices and they didn't want a reporter to do it […] they wanted somebody from *Top Gear* to do it because they felt it would pull in a bigger audience. So I'm finding it difficult to sell my stories to my own department. I have to pitch them to news programmes that don't have to fight for audiences as much.

Clearly, a shift in controversial coverage on public service television away from prime time current affairs and documentary formats to news analysis programmes corresponds to a decline in audience exposure. But Panorama *did* cover the Al Yamamah controversy and it did get significant coverage, as we have seen, across the television news spectrum. One key issue addressed in interviews for this book concerned why it was concentrated in late evening and news analysis outlets, a factor which by default limited its audience reach. For most respondents, the answer lay in the complexity and 'seriousness' of the story. Organisational features meant that this clearly made the story more suited to in-depth programmes, as a senior BBC news executive explained:

> It's not just about *Newsnight*, it's about *Today*, *World At One* – all of these shows have a questioning attitude. They are set up to examine and to challenge and to hold authority to account whereas the role of a news bulletin, although it does that to some extent, isn't quite the same as that and it also doesn't have the time. So it doesn't have the time to do a long and searching interview with somebody finding out how they'd justify what they'd done in the same way as a longer form show can do. I think that's true of all the long form shows wherever they are.

What's clear from this statement is that longer form programmes can go beyond the coverage of bulletins not just because of their relative time allocation in the schedule, but also because of their remit to 'come up with something that the bulletins haven't had'. This partly explains their relative autonomy from the centralised newsgathering processes at BBC and ITN:

> They do share more on the *One*, *Six* and *Ten*, and they do share more on the radio bulletins but a lot of the built programmes like the *Today* programme, *Newsnight*, *World At One* – all of those remain very, very independent in terms of their ability to generate newsgathering themselves.

This in turn contributes to a culture of elitism whereby longer form and later edition programmes attract 'the more senior editor type figures', who aspire to be less bound by the time and editorial restraints acting on mainstream reporters. Equally, the flagship status of longer form programmes has to some extent ring-fenced their resources:

> You have to have the time and resource to invest in actually doing the investigation and again, longer form programmes tend to have that time and resources in a way that other programmes don't.

So the people who are good at that sort of thing will gravitate towards the Newsnights and the Panoramas – that style of show.

Late evening broadcasts also have an additional resource advantage not just in the time they occupy in the schedule but also in the time they have to produce an edition over the course of a news day. As a leading political correspondent reflected: 'When you get to the *Ten O'Clock News* and you're doing a story for the Ten, you sometimes have – you have more time to think about what this really is.'

But alongside resource pressures, there has been a concurrent tightening of the editorial reins. This is partly the consequence of a growing 'climate of caution', a phrase coined by a senior political correspondent:

> I think a lot of people working in BBC news right now would relate to – I think I would call it a climate of caution. That's how I would describe it. It's not veto, it's not 'we're not doing this story because...', absolutely not [...] What there is I think is an increasing pressure to take care over language, to take care over the line – not to take a punt [...] I think I would say a culture of caution and compliance [...] a caution and a care that certainly I think sometimes, some people working in the organisation might feel has gone a bit too far the other way.

Most respondents – journalists and executives alike – cited the Hutton Inquiry in 2003 as the root of this new climate. Castigating the BBC for a 'catalogue of errors' in controversial reporting leading up to the death of defence intelligence expert David Kelly, the BBC's response included not only the establishment of a new editorial regime but the founding of an on-site College of Journalism which subsumed resources away from 'real journalism'. This has exacerbated an already well-established pattern of increasing budgetary constraints on journalists:

> There's a whole floor in White City devoted to COJO – the College of Journalism – channelled into journalism courses. Not output, courses. That, and there's been a diversion to enormous management salaries, there's been a diversion to the expansion of management, there's been a diversion to the proliferation of channels. All the money has been diverted away from operational output funds.

The problem has been compounded by successive editorial crises since the Hutton Inquiry which, despite having no link to the BBC's news output, nevertheless had a marked impact on it. Unlike the scandal which foregrounded the Hutton Inquiry, these crises provoked public attacks on the BBC emanating from commercial media rather than the government. Indeed whilst news executives were keen to emphasise the extent of the BBC's political independence, they were remarkably forthcoming in acknowledging a lack of independence from commercial pressure. In an era marked by an intensifying political war of words between the BBC and commercial organisations – notably News International – this raises important questions for how independence is defined in the context of public service broadcasters.

Although this climate has impacted on BBC news across the board, it has disproportionately affected central newsgathering operations in view of the privileged autonomy enjoyed by *Newsnight*. But a more significant factor in differential output relates to journalists' perceptions of their audience, as a senior reporter attested in connection with the Al Yamamah scandal:

> It's about very serious things and it's no secret that different audiences during the day across all different news outlets have different interests. Our research tells us the reality that people who tend to be watching the *Six O'Clock News* might be making their tea at the same time and trying to do different things and get their kids to bed whereas people tend to watch the *Ten O'Clock News* in a different way. They sit down and they want to watch the news and they therefore have a different – in theory they can have a different appetite for what they're about to find out about [...] just as different papers have different readerships.

For broadcasters, decisions over which stories to allocate to any given programme are taken by editors who are seen as making decisions 'on behalf of their audiences'. The prevalence of the story in the news analysis programmes was a reflection of its relative containment within the broadsheet press. This ensured that coverage of the controversy was broad and extensive but only within an upper tier of elite news outlets. It was in essence considered too complex and too 'serious' to be suited to day time or early evening programmes. In the context of proliferating news outlets, declining audience, and an increasing attention to audience targeting both in commercial and public service outlets, this raises difficult questions over the democratic value of news diversity. Controversy may be everywhere in the news but there are clearly different types of controversy aimed at different types of audience. The crux of the problem is that controversies that expose 'crimes of the powerful' are often the most complex stories to tell, a factor which inhibits its audience reach. This was articulated acutely by Bea Edwards, head of the US-based Government Accountability Project:

> It seems to me the major criminal activities around the world in 2010 had to do with very complex large scale white collar crime, tax evasions, secrecy jurisdictions, hiding money, money laundering – those things require a certain patience and intelligence and the media seem to be unequal to that task.

The Al Yamamah controversy suggests that some media *were* equal to that task. But the story's containment within largely elite-oriented news outlets begs the question of whether pluralist contestability can really be said to exist in the context of an establishment talking to, or even arguing with itself.

END OF STORY?

It remains for us to consider the potential long-term impact of the coverage and whether, as one campaigner suggested, the controversy left a legacy of 'a lot more awareness in a lot more quarters about how much influence arms companies generally and BAe in particular have within government'.

At the same time, campaigners did not go as far as to suggest that BAe were, in fact, a reformed company. On the contrary, any changes in practice instituted as a result of the controversy were considered likely to be cosmetic. According to Paul Ingram: 'I've no doubt that BAe are still involved in [...] deals under the wire.'

There were also potentially serious negative consequences for future judicial and media scrutiny of BAe's actions as a result of the legal outcome. Aside from absolving the government of wrongdoing, defeat in the House of Lords had a regressive effect on case law as one solicitor observed: 'It was a very disappointing result doubly not only because we lost but also because it seemed to set back the case law on where international frameworks can fit into domestic law.'

It seems reasonable on balance to conclude that the settlements were ultimately not so much a victory for BAe or the government, as a victory for 'the system'. But the fact that BAe was not charged with bribery and corruption – the central allegation on which the Al Yamamah controversy rested – is perhaps the most defining outcome of the story.

The case study does not then appear to live up to a liberal pluralist ideal in which official definitions are *always* contestable by both alternative sources and autonomous journalists; in which power does not, by default, have the final say; and in which media coverage does not ultimately serve the interests of elites. But neither does it wholly satisfy the conditions of radical functionalist theories. The coverage was clearly more substantial, prolonged and broader than either the Propaganda Model (Herman and Chomsky 2002) or Primary Definition (Hall et al. 1978) would allow for. Elite dissent may have been a necessary precondition for contestability, and it is likely that competitive forces in particular were instrumental indirectly in both stirring and sustaining media interest. But genuine journalist autonomy was alive and well during the height of the controversy and that no doubt played a part in bringing about a minimal degree of accountability. If not through legal sanction, it partly worked through a level of publicity and exposure that was clearly uncomfortable for official sources. Whether or not this induced a limited measure of reform in the politics and practices of the arms trade remains to be seen.

In any case, limited contestability also belied deep structural limitations in the news media imposed by a complex of organisational, cultural and instrumental factors. These erected elite audience barriers around the coverage and ensured that in mainstream outlets, framing was consistently more qualified in favour of official sources; that even at the margins it largely excluded fundamental questions raised concerning the system's capacity to hold power to account; and that both the media and alternative sources were, to varying degrees, ultimately acquiescent in an official source strategy to bring closure to the story.

Part II

Covering the Cover-Up

4
Whispers in the Press Gallery

BACKGROUND

The Hutton Report was the outcome of an inquiry set up to examine 'the circumstances surrounding and leading up to the death of Dr David Kelly'. Kelly, a government scientist and intelligence analyst, was the identified source for an allegation made on BBC Radio 4's *Today* programme that sparked one of the most vociferous and public attacks on the BBC from a sitting government in its 80-year history. The allegation, made by Andrew Gilligan, was that the government 'probably knew' that one of the claims on which it based its case for war with Iraq was inaccurate. The implicit charge therefore was that it had lied to both Parliament and the public in a bid to bolster support for an unpopular war.

Indeed, the extent of public mobilisation against the war prior to invasion was unprecedented (Freedman 2009). This owed much to the Stop the War Coalition – a strategic alliance that brought together disparate groups from religious associations to trade unions. It tuned in to a wave of protest across the world against what was seen as an increasingly belligerent US administration with imperialist ambitions. As well as popular resistance, the war had provoked a fracture in existing and longstanding international alliances. France, Germany and Russia were vehemently opposed, leading to deadlock in the United Nations and subsequent allegations that the war was illegal under international law. But what made the extent of anti-war protest unprecedented in the UK was the movement's appeal to 'the great moral mainstream' of public opinion, as John Pilger commented in a speech made at the demonstration. The largest demonstration ever in the UK was notable not so much for its numbers, as for its 'middle England' representation – a point that was highlighted in several news reports at the time.

It is against this backdrop that the government mounted its case for war based on Iraq's possession of, and willingness to use weapons of mass destruction (WMD). Although it was notionally endorsed by both sides of the Commons, leading Labour and Conservative MPs detracted; the Liberal Democrat Party opposed it outright;

key cabinet members resigned; and officials across the board made their discontent heard through various leaks and anonymous press briefings. In other words, the prospect of war drew lines both across and through the British political establishment, a situation that was broadly reflected in the pre-war press (although the majority of national newspapers supported the war). Perhaps indicative of the episode's uniqueness in British political and media history was the unholy alliance between tabloids representing opposite ends of the political spectrum: both the *Daily Mail* and the *Daily Mirror* waged prolonged anti-war campaigns.

However, such media outrage was limited to the pre-war build up and once military action commenced a closing of the ranks prevailed (Lewis 2006). It was not until after the invasion and subsequent regime change that wholesale fractures re-emerged. The catalyst for this was the failure to find WMD in Iraq and the deteriorating security situation inside the country. Gilligan's report coincided with both and as a result spread like wildfire across the global media. In the words of Alistair Campbell, the government's chief media strategist, 'this was a story that went right round the world. It was in virtually every newspaper in the world and we were accused of being liars'.[1]

But it was certainly not the root of the WMD controversy. The 'dodgy dossier' – a forerunner to the 'sexed up' sequel sparked by Gilligan's report – was found to have contained rampant plagiarism of a PhD thesis and sparked widespread allegations that the government had exaggerated the case for war. Both the sensationalism and political sensitivity of Gilligan's report rested on the fact that it implicitly accused the government of lying – the impeachable offence that taps deep into the Watergate consciousness.

Also significant in stoking government outrage – whether genuine or opportunistic – was the apparent lack of journalistic rigour in Gilligan's report. The essential feature of the live 'two-way' in broadcasting news is that the journalist becomes the interviewee. As a result s/he is relatively free of impartiality constraints that govern scripted reports. Gilligan's infamous charge that the government 'probably knew' appeared to lack substantiation, and thus provided a basis for the very public backlash led by Alistair Campbell.

Clearly, the stakes could not have been higher, nor could the controversy have involved more senior and powerful figures within the British state. In light of this, it is perhaps not surprising that the actual death of Dr Kelly – sudden and unnatural as it was – did not attract the spotlight of either the Hutton Report or subsequent media coverage. Instead, the report served as a quasi-legal adjudication on the conflict between the government and the BBC. This was illustrated by the BBC chairman's parting words following publication of the report, explaining the reasons for his resignation: 'I have been brought up to believe that you cannot choose your own referee'.[2] Hutton was not investigating so much as mediating between battling elite factions.

The insinuation of Gavyn Davies' statement was that the government *had* appointed their own referee in Lord Hutton, and as a result had won near complete vindication. The BBC, in contrast, was wholly castigated resulting in the unprecedented resignation of its two most senior figures. But rather than instigating closure, the report gave birth to a new controversy fuelled by allegations of a 'whitewash'. Given that the episode coincided with unprecedented levels of government investment in news management, it would not be surprising if journalists were sensitised to perceived threats to their integrity and autonomy. But what is significant here is not just the explicit criticism that the judgement was inaccurate and unfair, but the implied critique of the efficacy and legitimacy of the inquiry *process*. This is what distinguished coverage of Hutton from that of subsequent inquiries related to the Iraq War, making it acutely relevant for our purposes here.

A second distinct angle of criticism stemmed from the controversy surrounding the actual death of Dr Kelly. Evidence emerged at the inquiry casting doubt over official explanations of death by arterial bleeding, at the time widely accepted without question by the news media. This included the testimonies of two paramedics who had examined the body and maintained that the levels of blood at the scene were inconsistent with this type of death.[3] A campaign was subsequently launched by a group of senior medical and legal experts who argued that evidence for the accepted cause of death was unsatisfactory. More importantly, they argued that the inquiry itself had not properly dealt with the cause of death and the government's refusal to hold an inquest or release medical and police documents was an obstruction of due process.

The on-going campaign for a formal inquest into the death was based on apparent conflict of evidence, tampering of evidence, suppression of evidence, misinformation and obstruction of due process. It is worth saying something about each of these at the outset in order to justify the guiding and conservative assumption that the campaign was legitimate and its grounds compelling.

As mentioned above, the most striking aspect of evidence conflict was the discrepancy between the testimony of paramedics and the official pathologist regarding the amount of blood found at the scene. Given that the official cause of death was arterial bleeding, this evidence is arguably of the greatest material significance in the case. The crucial testimony in this respect was provided by paramedic Vanessa Hunt – the first medically trained person to encounter the body:

Q. Was there anything else that you know of about the circumstances of Dr Kelly's death that you can assist his Lordship with?
Hunt: Only that the amount of blood that was around the scene seemed relatively minimal and there was a small patch on his right knee, but no obvious arterial bleeding. There was no spraying of blood or huge blood loss or any obvious loss on the clothing.
Q. On the clothing?
Hunt: Yes.
Q. One of the police officers or someone this morning said there appeared to be some blood on the ground. Did you see that?
Hunt: I could see some on – there were some stinging nettles to the left of the body. As to on the ground, I do not remember seeing a sort of huge puddle or anything like that. There was dried blood on the left wrist. His jacket was pulled to sort of mid forearm area and from that area down towards the hand there was dried blood, but no obvious sign of a wound or anything, it was just dried blood.
Q. You did not see the wound?
Hunt: I did not see the wound, no.[4]

This testimony differed starkly from that contained within the official post-mortem report:

There was some bloodstaining over the right groin area and over the tops of both thighs. There was a heavier patch of bloodstaining over the right knee area [...] There was heavy bloodstaining over the left arm [...] There was bloodstaining and a pool of blood in an area running from the left arm of the deceased for a total distance of in the order of 2'–3'.[5]

Other aspects of evidence conflict are detailed later in the chapter. With regard to apparent tampering of evidence, two examples warrant a mention. The first concerns the testimony given at the Hutton Inquiry by Louise Holmes, a volunteer searcher who first discovered Dr Kelly's body. She described the body as lying 'at the base of the tree with almost his head and his shoulders just slumped back against the tree'. However, subsequent testimony by police described the body as lying flat with a gap of some measure between the head and the base of the tree. This suggested that the body may have been moved between the time it was found and the time it was examined. To be clear, the conflicting testimony did not prove the body was moved, but it underlined the case for an inquest in raising the very real possibility that evidence had been tampered with at the scene.

The second incident relating to possible tampering of evidence concerned the temporary disappearance of Dr Kelly's dental records, in the two days following his death. This was reported to police at the time by Kelly's dental surgery. According to the Attorney General, Dominic Grieve, who investigated the incident prior to rejecting a new inquest in 2011:

> Dr Kelly's notes should have been stored in a cabinet alphabetically but they weren't there. The dentist looked through about fifteen notes either side of where they should be but they were not found. Two other members of staff also looked but couldn't locate them.[6]

Two days later however, the dentist reported that the records were found 'in their right place'. According to a Freedom of Information response by the Thames Valley Police, a total of 15 fingerprint marks were found on the file, nine of which were either unusable or eliminated to a member of staff.[7] That left six clear DNA fingerprint marks from unidentified persons. The Attorney General makes no mention of this crucial finding in his report, simply concluding that he is 'unable to explain this aspect of the enquiry'.

With regard to suppression of evidence, this first became apparent in early 2010 when it was reported by the *Daily Mail* that medical records and other evidence had been classified under the Official Secrets Act for a period of 70 years.[8] Despite releasing the post-mortem report in late 2010, the majority of medical and police documents pertaining to Kelly's death remain, at the time of writing, classified on the basis of protecting the interests of his family. These include photographs taken of the body at the scene, the full reports by forensic biologist Roy Green and toxicologist Dr Alexander Allan, as well as witness statements submitted in absentia by controversial figures including Mai Pederson, an alleged US Army intelligence agent who was a close confidante of Dr Kelly (Baker 2007). It is a core contention of this thesis that given the conflicting and uncertain evidence surrounding the death of Dr Kelly – a senior public servant who suffered an unnatural death in extremely controversial circumstances – the public interest in disclosure would outweigh any emotional distress that it may cause for the bereaved.

With regard to misinformation, this appeared to emanate from both the official pathologist and journalists themselves:

- In his rebuttal to a letter by campaigners published in *The Times* newspaper in August 2010,[9] pathologist Nicholas Hunt referred to clots of blood found trapped inside the sleeve of Kelly's jacket said to have been noted in the post-mortem report.[10] But there was in fact no mention of this in the post mortem subsequently released, and the testimony of other witnesses confirmed that Kelly was found with his sleeve rolled up.
- In the summer of 2010, veteran journalist and broadcaster Tom Mangold posted a comment on his own article published on the *Independent*'s website that the lack of fingerprints found on Kelly's knife was attributable to DNA resistant tape found around the handle.[11] It was repeated by Andrew Gilligan in a subsequent article in the *Telegraph*.[12] But an FOI response from the police confirmed that there was no such tape or any paraphernalia on the knife.[13]

The emergence of such anomalies was no doubt partly attributable to the fact that Hutton's witnesses were neither cross-examined nor required to give evidence under oath. The persistent refusal by the government to hold an inquest in spite of such anomalies pointed to an apparent obstruction of due process. This was amplified by protracted delays on the part of official sources both in releasing information and responding to the few journalist queries that were raised. In an interview for this book, Alex Thompson – chief correspondent for *Channel 4 News* – provided a telling insight into this obstruction: 'When I asked the Ministry of Justice to simply answer the question why it has taken nearly a year to get the papers put in the public domain it took five press officers and nine weeks and I still didn't get an answer.'

These are just some of the problems highlighted by campaigners in respect of the official investigation and verdict. None of it proves that David Kelly was murdered or even that he did not commit suicide in the manner described by Hutton. But it does convincingly justify the assumption underpinning this book which is that the inquest campaign warranted serious journalistic concern in a way that was demonstrated in the previous case study. There we saw how journalists covering the Al Yamamah controversy routinely endorsed the case of campaigners calling for a reopening of the official investigation into BAe.

Like the Al Yamamah controversy, the inquest controversy centred on an alleged failure or subversion of due process. But it also draws our attention to 'non-decision making power' in the terms employed by Steven Lukes (2005). The Al Yamamah controversy developed around a high profile public announcement, namely the Attorney General's declaration to the House of Lords that the SFO Inquiry had been terminated. The inquest controversy, by contrast, offered no such spectacle and comparatively little response from official sources. It was not after all the Prime Minister or indeed the government that were at the centre of the controversy, but the security state – by its very faceless nature a much more difficult entity to challenge and scrutinise.

Together, these issues address the broader themes of the book by calling our attention to one of the core objectives of the liberal media project: to hold authority to account, particularly when non-media institutions of accountability apparently fail to do so. What is at stake here is once again not the original sin of the controversy ('sexing up/lying'), but the apparent undermining of the accountability system ('whitewash/cover-up'). This is what distinguishes coverage of the Hutton Inquiry proceedings from coverage of the outcome and it is for this reason that our analysis starts, in a sense, at the end: the Hutton Report marked a culmination of months of media fever over an establishment effectively at war with itself.

What follows then, is a discussion and analysis of the report's coverage on the prime-time terrestrial news programmes, as well as in-depth interviews with journalists, campaigners and state sources active on all sides of the debate. The news sample spans the period from 2004 (following publication of the Hutton Report) to June 2011 when the government rejected calls for an inquest into David Kelly's death. Overall, findings suggest that whilst the Hutton Report sparked outrage among journalists in the whitewash context, the controversy over the cause of Kelly's death was to remain side-lined for the best part of seven years. During this time evidence continued to surface which cast increasing doubt over the safety of the official verdict. Nevertheless, in a final response to a formal submission of evidence by campaigners in 2011, the government refused to reopen an inquest into the death. This raises important questions as to whether journalists were in some way complicit in an ultimate failure of accountability. What is certain is that apparent subversion of due process and excessive secrecy did little to prompt journalist concern, let alone outrage.

THE WHITEWASH FRAME

This was palpably not the case when it came to Hutton's verdict on the BBC. It was this aspect of the story which dominated television news bulletins and programmes during the first three days following the report's release. Journalistic attention was fuelled by government calls for a complete and unreserved apology from the BBC in the wake of Hutton's findings. The BBC capitulated within two days, resulting in the unprecedented double resignation of its two most senior figures. The event did not, however, precipitate a favourable outcome for official sources – the longer the story occupied the headlines and the further the BBC descended into crisis, the louder the cries of 'whitewash' became.

On the day the report was made public, all news programmes led with a narrative of the 'BBC in crisis'. Anchor introductions and backdrop images highlighted key critical words and phrases from the report casting the BBC as 'defective', 'at fault', and guilty of 'a catalogue of errors'. On the face of it, such coverage clearly played into the hands of official sources by 1) amplifying the report's criticism of the BBC, and 2) paying relatively little attention to the legitimacy or fairness of Hutton's conclusions. However, even in this crucial initial phase of coverage when the national news agenda was near exclusively given over to the story, the notion of whitewash became at times implicit in the language of reporters. They not only placed dramatic emphasis on the BBC's defeat, but importantly contrasted it with the government's apparent victory. As Nick Robinson observed for one ITV news bulletin: 'If Tony Blair had written this report himself I can barely think of a single phrase that he would have disagreed with.'[14]

Given the dominant critical narrative that epitomised broader coverage of the WMD controversy, such statements were clearly designed to do more than just celebrate Blair's 'bounce back'. They effectively sowed the seeds for the whitewash frame that was to emerge on the following day.

There was a marked difference on the first day of coverage between the live commentaries of correspondents and the scripted language of reports and anchor introductions. Whilst the latter highlighted the damning aspects of the report, the former tended to highlight reaction to it. Recurring words such as 'shock', 'anger' and 'upset' were used to describe the response of BBC staff 'on the shop floor'.[15] The emotive language strongly conveyed a sense of unjust 'injury', implicitly questioning the fairness of Hutton's report. Equally, reporters tended to place emphasis on their own sense of surprise at the report's conclusions: 'none of us, none of us expected that 100 per cent, no ifs, no buts, Tony Blair and his team would be in the clear'.[16] The implied criticism here is that the report's findings were not necessarily in keeping with the evidence heard by journalists at the inquiry.

The discourse of public service broadcasting qualifies its editorial approach as one in which journalists report other people's views rather than put across their own. However, on close analysis we find that these are not necessarily mutually exclusive. For reporters on ITV's late evening broadcast as well as on the *Channel 4 News*, the implied criticisms alluded to above quickly became explicit. Tom Bradby introduced his report with a clear indication of the gap between journalists' understanding of the controversy and Hutton's conclusions: 'For us this was a very complex issue, but not for Lord Hutton'.[17] In the two-way following the report, he articulated this further by asking, 'does [Lord Hutton] really understand the conditions under which the fourth estate has to operate?'

This was a reference to the difficulties inherent in sourcing whistleblowers from within the security state, protecting them, and conveying their message to the public:

> For someone like Kelly to go and talk to someone like Gilligan, express his reservations, was a difficult and some might think brave thing to do and I think the difficulties of all those contacts, the difficulties of finding out what's really happening in the intelligence community – all of that completely absent from the report.[18]

Initially, at least, the most vociferous allegations of whitewash stemmed from journalists themselves. The initiative that journalists took in challenging the official script was captured in a two-way statement by Nick Robinson: 'Only the smallest quietest backbenchers have dared say that word that I suspect you'll hear in the next few days: the word "whitewash".'[19]

The point was made even more emphatically by Eleanor Goodman on the *Channel 4 News*: 'While the word "whitewash" was liberally spread around the press gallery, nobody uttered it in the House of Commons.'[20]

This demonstrates that television journalists pre-empted criticism of the report that was to stem in the ensuing days from elite sources. In several live exchanges they offered both guarded and overt criticism of the findings on multiple grounds: namely imbalance, inaccuracy and an attack on journalism. This latter frame was given relative prominence on *Channel 4 News,* with Jon Snow summing up the mood in a live interview with former Foreign Secretary Robin Cook: 'This seems really in the end to distil down to a clash between the media and the political classes and the political classes have come off whiter than white.'[21]

BBC current affairs presenter Andrew Neil, appearing on *Channel 4 News* as an interviewee, described Hutton as 'the anti-journalist judge'. His attack came with a warning for the long term implications of the report for independent journalism:

> We've had a judge who gave the government, officials, ministers, anyone in the establishment the benefit of the doubt at every turn and yet at every turn the BBC was given no benefit of the doubt at all and I think that will lead to a kind of anti-journalist climate which will mean that we will not be able to find things out that we should.[22]

On the second day of coverage, the notion of the Hutton Report as an 'attack on journalism' prompted unusual expressions of solidarity between broadcasters. As Tom Bradby attested on an ITN bulletin:

> I have to say, and I never thought I'd say this, I've had more or less 15 years of competing against the BBC – the idea of beating the BBC is what propels me out of bed in the morning. But I have to say there's a degree of sadness really here today about this whole thing [...] I think in the wider journalistic community there's some anger building. In some sections it's almost outrage at this report.[23]

If officials had hoped commercial media would instinctively endorse Hutton's critique of the BBC, they had grossly miscalculated. Indeed, all ITV news programmes on the day after the report was published featured headlines dedicated to whitewash claims. What had been the preserve of unscripted live two-ways was now the exclusive subject of lead reports.

These reports were second on the bill to the 'BBC in Crisis' headline, given added fuel by the resignation of Greg Dyke. But even here the language of reports invoked the whitewash angle by highlighting the sense of outrage amongst BBC staff who were described as 'militant', 'shocked' and 'upset'. Once again, the language was notably stronger in the two-ways. Tom Bradby went as far as to draw a parallel between what was on the minds of BBC staff and the public at large: 'I think the big question tonight is that [the government is] still I think up in front of the court of public opinion. And what do they think tonight? I think there are real question marks over that.'[24]

The contrast between the report and public opinion was to be a recurring theme in the whitewash frame. During the first two days of coverage there were seven references to public opinion made across all programmes citing independent or viewer polls, or viewer feedback. Virtually all of these suggested strong public disquiet. In coverage of the Commons debate of the report a week after it was released, journalists gave significant voice to those of protestors. More importantly, despite numbering only a handful, they were cast as representative of public opinion. Referring to a heckler who interrupted Tony Blair at the despatch box, ITN reporter Jon Ray remarked: 'As for the court of public opinion, well today Mr Blair found himself shouted down.'[25]

This marked the culmination of a key shift in framing emphasis that began following Dyke's resignation. Up until that point, government ministers were cast as unqualified victors so delighted with Hutton's findings that they probably wanted to 'hug him', in the words of Nick Robinson.[26] A day later however, Robinson along with others began to question whether official sources had gone too far for their own good in pressing for the full apology from the BBC (and hence double resignation): 'I wonder if [Tony Blair] quite wanted to be where he is: having to insist that he doesn't want to attack the independence of the BBC. Never before have the two figures at the top gone.'[27]

Coverage of the 'BBC in crisis' frame, along with the associated 'attack on journalism', had created a new crisis for the government in which it had to assert its support for the BBC's independence and defend itself against the escalating whitewash claims. During a relatively brief live interview on *Channel 4 News*, Secretary of State Tessa Jowell mentioned the word 'independence' or 'independent' no less than ten times in what was clearly an attempt to dampen some of the more vitriolic comments from the Prime Minister in preceding days.[28] If nothing else, it was indicative of the fact that official sources were by no means leading or controlling the news agenda.

It was also no doubt an attempt to draw a line on the coverage, aided by the BBC's issuing of a 'full and frank apology', as well as suggestions of story fatigue. The notion of fatigue was articulated explicitly by Jon Ray following the Commons debate on 4 February: 'If you think you're sick of the Hutton affair just remember this: it will only take one more disaffected member of the intelligence services to come forward and we could be going round this whole weary circuit all over again.'[29]

Former intelligence officer Brian Jones had come forward on the day of the Commons debate, claiming that he and others had raised objections to the dossier but were overruled. Ray's comment that such voices of disapproval could prompt a re-run of the 'whole weary circuit' was in a sense played out in the Butler and Chilcot Inquiries that were to follow Hutton. These examined respectively the intelligence failings and the basis for going to war – two issues at the heart of the wider WMD controversy but not addressed by Hutton.

SCHEDULE BOUNDARIES

In contrast to the preceding case study, the research did not find meaningful distinctions between coverage on the main bulletins and the extended analysis programmes, or between early and late evening editions. However, *Channel 4 News* did provide a degree of context that was not evident in other output. In addition to pursuing the 'attack on journalism' frame in live studio interviews, reports offered unguarded questioning of the Hutton Report in two ways. First, detailed attention was given to discrepancies between findings and evidence. This was framed broadly as a stark contrast between Hutton's 'whiter than white' appraisal of government, and the picture that emerged during the Inquiry. As Gary Gibbon reported: 'In Lord Hutton's hearings an unprecedented light was shone on Number 10 – a very informal, sometimes macho environment, where officials talked of playing chicken with the BBC, destroying enemies and getting names out.'[30]

But importantly, this report also drew attention to specific evidence that appeared to conflict with Hutton's conclusions, mainly in respect of the intelligence dossier that was the subject of Kelly's engagement with the media. In particular, we were reminded of the prime ministerial aide who persuaded the head of the Joint Intelligence Committee to withdraw a caveat that Iraq would only use its WMD if attacked. Such evidence – undisputed by official sources – contrasted sharply with Hutton's conclusions that the dossier was not 'sexed up'. It therefore gave substance to whitewash claims that were merely alluded to in ITV or BBC broadcasts.

The second distinct aspect of context provided by *Channel 4 News* was observed in the full explication of Gavyn Davies' resignation statement. Despite the resignation being a centrepiece of lead headlines on all evening news broadcasts, extracts from the statement were limited to opening remarks which were notably tamer than the scornful critique further on in the statement. This was expressed by Davies through a series of questions that were read out in full by *Channel 4 News* anchor Jon Snow:

> First, is it clearly possible to reconcile Lord Hutton's bold conclusions on the production of the September dossier with the balance of evidence that was presented to him during his inquiry? Second, did his verdict on Mr Gilligan's report take sufficient account of what was said to Dr Kelly on tape by Susan Watts? Finally, are his conclusions on restricting the use of unverifiable sources in British journalism based on sound law and if applied would they constitute a threat to the freedom of the press in this country?[31]

Whilst the first two questions challenge the findings on the basis of evidence at the hearings, the final question goes further and focuses on the legal reasoning underpinning the judgement. This theme was explored in a report two days later by Mark Easton. In it, he revealed an error at the heart of Hutton's legal argument 'that false accusations of fact impugning the integrity of others, including politicians, should not be made by the media'.[32] Easton points out that Hutton relies on the libel case of *Reynolds* v. *The Times* to back up his argument:

But that case is famous for saying the opposite – that justification for publishing an accusation is not whether it's true or false but whether it's responsible – a balance between protecting reputations and freedom of expression. Curiously at the back of his report Lord Hutton prints part of the Reynolds judgement but not the bit that most lawyers think is important.[33]

No such assessments were made in other television news programmes. Indeed, the weight of criticism where it surfaced was founded on the overall imbalance of the report, rather than its legal basis. The fact that Gilligan was judged to have made 'errors' and the management 'defective' was, in a sense, accepted at face value.

Nevertheless, as already suggested, it would be wrong to infer that this discrepancy reflects a gap between the ideological resilience of bulletin and analysis programmes that was evident in the Al Yamamah controversy. After all, what was most ideologically sensitive about this controversy was not the suggestion of erroneous judgement, but the implicit reference to a corrupted system of accountability. In other words, what is deeply controversial about a whitewash is not the outcome itself, but the suggestion that the outcome was in some way prefigured, or inevitable. In this light, the very mention of the word or suggestion of whitewash provides base line evidence of contestability. Specialist outlets like *Channel 4 News* might merely have used their relative time and resource advantage to probe deeper into the detail of the report.

The analysis did, however, find significant differentiation along institutional lines, namely between the output of BBC and ITN newsrooms, with the former exhibiting considerably more caution.[34] During the feverish first two days of coverage, the lunchtime and early evening BBC bulletins made little suggestion of any criticism of the report, and at times actively endorsed it. Frank Gardner, one of the BBC's security correspondents, described Hutton as 'a man with impeccable reputation for fairness – his report carries huge weight'.[35] This was in complete contrast to characterisations of Hutton as an establishment stooge expressed by sources within reports, notably Conservative MP Boris Johnson: 'Law Lords tend to come down very firmly on the side of the government and of the establishment. They've all done that in the past and Hutton has proved no exception.'[36]

Endorsement of the Report's main findings was apparent even in the words of *Newsnight*'s notoriously antagonistic anchor, Jeremy Paxman:

A mistake was made and the thing was mishandled and I don't think you'll find a person around here that doesn't accept that that was the case [...] Personally I'm very happy to accept that Lord Hutton does not accuse [the government] of doing anything wrong as regards to this dossier.[37]

The unqualified acceptance of Hutton's findings was further underlined by references to them without mention of the report itself. Former BBC Chairman Gavyn Davies was described by Duncan Kennedy as having been 'forced out for heading a news organisation that had effectively failed at every level'.[38] In contrast, ITN journalists were far more likely to add caveats such as 'according to Hutton' when mentioning key findings of the report.

Where criticism was alluded to by BBC journalists, it was often couched in terms of the supposed narrowness of the report, rather than imbalance. In this sense, the BBC coverage invoked a much softer version of the whitewash frame than their ITN counterparts. Where ITN journalists talked explicitly of whitewash in live two-ways, their BBC colleagues went only as far as criticising the limitations of the terms of reference. As Guto Harri remarked: '[Hutton's] managed to shunt away a lot of the controversy – he's made it clear his report is not questioning the reliability of intelligence; he's not questioning the basis on which Britain went to war.'[39]

The problem according to this framing was not that Hutton got it wrong, but that he didn't address the burning public interest issues. According to Paxman: 'He chose to define the word "circumstances" very narrowly – no investigation into whether or not WMD existed in Iraq or why intelligence doesn't seem to have matched reality.'

As well as offering a more cautious critique, there was a notably more limited context in the framing of BBC reports compared to those of ITN. When ITN journalists talked of the Hutton Report as an attack on journalism, BBC correspondents tended to limit the context to the key figures involved. A *Six O'Clock News* report by Nick Higham clearly set the frame of reference around Andrew Gilligan: 'He's the reporter who became the story. It was his conversation with David Kelly that led ultimately to today's report and a bleak day for the BBC.'[40]

Whilst this is true at least in a chronological sense, by not providing broader context such as why the report was considered so controversial and damaging to the government, we are left with the impression that the consequences of the Hutton Report were wholly traceable to a single piece of journalism.

A further limitation was observed in the tendency of BBC reporters to stick much closer to impartiality codes than their ITN counterparts, restricting themselves to reporting the views of others rather than expressing their own: 'Mr Blair doesn't think it was a whitewash'.[41] Even in live two-ways, the notion of whitewash tended to be subsumed within the context of the BBC in crisis, in one instance delicately preceded by the phrase 'not everyone accepts the Hutton Report'.[42]

This often manifest in a mixed picture of conflicting opinions. In terms of public opinion discussion, it was not simply a case of being faithful to the evidence provided by pollsters. Particular aspects of language used in the reporting of opinion polls had a marked effect on the tone of coverage. For instance, Laura Trevelyan mentioned in a report broadcast on the *One O'Clock News* that '49 per cent of people think the BBC criticism was fair'.[43] The same statistic could just as accurately and faithfully have been read as 'more than half of people think the BBC criticism was *un*fair', with a clear difference in emphasis. Nevertheless, the report did go on to state that 'only 36 per cent found the verdict convincing and almost half said the report was a whitewash'. In addition, the broadcaster made reference to newspaper headlines that were generally critical of Hutton. But the overall picture was of a mixed response to the Hutton Report that was sharply at odds with the resounding public outrage alluded to by ITN broadcasters.

In general, BBC news programmes did not convey the same sense of indignation that was apparent in ITN broadcasts, in spite of the visible outrage of its rank and file staff. This was not necessarily symptomatic of a tightening of the reins by the caretaker management. Ironically, it was perhaps more likely a reflection of the journalism department seeking to assert its independence from the BBC as a whole. By distancing themselves from the outrage expressed by the former management, as well as rank and file staff, BBC journalists carefully avoided what could be labelled as 'flag flying' reportage.

From a contestability perspective however, this is a moot point. For one thing, the weight of criticism implicit in whitewash allegations may be just as, or more significant when couched as the views of others, as when it is expressed as editorial opinion. Moreover, the invocation of whitewash did not have to be explicit for it to be significant. It was conjured, for instance, through the expression of surprise at the overwhelming one-sided nature of the Hutton Report. In the words of Andrew Marr, 'the real 700-page report couldn't be all one way could it? Oh yes it could'.[44] Ironically, had journalists given more attention to the limited criticism of the government that was in the report, as the political opposition did in Parliament, the whitewash frame might never have surfaced to the extent that it did.

Clearly, this frame was a demonstration of outrage that caught official sources off guard and was on the whole, a robust defence of journalist autonomy in the face of an unprecedented assault. The implicit charge was not just that the report was imbalanced and unfair, but that it was in some sense *illegitimate*. However, this latter context was not explored in-depth even by *Channel 4 News*. Without it, the coverage remained irrevocably bound to Hutton's 'interested parties', namely the government and the BBC and latent questions over the legitimacy of the public inquiry went largely unaddressed. More significantly, the intensity of the coverage burned out very soon after government sources began to talk of 'drawing a line' on the conflict. Following the Commons debate on 4 February – less than one week after the report's release – the whitewash frame disappeared from the television radar.

THE INQUEST CONTROVERSY

Despite closure of the whitewash frame, the Hutton Report was to resurface in television news through a different guise. This involved an enduring campaign to re-open a formal inquest into David Kelly's death. In contrast to the whitewash frame, the inquest controversy never achieved headline status. But whilst the former coverage was condensed within a single week, the inquest controversy was to endure more than six years of prevailing media silence, only to resurface significantly in the summer of 2010. Throughout this period, ITN ran almost twice the number of BBC reports (see Figure 4.1). The other key distinction of the narrative was that it was largely construed as a debate among experts rather than a political controversy. It is perhaps in view of this that it earned the moniker of 'the medical controversy' in television news reports. This was a reflection of the pre-eminence of senior doctors who fronted the campaign for an inquest, but it was also a diversion away from the campaign's central focus: the failure of the official investigation.

Before assessing the media coverage of this aspect in depth, it is worth highlighting a distinction between the inquest campaign

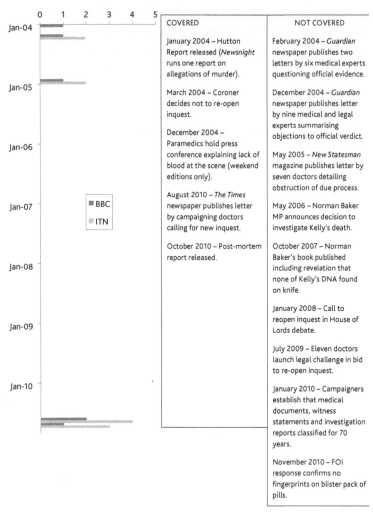

COVERED	NOT COVERED
January 2004 – Hutton Report released (*Newsnight* runs one report on allegations of murder).	February 2004 – *Guardian* newspaper publishes two letters by six medical experts questioning official evidence.
March 2004 – Coroner decides not to re-open inquest.	December 2004 – *Guardian* newspaper publishes letter by nine medical and legal experts summarising objections to official verdict.
December 2004 – Paramedics hold press conference explaining lack of blood at the scene (weekend editions only).	May 2005 – *New Statesman* magazine publishes letter by seven doctors detailing obstruction of due process.
August 2010 – *The Times* newspaper publishes letter by campaigning doctors calling for new inquest.	May 2006 – Norman Baker MP announces decision to investigate Kelly's death.
October 2010 – Post-mortem report released.	October 2007 – Norman Baker's book published including revelation that none of Kelly's DNA found on knife.
	January 2008 – Call to reopen inquest in House of Lords debate.
	July 2009 – Eleven doctors launch legal challenge in bid to re-open inquest.
	January 2010 – Campaigners establish that medical documents, witness statements and investigation reports classified for 70 years.
	November 2010 – FOI response confirms no fingerprints on blister pack of pills.

Figure 4.1   Number of news editions covering the inquest controversy, January 2004 to December 2010

Source: National film archives

and the conspiracy theories that it gave rise to. The former was concerned principally with the safety of Hutton's official verdict of death, and tangentially with obstruction of justice and possible cover-up. At its heart were not assertions as to how Dr Kelly *did* die, but merely that he was highly unlikely to have died in the manner that was officially claimed. Moreover, the campaign pointed to a host of problems and limitations in the official investigative process, as well as subsequent withholding of information. The primary concern of campaigners then, was to push for this apparent failure of justice to be redressed through a proper inquest.

Conspiracy theories were based on the concerns of these campaigners, but included speculative assessments as to how Dr Kelly died, based on circumstantial evidence that pointed to the involvement of third parties. One such theory was notably put forward by Norman Baker MP, who went on to become a government minister in 2010. He published a book in 2007 in which he suggested that Kelly was murdered with the knowledge and connivance of the British security services. However, in one important respect, the inquest campaign was more far reaching in its challenge to state power than such conspiracy theories. The latter are first and foremost associated with the alleged 'original sin', and the particular individuals and institutions that may have been involved. The inquest campaign, on the other hand, was concerned purely and solely with systemic failure of accountability. It was this aspect of the campaign that invoked public interest concerns and meant that, from a news value perspective, the controversy was about much more than the death of one man.

Perhaps the most significant limitation in the coverage stemmed from the tendency of journalists to overlook this distinction. Those who questioned the official verdict were all too readily dismissed as conspiracy theorists, a term which carries the weight of stigma through its association with tabloid and internet sensationalism. The problem was typified in an anchor introduction to *Channel 4 News* which reduced the debate to one between officials and conspiracy theorists only: 'The full post-mortem was published in an attempt to end the speculation about how he died. But the conspiracy theories persist.'

This framing was typical of the coverage relating to the inquest campaign – particularly when the story first surfaced sporadically in 2004. As will be demonstrated, it was also to prove crucial in keeping the story off the agenda of 'serious' news outlets.

In researching stories left off the news agenda, a requisite challenge is to establish the grounds on which they *should* have been paid more attention, should such grounds exist. In other words, how can we be sure that the controversy was intrinsically worthy of greater exposure, or that its marginalisation wasn't simply an accidental bi-product of randomness in the news selection process? Clearly the uniqueness of the story makes it difficult to identify comparatively similar controversies that received wider media attention. On the other hand, the news value of the inquest campaign rested above all on its perceived credibility, rather than any inherent characteristics of the narrative. In other words, the controversy becomes more compelling as a news story if its fundamental premise is believed by journalists, namely that the official verdict of death was unsafe. Few would argue that even if there *was* sufficient evidence to cast doubt over the official verdict, the story would not warrant wider journalistic attention than it received. Journalists themselves were unanimous on this point during interviews for this book. But it prompts a key question: was the evidence in favour of the official verdict given more prominence in news reports than that which cast doubt over it? Table 4.1 displays an overview of conflicting evidence in relation to the cause of death presented at the Hutton

Table 4.1   Conflicting evidence in relation to the official verdict of Dr Kelly's death

Suicidal tendencies	EVIDENCE FOR	Pressure of being publicly 'outed'.
		Shame of having breached civil service code.
		Depression over a life's work in ruins.
	EVIDENCE AGAINST	No evidence of depression or intent to commit suicide.
		Expressions of optimism in private communications leading up to death, plans to meet with daughter and travel to Iraq.
Arterial bleeding as principal cause of death	EVIDENCE FOR	Pathologist testimony notes incised wound on wrist, severed ulnar artery and the presence of blood at the scene.
		Body observed as lying flat surrounded by knife and wristwatch.
	EVIDENCE AGAINST	Paramedics find minimal blood and no visible wound.
		Senior medical experts describe death caused by severed ulnar artery as 'virtually impossible'.
		Wristwatch not positively identified as belonging to Dr Kelly and no DNA found on the knife.
Ingestion of pain killers secondary cause	EVIDENCE FOR	Blister pack of 30 co-proxamol tablets found next to body with only one pill left.
		Silent heart condition identified in post-mortem.
	EVIDENCE AGAINST	Toxicology report finds levels of co-proxamol less than a third of that considered fatal.
		Only one pill found in stomach contents.

Sources: *The Hutton Inquiry: Transcripts* (2003), http://webarchive.nationalarchives.gov.uk/20090128221550/http://www.the-hutton-inquiry.org.uk/ (last accessed on 14 March 2011); Thames Valley Police, *Information Disclosure Logs*, www.thamesvalley.police.uk/aboutus/aboutus-depts/aboutus-depts-infman/aboutus-depts-foi/aboutus-depts-foi-disclosure-log/aboutus-depts-foi-disclosure-log-investigate.htm (last accessed 6 June 2012).

Inquiry and subsequently. Figure 4.2 illustrates the number of times evidence for and against the official verdict was cited in the sample of news programmes analysed.

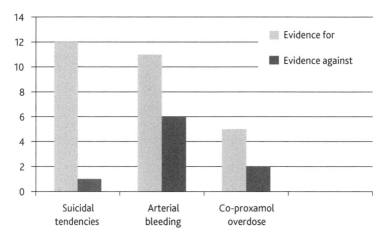

Figure 4.2   Number of citations in news programmes of evidence for and against official verdict

Source: National Film Archives

The data suggest that conflicting evidence cited in reports was weighted heavily in favour of the official explanation of death. Most significantly, journalists overwhelmingly endorsed Hutton's conclusion that Kelly was suicidal at the time of his death. In fact, conflicting evidence heard in relation to Kelly's mental state was, if anything, skewed against the view that he was suicidal. The only relevant witness who considered him to be so was a consultant psychiatrist who had never actually met Kelly, let alone interacted with him during his final days and hours. His testimony was based in large part on that of other witnesses, namely Kelly's close family. But whilst they had spoken of him as 'withdrawn' and 'subdued', this was primarily in the context of the period leading up to his appearance before the Foreign Affairs Select Committee on 14 July 2003. Following that, Kelly's daughter and son-in-law, with whom he was staying at the time, described his demeanour repeatedly as 'normal', 'calm', 'relaxed', 'relieved', and eating and sleeping 'very well' right up to the day of his disappearance. According to his sister, Susan Pape, who spoke to Kelly by telephone two days before his death:

In my line of work I do deal with people who may have suicidal thoughts and I ought to be able to spot those, even on a telephone conversation. But I have gone over and over in my mind the two conversations we had and he certainly did not betray to me any impression that he was anything other than tired. He certainly did not convey to me that he was feeling depressed; and absolutely nothing that would have alerted me to the fact that he might have been considering suicide.[45]

Although Kelly's wife had described him as 'shrunk into himself' and 'heart-broken' on the day he died, she did not consider him suicidal at the time, and stressed that 'he had never seemed depressed in all of this'.

Clearly then, the coverage of evidence relating to David Kelly's state of mind prior to his death did not reflect the balance of evidence heard, and if anything, was inversely proportionate to it. This picture is even more acute if we consider the immediate aftermath of the Hutton Report's publication and the week of headlines that followed it. During this period, evidence in favour of Kelly being suicidal was cited seven times within the sample, whilst evidence against received no mention at all. Moreover, at every turn television news reported Kelly's suicide by arterial bleeding as fact. Indeed, it was the one finding of Hutton's report that was regularly stated in all outlets without any caveat or qualification (see Table 4.2).

Table 4.2   Number of times key Hutton findings reported without caveat or qualification, 28–30 January 2004

BBC management at fault	Gilligan allegation inaccurate	Cause of death suicide from incised wounds
4	2	17

Source: National Film Archives and BBC Online

This suggests that the controversy's failure to gain news traction, particularly in the crucial post-Hutton phase, was not simply the result of story selection randomness. Nor can it be dismissed as a reflection of the controversy's relative news value (compared to the whitewash frame) given that evidence in favour of the official explanation of death was repeatedly cited and elaborated on. The imbalance in coverage was at least partly attributable to a systematic tendency of journalists to overlook evidence that undermined the official verdict.

Instead of giving voice to those challenging the official explanation of death, journalists were at pains to point out the extent of public 'shame' and 'humiliation' that Kelly experienced as a result of being outed as Gilligan's source. The Hutton Report itself strongly criticised Kelly for his breach of the civil service code and official procedure in talking to the media. In the words of investigative journalist Tom Mangold, 'David knew he had made a mistake in indulging in political and intelligence gossip with Andrew Gilligan'.[46]

There is, however, a clear gap between alleged professional misconduct and what was characterised by Hutton as a 'public disgrace'. A cursory glance at media coverage in the short period between his outing and death suggests the contrary; that the dominant media narrative cast him as the victim rather than villain in the on-going battle between the government and BBC. The coverage certainly gave no indication of the kind of humiliation and shame that was espoused in news commentary following the Hutton Report. Indeed, in the post-Hutton coverage there was a clear tension between acknowledging the criticism of Kelly's character offered in the report – 'a difficult man to help' – and adopting the hitherto dominant frame that characterised him as a heroic and human casualty of an institutional war.

We have seen that journalists' neglect of evidence undermining the official verdict was not a reflection of the balance of evidence heard during the Hutton Inquiry. Throughout the duration of the hearings, all news outlets within the sample had dedicated reporters in attendance, with unfettered access to the testimonies and evidence presented. What's more, the Hutton Inquiry was in one way unprecedented in its openness – full transcripts of the hearings were published online as they progressed. Much of the contradictory evidence heard in relation to Kelly's death was therefore easily accessible to all journalists, regardless of whether or not they attended the hearings.

This raises the question of why conflicting testimonies, particularly in relation to the amount of blood found at the scene and the position of the body, did not receive significant attention by news broadcasters. Even the testimony of official experts which cast an element of doubt over the official explanation of death barely gained traction in the news. For instance, Hutton's conclusion that Dr Kelly had swallowed 29 co-proxamol tablets was based solely on the fact that a packet which held 30 tablets was found in Dr Kelly's pocket at the time of his death, with only one tablet remaining. The toxicology evidence heard at the Inquiry stated that less than a fifth of one tablet was in fact found in Dr Kelly's stomach and chemical levels detected in his urine suggested a dosage of less than one third of what could be considered potentially fatal.[47] Despite this, a co-proxamol overdose was widely reported as a possible secondary cause of death.

Nor can the exclusion of alternative frames be explained by an absence of campaigners voicing concerns over the official verdict. During 2004, there were at least three letters by medical experts published in the *Guardian* newspaper. All of these were similar in content to a letter published in *The Times* which did spark renewed coverage some six years later.

The paucity of coverage was perhaps even more surprising given the weight of elite endorsement of the inquest campaign. It was led by senior medical and legal experts and backed by a former front bench MP (who became a senior government minister in 2010). When the controversy was first covered by *Channel 4 News* in March 2004, the eminence and seniority of those behind the campaign was highlighted. In the words of the programme's chief correspondent, Alex Thomson: 'Tonight for the first time on TV some of Britain's leading medical specialists believe Hutton was wrong [...] these are senior experienced medical professionals – they're not wacky conspiracy theorists.'[48]

The phrase 'for the first time on TV' is indicative of the slow reaction of news broadcasters to the questions surrounding Hutton's official verdict. He went on to list some of the key unanswered questions that have given rise to allegations of cover-up:

> Dr Kelly's dental records went missing: why? Mysterious detectives at the scene are unaccounted for. Who are they and why? His body had apparently been moved before examination. By whom, what for? [...] So far Lord Hutton's inquiry has failed to answer these questions. Only a coroner's inquest could do so. But even the basic medical conclusions of Lord Hutton about his death are now under question.

What is revealing about this statement is that the unanswered questions cited did not stem from, and were not dependent on the views of scientific experts. Yet much of the report went on to focus on the apparent conflicting views between medical professionals on the one hand, and forensic experts on the other. When the story resurfaced in 2010, it continued to be framed principally as a conflict between experts, effectively absolving journalists of their responsibility to question or challenge the official verdict directly. This was epitomised by the opening words of a report by Lucy Manning for ITV News: 'Some as the Hutton inquiry found think David Kelly killed himself but some think the evidence just isn't there, others that there was some sort of cover-up.'[49]

In contrast to the demonstrations of outrage in the whitewash frame, this spectacle of expert debate enabled broadcasters to draw attention to their role as impartial arbiters. In August 2010, ITV's *News at Ten* ran a special feature in which a representative both for and against re-opening the inquest were given a platform to air their views.[50] The introduction seemed to emphasise the broadcaster's self-appointment as referee: 'on tonight's ITV *News at Ten* we hear from both sides in that debate'. The implication is that expert opinion was broadly split between protagonists and antagonists in relation to the inquest campaign. But in fact all scientific experts who appeared in television reports – including forensic specialists and the official pathologist who endorsed Hutton's verdict – were in support of an inquest. According to Dr Margaret Bloom, a leading figure in the campaign, opinion within the medical field was overwhelmingly circumspect in relation to the official explanation of death: 'I've never met anyone [in the medical profession] who really thought it was very likely that he slit his arm or artery and that's what killed him. It's not medically very likely. Nor have I met anyone who was satisfied with the process as it stands.'

This suggests that the expert debate was not as evenly balanced as it was framed in television news, although this framing did to an extent liberate campaigners from the conspiracy theory tag. However, in subtle and significant ways, broadcasters abandoned even their notional neutrality in favour of the original verdict. The manner in which reports concluded was often particularly suggestive. In a way reminiscent of the immediate post-inquiry coverage, Liz MacKean closed her *Newsnight* report with a suggestion of what might have driven Dr Kelly to suicide: 'There can be no doubt about the calamitous effect on David Kelly himself – a man used to the shadows who found himself in the unblinking public gaze.'[51]

LIFTING THE LID

Whilst the initial coverage in August 2010 was framed as a debate between experts, subsequent coverage was overwhelmingly given over to official responses and their apparently 'debunking' effect. As already mentioned, the coverage had been sparked by a letter published in *The Times* newspaper,[52] prompting two official responses. The first consisted of a statement released by the original pathologist Dr Nicholas Hunt, re-emphasising that the death was a 'text book' case of suicide. The second response was the release by Justice Minister Kenneth Clarke of the official post-mortem and toxicology reports. But campaigners pointed out that there was nothing in the documents released that was not already accessible in the Hutton transcripts:

> Anyone that has read the account on Lord Hutton's website of Dr Hunt's evidence will appreciate that there's nothing new that's been seen in his post mortem report [...] It simply puts into words that which was said by Dr Hunt and Dr Allan and has taken the matter no forward at all.[53]

Journalists nevertheless routinely indicated that the report helped explain away a lot of the lingering doubt.

The event was characterised by official sources as the end of secrecy in relation to Kelly's death, a point that was readily accepted by broadcasters. Reports were typically introduced by anchors with reference to 'previously secret evidence' that had been released. But the released documents were only part of the classified documentation that campaigners were seeking access to, and by no means the most pertinent. Of the 1,158 police documents submitted to Hutton, only 260 had been published at the time of writing. Many of the remaining classified documents include medical reports as well as supplementary witness statements.

Although some news reports did feature campaigners emphasising this point, it did not prevent correspondents from placing emphasis on the *declassification* of evidence. In the words of Simon Israel for the *Channel 4 News*, 'today that secrecy was lifted'.[54] The event had helped to resolve what was perhaps the most troubling aspect of the controversy from a journalistic point of view: the withholding of information by the state. Lifting the lid demonstrated that the state had nothing to hide after all.

Importantly, it also came with an explanation as to why information had been withheld in the first place. According to Lucy Manning, for ITV's *News At Ten*, 'Lord Hutton said today he wasn't trying to conceal evidence by keeping the post mortem secret, he was just protecting Dr Kelly's family'.[55] This explanation was not challenged in any of the news programmes that covered it. In particular, at no point did broadcasters raise the crucial question of whether the public interest outweighed that of the family. By accepting the official maxim without question, journalists effectively absolved themselves of their duty to pursue the matter further.

It did not, however, explain why in the seven years of controversy to date, the job of pressing for access was left almost exclusively to campaigners. In contrast to the preceding case study, the inquest campaign resoundingly failed to induce the usual defensive reflex of journalists in the face of official attempts at information control. This was true even amongst those journalists who consider the act of 'uncovering the cover-up' a core component of their self-defining role.

When campaigners made a formal legal submission to the Attorney General in March 2011, the event was not picked up by television news within the sample analysed. It was not until the Attorney General refused the inquest – marking the third occasion in which an inquest had been formally denied by the government[56] – that the story momentarily resurfaced. It attracted relatively brief reports of just over two minutes on *Channel 4 News* and the BBC *One O'Clock News*. But neither of these went into any detail about either the reasons for an inquest put forward by campaigners, or the Attorney General's justification for his refusal. As a result, news audiences were effectively excluded from the terms of the debate and the particular outstanding issues of controversy.

Instead, both reports adopted what was by this stage one of the key frames advanced by official sources and their supporters. Its central proposition was that on-going speculation and challenge by campaigners was inevitable in light of the intense political controversy that had surrounded Kelly. Matt Prodger concluded his BBC news report with this emphasis: 'Given the intensely political nature of the storm which surrounded David Kelly it's no surprise that the controversy has continued and is likely to do so.'[57]

The implication here is that the arguments in favour of an inquest were politically motivated and more acutely, on-going controversy is to be expected in light of the broader context of the death. Once again, both journalists and audiences are effectively absolved of paying further attention to the controversy by the subtle framing adopted. This drew a line on the story in such a way as to devalue the case of campaigners and draw attention away from outstanding questions in relation to the failure of due process.

Although revolving around the same events, the whitewash frame and the inquest controversy were to an extent, mutually exclusive stories. The former was in some way contingent on acceptance of the official verdict of death. In arbitrating between the government and the BBC, Hutton was in effect casting a judgement as to which institution was more responsible for Kelly's death, implying that it was his public 'outing' in the midst of that battle which drove him to suicide.

In any case, we have seen that Hutton's vindication of the government and castigation of the BBC was an insufficient condition in explaining the lack of journalist attention to the inquest campaign. This consisted in an active endorsement of evidence in support of the official verdict (and to the neglect of the contrary); a relatively extreme adoption of impartiality codes that relegated the controversy to an 'expert debate'; persistent favouring of official responses over new evidence produced by campaigners; and the failure to draw attention to existing evidence that continues to be withheld. Thus, even when the inquest campaign briefly surfaced in television news, journalists on the whole paid deference to official dictum. This was particularly noticeable in the introductions and conclusions to reports where framing was at its most explicit.

5
The Basis of Belief

The preceding analysis suggested a resounding failure of journalists to 'uncover the cover-up'. We now need to determine why that failure occurred. Clearly this starting position is an antagonistic one, at least in respect of the core subjects of my research: broadcast journalists. But although the analysis is focused on and critical of journalism, it does not follow that the problem is rooted in journalism alone. It is perhaps significant on this point that the coverage has not attracted the attention of some of the most radical and outspoken media critics.

Of course, just because the case has not attracted attention from mainstream journalists or their critics does not mean it is intrinsically worthy of that attention. In the preceding analysis, I attempted to show that active selection and prioritisation of evidence in favour of the official verdict was at least as significant in marginalising the story as its considered news value or random factors. This view was given added weight by interviews with journalists who overwhelmingly maintained faith in the official verdict. It was this fact above all else which accounted for how they valued the story in terms of newsworthiness. In the words of one investigative journalist, 'I think he killed himself. And if I think that it means I don't think there was a cover-up'.

This suggests that the considered news value of the story was intimately related to whether or not journalists subscribed to the official explanation of death, rather than the controversy's inherent news currency. Much of the following discussion is therefore concerned with epistemological considerations in attempting to understand why the official explanation of death was so believable, in spite of existing and growing evidence to the contrary. The conclusions reached are not intended to pass judgement on any of the journalists or sources that kindly gave of their time and insights, nor indeed other individuals or groups with whom they are associated. My concern in this chapter is not simply to critically assess journalists, but to understand the structural and instrumental factors that both advance and constrain their work.

THE ORIGINS OF OUTRAGE

But we ought first to consider why the Hutton Report provoked considerable and remarkable outrage among news broadcasters, even within the confines of the whitewash framing. What seems clear at the outset is that the controversy fed on the charisma of media personalities at the forefront of the battle between the government and the BBC. Greg Dyke had been a relatively high profile Director General at the BBC ever since he assumed the role in 2000 with an infamous promise to 'cut the crap'.[1] Alastair Campbell, the Prime Minister's chief media strategist, was without doubt a more outspoken and public figure than any of his predecessors. Moreover, his own professional experience within journalism helped to ensure that his public utterances were always newsworthy. David Cohen, feature writer for the *London Evening Standard*, provided a snapshot of the personalities that coloured the WMD controversy:

> The characters involved: Alastair Campbell, ex journalist – so there may be 'fuck him' sort of feelings – and also he's very aggressive so the way he responds is News. He responded in a very colourful, incandescent way. And then you've got [Andrew] Gilligan – very controversial, in many ways not well liked and accused by his home bosses of reporting in primary colours so of being out to make his name.

As discussed in the previous chapter, it was Gilligan's infamous two-way on Radio 4's *Today* programme that was at the centre of the conflict which the Hutton Report was to eventually adjudicate on. In an interview conducted for this research, Gilligan used the kind of 'straight talking' language that was not dissimilar to that associated with both Campbell and Dyke. His insights also pointed to the media personality war in which he was embroiled:

> I think [the government] were genuinely mad. I think Alastair Campbell had genuinely lost it. I was amazed at quite how deranged a figure he was because it was so – it seems like a useful diversion for the government's central difficulties about the dossier but it very swiftly became very personal.

This indignation towards Campbell was shared by broadcast journalists across the board. Alex Thomson, chief correspondent of the *Channel 4 News*, lamented how an organisation the size of the BBC, 'the biggest journalistic institution on the planet', could be 'so comprehensively intimidated and done in by one bully of a press officer in the government called Alastair Campbell.'

Journalists interviewed for this book from both ITN and the BBC used uncharacteristically extreme language in relation to Campbell, described as 'animus' and 'manipulative', as well as referencing the 'absurd' and 'ludicrous' outcome of events which culminated in the Hutton Report. This was not just a response to Campbell's media personality. More significantly, it was a symptom of genuine journalist outrage sparked by the WMD controversy and cemented by the official outcome that was the Hutton Report.

Another driving force concerned the controversy's implication that the government had at best misled (intentionally or otherwise) journalists, parliament and the wider public over the justification for war. To many of those journalists who had supported the war, the failure to find WMD in Iraq and the evidence that the case had been 'sexed up' by Campbell and Blair had damaged their own professional reputations. One journalist in particular has publicly and repeatedly expressed 'shame and regret' for the position he had taken and much of his angst since has been directed at Blair for not doing the same.[2] For those journalists that had opposed the war, the failure to find WMD added fuel to the fire of their opposition. It coincided with evidence that was emerging from intelligence sources that the government had 'sexed up' the WMD case to begin with. This created a deep-seated anger stemming from a sense of powerlessness amongst journalists. It was encapsulated by Paul Lashmar, award-winning investigative reporter:

> Journalists wrote stories in the UK about WMD. A lot of people were questioning WMD and the justification for going to war but they didn't stop anything. And the fact is [...] no matter how much journalism there is around, it's the power of the executive and Tony Blair as it was then to do what they want. Despite all the investigative journalism that took place at the time, we went to war.

Another basis of outrage consisted in a shared sense that the Hutton Report was an attack on journalism as a whole. According to Robin Elias, managing editor of ITV News, journalist outrage was a response to perceived pressure not just on the BBC, but 'on everybody else around that time'. This helps to explain some of the implicit messages of solidarity offered by ITN correspondents in live two-ways, as discussed in the previous chapter. Indeed, the analysis found that contestability was more evident on ITN news programmes than on BBC. Clearly, this had much to do with the BBC itself being in the eye of the political storm. But it also owes something to the subtle differences in the way in which each organisation perceives and articulates its journalistic role. In contrast to the assertion of one BBC journalist that 'the BBC doesn't criticise things we report other people's criticisms', a senior ITV news executive appeared to have a very different take on the notion of impartiality:

> There is a moral code if you like. We know when things are unfair, if a section of society is being badly treated. So I think your moral compass does come in and that's a very difficult thing to define. But I think that's what makes a good news organisation.

But as well as self-interested responses, the controversy also invoked a strong sense that the Hutton Report was simply morally unjustified. According to Alex Thomson,

> [The government] were found out in appointing someone who had spent most of his career as a stooge from the days when he had the misjudgement to be a junior QC on the much discredited Widgery Tribunal over Bloody Sunday in 1973, right through to the now named after him Hutton Inquiry. We knew exactly what we were getting. It was a whitewash. It was plainly a whitewash worthy of some West African dictatorship and it's the business of journalism to expose that nonsense.

The reference to 'West African dictatorship' is significant here. Journalists are clearly sensitive to controversies that 'blow a hole' in the perceived notion that political corruption is something that happens outside of Britain rather than within it. Britain's reputation for clean politics was seen as its 'unique selling point' by Gary Gibbon, political correspondent for *Channel 4 News*, even in respect of other EU countries. He articulated this sensitivity by drawing attention to the recent imprisonment of David Chaytor for defrauding MP's expenses:

> The fourth estate has many flaws and corruptions of its own, but it tends to hold the political governing establishment to very high standards of probity and when we lock up an MP for 18 months

for twelve-thousand-pounds-worth of expenses over three years [...] people in Italy, France, Spain – their eyes pop out. They just cannot believe the small change of cab receipts as they would see it, because they are doing it on a colossal scale which is not only monetary [...] I think that's what gets journalist's backs up because they see on occasion that there is massive corruption. It blows your perception of your nation and you know it doesn't go anywhere good.

In many ways, the outrage exhibited by journalists in relation to the Hutton Report was not dissimilar to that which was found in relation to the Al Yamamah controversy. Both were concerned ultimately with a sense that the supremely powerful can elude justice, in Britain just as much as anywhere else. In this case, the Hutton Report was perceived as the means by which Tony Blair and Alastair Campbell could get away with exaggerating, if not fabricating the case for war.

But there was one important distinction in the controversy surrounding the Hutton Report: unlike the BAe case, it was built on the fault lines of party political conflict. Whilst journalists played a lead role in questioning the report, no doubt spurring on the political opposition to follow suit, this framing clearly owed much to the wider brewing controversy over the absence of WMD's in Iraq. This in turn owed its narrative gravitas to the deep split in both elite and public opinion that emerged during the run-up to the war in 2003. According to a former senior intelligence official, contestability in this case can be traced all the way back to the end of a Cold War political consensus:

Issues around defence, the deterrent, the use of force, are no longer part of a post war consensus as there was during the Cold War essentially. So you're liable to find whatever is said will be taken and used as a political football [...] There are more leaks so information arrives and questions suddenly get asked, issues suddenly appear in the newspapers [...] The public is generally, and certainly the media are less deferential.

Added to this, and in line with the previous case study, outrage was infused with a perception among journalists of a public desire to 'put Blair on the rack'. By the time the Hutton Report came out, Tony Blair had been prime minister for six years during which time he had presided over three military conflicts and two further engagements of British troops abroad – more than any other prime minister in history. The WMD controversy placed Blair at its epicentre and with it, fuelled the innate journalistic drive 'to bring down a prime minister'.

It was therefore the political context above all which accounted for the extent of journalistic outrage and contestability in coverage during the aftermath of the Hutton Report. It is perhaps partly because of this that the story dropped so quickly from the news agenda once the political arguments went quiet.

COLLECTIVE FAILURE

As discussed previously, journalists commonly express a range of self-conceptions as to their function in liberal democratic terms. At one end, some adopt a passive view in which their goals are, according to a senior BBC news editor, not 'to animate change' but 'to bear witness and bring things to light'. At the other end of the spectrum, journalists consider their role in a much more active sense. According to Alex Thomson of *Channel 4 News*: 'Journalism should be at its best the highest performance watchdog that we've got. Because most of our official watchdogs are paper toothless tigers anyway by virtue. It comes with the turf.'

From this perspective, journalism is not limited to bearing witness, but is concerned ultimately with 'changing the world'. 'The best form of journalism – the things that when one eventually retires one will look back on say "yeah I was pleased with that" is your journalism and breaking stories which change the world and change it for the better. Full stop.'

But even from this perspective, most journalists acknowledge that their capacity to bring about change, to ensure that the powerful are adequately and meaningfully held to account, is at best limited and at worst severely impaired. For Andrew Gilligan, the limit is a clear professional distinction between journalists and legal professionals: 'Obviously I can't be the one to deliver justice. That is other people's jobs. But it's nice to see your stories have results'. For others, the limitation exists primarily in the public response to campaigning journalism and the need for the media to ultimately 'reflect the public mood', however much it tries to influence opinion or mobilise resistance. At the time of writing, the Iraq Inquiry headed by Sir John Chilcot is yet to deliver its conclusions, but there was a strong sense expressed by journalists that the battle has already been lost.

For Gary Gibbon, this was reflected in an inevitable decline in public interest as the events in question recede further into the past:

> Just one year on from his first appearance at Chilcot, at Blair's second appearance there were 50 people from the Socialist Workers Party outside. The year before that when he came it was still a Labour government which added a bit of edge to it and there were quite a few more demonstrators. But nothing like as many as there would have been the year before that or the year before that.

The capacity of official sources to use timing as a means of deflecting accountability will be discussed further below. The key point here is that whilst journalists may have lost the battle over the WMD controversy, they did not even wage a fight over the inquest campaign. Even within the most passive conceptions of their democratic function – that of 'bearing witness' – there was an acute failure to bring the obstruction of justice, and other attributes of cover-up, to the attention of mainstream audiences. Norman Baker – a government minister who investigated David Kelly's death whilst in opposition – highlighted the sheer lack of investigative impulse shown by the vast majority of professional journalists:

> Journalists make their own judgement but I suggest to you that if the entirety of Fleet Street has to wait until I submit a Freedom of Information request to demonstrate that there were no fingerprints on the knife allegedly used by David Kelly to kill himself, that's a collective failure of Fleet Street not to find that out. Why is it left to one MP to find that out? That's just one example.

So what accounts for this collective failure? One possibility is that journalists were 'chilled' by the climate of caution that emerged post-Hutton, and were discouraged – consciously or unconsciously – by perceived professional risks associated with the story. The discrepancy in levels of coverage between ITN and BBC appears to support this idea. But it does not explain why journalists were comfortable adopting adversarial roles in the whitewash frame which, as we have seen, did not smack of a journalism that had been quietened or subdued by the government.

We can further discount the effect of resource pressures on journalists, at least as a direct source of containment. Much of the evidence that has cast doubt over the official verdict was publicly accessible online through the Hutton Inquiry transcripts. Further evidence has been obtained largely by non-professional campaigners collaborating through a network of online blogs. Clearly, this was not the kind of controversy that demanded intensive, resource-draining investigative journalism.

What was missing was the kind of campaigning journalism that was evident in the whitewash frame. According to Andrew Gilligan, the distinctive feature of this type of journalism is simply that you cover the stories 'and keep coming back to them'. But it is not limited to the print domain, as one senior ITV news executive explained: 'We've taken up certain causes, certain issues that we've taken ownership of I think, and we like to promote. We like to follow those through and we think those are the issues that strike a chord with the public.'

Channel 4 News goes further than this and campaigns not simply on issues that resonate with their audience, but also on ones that require audiences to be 'pushed'. According to Garry Gibbon: 'It's about what is the tolerance levels of the audience and what are the things you've got to tell them and Channel 4 has traditionally pushed the tolerance of its viewers.'

The question we are left with is, why did journalists not consider the inquest campaign a story worth fighting for? The surface answer, as we have seen, is that journalists believed the official explanation of death. Of the twelve interviewed for this case study, representing a cross section of the mainstream media, all but Miles Goslett – a freelance journalist who campaigned for an inquest with the help of the *Daily Mail* and *Mail on Sunday* – adopted this position. It stands to reason that if these journalists *did* believe that the official verdict was unsafe and that there had been some degree of official cover-up, then they would have considered it a far more important news story. But in most cases their position was followed or preceded by a caveat such as that offered by Paul Lashmar: 'I haven't done a forensic analysis of it so I'm probably not the best person to ask'.

Indeed, one of the most consistent findings that emerged during interviews was that journalists on the whole were simply not cognitive of the evidence on which the inquest campaign and allegations of cover-up were based. Some did comment on the controversy concerning the lack of blood found at the scene, but few exhibited awareness of the various forensic anomalies and unanswered questions at stake. What seems clear is that although understanding of the case did not require intensive investigation, it did require some degree of time and attention. According to Miles

Goslett: 'You've got to have the time and inclination to drill down, familiarise yourself with large amounts of information, think about everything pretty carefully and so on. And of course most journalists don't have the time or the inclination to get involved in that.'

It follows that if more journalists had taken the time to review the evidence, they might have adopted a different position and the story might have gained more traction as a result. The crucial missing ingredient then, was a lack of interest in the case. Returning to Norman Baker's question, we might fine-tune it further and ask why did the inquest campaign fail to spark widespread journalist curiosity?

ACCOUNTABILITY DISTRACTION

A recurrent theme that emerged from interviews with campaigners was the view that the Hutton Report succeeded in *distracting* journalists from its original focal point: the death of Dr Kelly. The conflict between the government and the BBC was a headline-grabbing narrative and it was a natural reflex on the part of most journalists to consider Hutton's verdict in the terms of that conflict. The Hutton Report itself devoted less than five per cent of its contents to the investigation and cause of Kelly's death.[3]

The Inquiry that preceded the report was an all-consuming news spectacle that intensified in the build-up to the report's publication. It resonated powerfully with news values not just in the charismatic and powerful figures it revolved around. As we saw in the previous chapter, the proceedings fuelled the media's appetite for information disclosure, particularly in respect of the normally hidden inner workings of government. Moreover, as Paul Lashmar pointed out, the inquiry provides this material as ready-made fodder: 'if you've got an inquiry someone's doing the donkey work and breaking the news for you'.

But the very transparency of the Hutton Inquiry and report that followed may have impeded the inquest controversy as a news story. According to Miles Goslett,

The Hutton Inquiry was so open that it was closed. It took place in front of television cameras – not the hearings themselves – but you would see Blair getting out of the car and going in to give evidence and so on, and in that respect [...] it just deflected attention away from why they weren't having an inquest.

Journalists interviewed for this book used relatively animated language to describe the build-up to the report's publication which, in the words of Alex Thomson, 'unfolded day in day out like some sort of massive slow motion car crash'.

But importantly, the dominance of the whitewash frame didn't preclude reflection on the cause of death all together. Some journalists who followed the proceedings closely gave serious consideration to the possibility that Kelly did not commit suicide. They stressed the intimacy they experienced with the proceedings when foregrounding their conclusions that the official verdict was safe after all. According to Gary Gibbon:

> I was there for every day of Hutton. I heard the post-mortem examination being read out by the guy who did the post-mortem examination. I heard the medical evidence [...] You lived in [David Kelly's] world and mind for the whole of that summer as you sat through the inquiry and I'm personally convinced on the basis of everything I heard that he did what the post mortem said he did.

For some, the sheer length and transparency of the inquiry seemed to evoke a perception of thoroughness that was in stark contrast to the perspective put forward by medical and legal experts of 'a rubbish investigation'. But the 'closeness' of journalists to the proceedings might have been more of an impediment than an advantage. Miles Goslett highlighted the analytical advantages that stemmed from a certain degree of distance from the locus of coverage:

> It began as a Westminster story and I don't work in Westminster and I've recently been thinking about that and thinking that I'm actually quite glad I don't work in Westminster. Because when you work that close to power you can't actually see what's going on. You've got to stand back from it. So what began as a political story carried on being a political story. Because the inquiry took place in London; because it was dominated by star attractions like Alastair Campbell and Tony Blair; it remained a Westminster story.

But as the political fracas settled down and without the fuel of disclosure provided by proceedings, it did not take long for the Hutton Report to recede from the headlines. The notion of the whitewash frame as a diversion does not therefore explain the subsequent neglect of the inquest campaign, particularly when new evidence surfaced or when other seemingly newsworthy events occurred (such as the publication of Norman Baker's book or the announcement that the group of doctors had begun a formal legal challenge). There was however a sense expressed in some interview responses that pointed to the potential for journalist mistakes to be self-perpetuating. According to Norman Baker:

> I think they bought the narrative on day one from the government that this was a suicide of course and the real issue was the political battle between the BBC and the government, and having bought that argument on day one it's rather difficult to go back and say well actually we didn't look at it properly, we'll look at it now.

As time went on, the very notion that the inquest controversy could be 'worth looking at' raised implicit questions as to why journalists had not looked at it sooner. It is plausible that this in turn made the story less attractive as journalists avoided what threatened to bring them into disrepute. It is of course difficult to substantiate such inferences and there certainly seems little reason to doubt the sincerity of those journalists who simply believed that Kelly committed suicide and hence, that there wasn't much weight in the inquest campaign as a news story.

Perhaps a more convincing explanation than self-defence was a sense in which the inquest controversy was just too 'obvious' to attract the attention of serious news journalists, particularly those who based their reputations on deep and complex investigations. By the time the Hutton Report had come out, initial questions concerning the verdict had already been raised. In the midst of the openness and media fervour that followed, the inquest campaign – neglected as it was – did not amount to the coveted 'untold story'. Paul Lashmar epitomised this sentiment that the good journalist goes to places other people can't reach: 'it's the journalist's job to get facts that no one else can'. The facts underpinning the inquest campaign were, as we have seen, very much in reach.

HERD MENTALITY

Accessibility might explain the story's lack of appeal to serious investigative journalists, but it does not explain the corresponding neglect by frontline daily reporters. We might expect cash-strapped news producers to capitalise on the fact that campaigners had been doing the 'donkey work' of investigating and soliciting new information about the case. But rather than an instinct to tell the untold story, it was a herd mentality amongst reporters and editors which kept the inquest campaign in the shadows of the television spotlight. It was encapsulated in an emphatic appeal by one BBC journalist to the line taken by other news organisations:

> I think our approach is like most of the papers, most of the broadsheets and most of the [tabloids] actually – it's only really the *Mail* that continues to be publishing stories with any regularity about it [...] I think there's kind of a general view that actually the *Mail* hasn't really turned up any new information, that it hasn't really fundamentally advanced the story. They have a particular interest in continuing to do it [...] ITN hasn't touched it, Sky hasn't touched it, most of the papers haven't touched it.

Journalist responses repeatedly gave the impression that an important element of newsworthiness is the degree to which others consider it newsworthy. The more a story is repeated and circulated, the more news currency it gains, until it reaches the point of saturation. The absence of the inquest campaign from the mainstream news agenda, in part for reasons already explained, only added to its marginalisation. An insight into the self-perpetuating effects of mainstream marginalisation was provided by Robin Ramsay, who worked at *Channel 4 News* on an in-depth investigation in the 1980s. His reflections depicted a daily news agenda legitimated by the *Today* programme:

> I used to drive in the morning with the journalist I was working for and he had Radio 4 on and you get into *Channel 4 News* and I discovered that everybody working there listened to the *Today* programme [...] You get to your editorial meeting at 9.30 with a cappuccino in your hand and you sit there and say here's an interesting story and why is it a story? It was on the *Today* programme and that makes it legitimate. So breaking that circle is very, very difficult to do.

In a multi-platform, multi-media news age, such reflections may seem out of date. Surprisingly, however, several journalists repeatedly referenced the *Today* programme in ways that suggest it continues to be a legitimising force. According to a senior television news editor:

There's no doubt that across all newspapers, radio and television there's a sort of a consensus that we follow. My first news hit of the day is the *Today* programme at six a.m. and today was New Zealand followed by Libya and I'd be surprised if that isn't the order for us for the rest of today. Not because they set it out but because there's a sort of an obvious logic to it if you like.

The last sentence is particularly interesting and there is little basis on which to doubt its sincerity. Just because journalists rely on input from *Today* and other news outlets in order to gauge the headlines of any given day, does not mean they follow them in blind faith. But what this sentence does reveal is a certain blind faith in a universal intuition, or what some journalists described as a 'self-correcting' mechanism in newsgathering. According to this view, story anomalies might surface sporadically on mainstream news, but a collective consciousness ultimately ensures that the stories of greatest weight and import occupy the bulk of the news agenda.

INSTITUTIONAL INSECURITY

Indeed, in spite of the proliferation of news outlets, there is a growing consensus between newsrooms as to which stories 'matter'. But this is not purely a function of faith in the logic of the news market. According to Alex Thomson, the trend is in part a consequence of declining and fragmenting audiences, as well as advertisers:

It's about the institutional insecurity of a business that's seeing its audience diminish because they are fragmenting for all sorts of reasons, because advertising's fragmenting for all sorts of reasons. This has led in my view to a profound lack of confidence and consequently too many news programmes are chasing the same stories and the same agenda, almost in the same order very often.

For some, this 'insecurity' exists not only at the macro institutional level, but also at the micro individual level. Here again, resource issues can be found to play an indirect role in homogenising output. Insecurity has been fostered by waves of redundancies and cuts within journalism, combined with a long term rise in property prices, and exacerbated by the financial crisis of 2008–10. According to one senior BBC news editor, this has made journalism increasingly risk-averse:

We definitely have more of a yes-man or -woman culture now [...] There's a generation of people now that are very keen to rise, will do what they think the editorial bosses want them to do, and are less awkward in terms of how they interpret directives from the top. So all of that doesn't add up to a particularly healthy picture I think. You end up with an output that is too homogenised, too reactive and I think probably not questioning enough.

Institutional insecurity has not, however, manifest in direct editorial control of journalists who seek to breach the news agenda consensus. Whilst Miles Goslett did reflect on a degree of editorial pressure over his pursuit of the inquest story, this did not amount to any form of 'don't go there' direction. Rather, it consisted in a 'half hearted' lack of encouragement from both editors and other journalists who warned of being 'associated with a failure'. Goslett left the *Mail on Sunday*, where he was a staff writer until April 2010, in order to pursue the story as a freelancer.

What is clear is that the controversy did not erect a significant barrier between journalists and their editorial management. Those journalists who chose not to pursue the story were literally on the same page as their editors and most of their colleagues. But institutional insecurity can foster a growing consensus of what is acceptable copy for the daily news agenda and in many ways this bears the hallmarks of a 'safe zone' of daily news. Norman Baker expressed this as a tacit restraint weighing on politicians and journalists in equal measure:

I think there is a general feeling in politics and indeed the media that you stay within a safe zone. There's a segment of the circle if you like that is safe and where you can operate within and where your opinions can be held within that. Once you move outside that safe zone then you put yourself up to attack, ridicule and generally endanger your reputation.

What are the story criteria for inclusion in the safe zone of news? They certainly do not, as we have seen throughout this book so far, preclude active and vociferous questioning of the government or indeed any notion of establishment elites. But we can in this case point to two related blind spots that gave rise to perceptions of the story as being 1) too 'risky' and 2) 'unrealistic' for inclusion within the mainstream news agenda.

THE RISK FACTOR

One of the most common responses as to why the inquest controversy did not receive more traction in the news concerns the supposed 'lack of evidence'. As we saw in the previous case study, serious news controversies feed on documentary evidence sourced either through public disclosure or investigative journalism. Martin Day, senior partner in the law firm that represented campaigners, himself pointed to an assumed insufficiency of credible evidence to justify coverage by serious news outlets: 'I think the broadsheets wanted to see some real hard evidence before they felt it was worth accosting their readers with it [...] I think it falls somewhere in between the two. It looks like there is just about enough evidence to make it worthwhile.'

The need 'for real hard evidence' is particularly acute in television news which, according to Miles Goslett 'doesn't really tend to deal with speculative stories in the way that newspapers do'. For Andrew Gilligan, the contrast is most striking between the BBC and newspaper editors who are 'less inhibited by a sense of gentility'. But appeals to evidence were evoked equally by respondents from across all news outlets. According to one senior ITV news executive: 'I don't think you find many stories especially on mainstream television that are based on rumours. I think you can have the skids under people that are based on rumours and then as you get substance it can make them more viable. But I think we're pretty evidence-based.'

The relative caution of television news, and indeed broadsheet newspapers, is no doubt for good reason, and all the more so in a digital news environment saturated by information 'noise'. But television news outlets are not, by their own acknowledgement, *always* bound to the rigidity of 'real hard evidence' in a consistent and equal manner. The same ITV news executive who made the assertion above followed it with an important qualification. The example cited concerns coverage of the long-running scandal over illegal wire taps used by journalists at *News of the World*:

[The *News of the World* hacking scandal] is an interesting case actually because that was based on suspicion [...] No one could believe that as editor of the *News of the World* [Andy Coulson] didn't know what was going on. If we actually thought, no, probably nothing was going on, that story would have evaporated but it chipped away. And actually there wasn't evidence against him. Eventually there was because a couple of former employees came out and said, no, he must have known.

Clearly, newsgathering is not an exact science. The degree to which evidence may be considered sufficient or not to run with a given story varies from case to case as much as from outlet to outlet, and often depends on particular story contexts. There is a thin line between caution that results in news that is more reliable and over-caution that results in news that is less scrutinising. But the reality is more complex than this. We have already seen how over-caution can also affect reliability, resulting in an implicit framing bias that favours a particular view. We have also seen how a range of institutional insecurities may be fostering an ever more cautious approach in broadcast news.

Any such trend has certainly been exacerbated by increasing sensitivity to perceived legal risks. The UK has long had in place what many consider the most restrictive legislation on journalists in the western hemisphere. According to Robin Ramsay, the Official Secrets Act 'made it an offence for anybody almost to tell anybody almost anything that they gained from their government job'. Perhaps even more of a restraint is the notoriously stringent UK libel laws. According to Phillip Knightley, an award winning investigative journalist specialising in war reporting, propaganda and espionage, the British system of libel is 'vicious and favours the wealthy over the ordinary'.

Perhaps the strongest indication of the cautionary effect of perceived legal risks was provided by a senior television news executive:

When I was programme editor some years ago – about ten years ago – there would be a lawyer on the end of the phone that I could speak to whenever I liked but I would very rarely do it. It was one guy, a barrister [...] Now there is a duty lawyer in the building throughout the day, right through to half past ten at night. So that's an indication that we're more cautious. That might be just down to the fact that our insurance premiums have gone up for libel and we need to be more careful. But I think we're more – as an organisation we're probably more aware of regulation and legality than we were. I'm not sure why that is.

As intimated in the above quote, it is not clear why news organisations appear to be increasingly sensitive to legal risks. The trend is certainly not matched by a corresponding expansion of the regulatory regime governing broadcasters. According to Alex Thomson, journalistic organisations are 'terrified of money and they're terrified of lawyers and we're terrified of money, money, money'. Often this fear results in an exaggerated perception of both the legal risks as well as estimation of costs:

> I had a story recently where there was a possibility of an injunction from the MOD and the advice I got in no uncertain terms was we do not want this to go to an injunction. We don't want to be injuncted over this because it's going to cost us a lot of money. I'm not convinced it does cost a lot of money. I was quoted a six-figure sum by somebody in ITN who I better not name. I don't think it costs you six figures to get an injunction overturned by asking a judge to overturn it.

But regardless of whether or not the legal advice is proportionate, news organisations have clearly become increasingly risk averse in recent years. The reasons for this are likely to be the same as those already discussed in relation to institutional insecurities. The consequence is that some stories that may be 'known truths' will be excluded from the news agenda if they are deemed to lack sufficient 'proof'. Alex Thomson again:

> There are endless examples one could give, I'm sure, of well-known truths which do not make it into the public domain [...] They may well be known to be true but not provable and that makes it difficult because if you can't mount a defensive justification you aint going to win any defamation trial. Who wants to risk that?

THE UNREALITY FACTOR

As we have seen though, journalists did not steer away from the inquest campaign simply because the case wasn't provable. Rather, the perceived lack of evidence made the implicit allegations of cover-up seem less credible to journalists themselves. A crucial question then concerns which *kind* of evidence was assumed to be lacking and why? For many respondents, belief that Dr Kelly committed suicide appeared to be based on a rejection of the directly opposing conclusion that he was murdered. Much of this reasoning was based on the lack of apparent motive for murder, as Paul Lashmar explained: 'I just don't see any evidence in the David

Kelly thing that convinces me that someone decided to bump him off because it all came out anyway – well most of it. What did it achieve?'

This appeal to the lack of evidence for murder is perhaps an understandable response by those whose 'gut instinct' was to favour the official verdict. But in effect, this puts journalists on no firmer ground than those who consent to murder theories. Both groups based their beliefs in one possible outcome at least partly on the perceived lack of evidence supporting the other. There seemed to be a common misconception amongst some journalists that the inquest campaign revolved around an implicit or explicit rejection of any *possibility* of suicide. There are certainly many who believe that Dr Kelly was murdered, including Norman Baker. And even the most moderate of campaigners espouse the view that he was highly unlikely to have killed himself in the manner described by Hutton. But the legal campaign for an inquest rested on concern about the *process* which led to the conclusion of suicide. It was this, over and above the statistical unlikelihood, that made the official verdict unsafe in the eyes of campaigners. This somewhat moderate position does not make great news copy as Dr Michael Powers QC – a lead figure in the inquest campaign – suggested:

> From what I've seen, the evidence of murder is really no better than the evidence of suicide. It may put me in a rather grey, less interesting and rather boring middle ground. But simply because you can't prove suicide doesn't mean to say that you can prove murder. They've both got to be proved positively and you may not be able to prove either positively.

We saw in Part I how the ambiguity of the BAe plea bargain settlements to some extent restricted the story's headline appeal. It is self-evident that any form of uncertainty lacks news currency. But in this case there was a clear reluctance on the part of journalists to even acknowledge uncertainties in the evidence on which the official verdict was based. Although most journalists qualified their positions by declaring a lack of interest in or expertise on the issue, virtually all nevertheless expressed confident assertions about how Dr Kelly died. The agnosticism expressed by Phillip Knightley was a notable exception:

> I don't know, honestly I don't know [...] I hadn't looked at that and reported it closely. I should have but I didn't. I'd hesitate to say

that it was conspiracy or a cover-up but it's always possible. I was suspicious of Dr Kelly's death for a long while and then recently information made me less suspicious but I still don't know.

Perhaps the most significant force of containment in this context is the story's susceptibility to the label of 'conspiracy theory'. This taboo, which operates within journalist and academic circles alike, has some sound basis. It discriminates against conjecture often associated with tabloid sensationalism or internet subcultures that respond to secrecy or uncertainty with unfounded reasoning. Conspiracy theorising has also provided the foundation for racist and extremist ideology upon which acts of terror, genocide and ethnic cleansing have been predicated.

Such a cautionary approach, however, has led to an outright rejection of the idea that particular groups of powerful people might make, in the words of terrorism expert Jeffrey Bale (1995), 'a concerted effort to keep an illegal or unethical act or situation from being made public'. Yet both historical precedent and contemporary events suggest that such instances are a regular feature of politics. The Chilcot Inquiry into the Iraq War, for instance, has surfaced considerable evidence that the decision to invade was taken in secret and long before it was publicly announced and justified.

The problem amounts to an 'intellectual resistance' with the result that 'an entire dimension of political history and contemporary politics has been consistently neglected' (Bale 1995). The research for this book uncovered such a resistance amongst not only journalists, but the full range of professionals interviewed for this case study. Some respondents simply dismissed any notion of cover-up with characteristic derision, employing words like 'nonsense', 'insanity' or 'laughable'. Others expressed a reluctance to engage with evidence of cover-up simply because it appeared to be based solely on anomalies which can be manipulated to fit any theory, as Paul Lashmar explained: 'There is a point with all good conspiracies that you reach where there is so much material out there that you can read it in any way that you want.'

It is a measure of the complexity of this case study that several respondents *did* profess belief in some sort of intentional cover-up whilst at the same time subscribing to the suicide verdict. The common thread was a tendency to couch the notion of cover-up in terms of 'cock up' rather than 'conspiracy'. That is to say, if a cover-up had taken place, the likely intention was to conceal professional failings rather than unethical or criminal behaviour.

In a related sense, the cover-up was seen by some as simply a manifestation of 'secrecy for secrecy's sake'; a culture of information control so pervasive as to be employed even when it was not necessary. According to Alex Thomson, the sheer 'obviousness' of the state's behaviour made the notion that it was anything other than bureaucratic 'neurosis' somewhat incredulous:

> If there had been a cover-up it is hard to imagine a state behaving in a more obvious way of sending the signal that there had been a cover-up [...] from apparently moving the body, from non-disclosure of materials, from obsessive secrecy surrounding the whole thing. But then again obsessive secrecy is the culture that we live in and it's every bit as bad as it ever was and if anything it's getting worse. Does the obsessive secrecy and general kind of official neurosis exhibited by the Ministry of Justice and many other officials in this case tell us anything about the potential for conspiracy? I think probably not. Does it tell us that we're a pretty sick state when it comes to secrecy for secrecy's sake? Absolutely.

Although a belief in cover-up doesn't require subscription to any murder theory, it does invite consideration of the *possibility* that David Kelly might have been murdered, and that the state may have been in some way complicit. But this possibility is precisely what seemed to invoke outright dismissal of the inquest campaign among some journalists. On occasion, the implication of cover-up was exaggerated so as to invoke an obvious aura of absurdity. According to Paul Lashmar: 'I don't think there are MI5 or MI6 assassins wandering around Britain bumping off people who don't agree with the state, which is the sort of implication.'

At the heart of statements such as this lies a basic assumption that British security services do not carry out or cover-up extra judicial killings, at least not on home soil. In this case, the very possibility that an agent of the state might have been complicit in the assassination of one of its own public servants seemed to provoke a presumptive reflex among journalists that led them to discredit the notion of cover-up altogether. Although Robin Ramsay himself expressed faith in the suicide verdict, he articulated this instinct in terms of an 'intellectual hegemony':

> Inside all our heads and inside the heads of editors is a notion of how the world works and if you pitch at them something which says your understanding of how the world works is

false or inadequate they will reject it. In a way this is merely describing how a kind of intellectual hegemony works. It is the conventional view amongst political journalists in this society and political editors in TV stations and newspapers that the world is dominated by cock-ups and not by conspiracies. That's their fundamental view [...] these are almost bed rock beliefs.

OFFICIAL SOURCE STRATEGIES

Whilst the perceptual blind spots identified above clearly played a central role in keeping the inquest campaign out of the news spotlight, we cannot discount the possibility that they were aided by instrumental factors – namely official source strategies. Before considering these in depth, it is worth discussing the distinct facets of journalist-source relations in the context of the security state.

Much has been written about the relationship between journalists and official sources which in liberal pluralist accounts is generally characterised as one of mutual dependence (see Chapter 1). In the case of security service sources, it is perhaps better described as mutual 'benefit'. Journalists gain from insider knowledge that few of their colleagues or competitors have access to. They are given stories that by their nature cannot be independently verified. They are therefore not perceived to *require* verification which may involve timely and costly investigative work. Security service sources for their part can remain out of the public eye whilst being given an unchallenged platform for their views and stories.

But despite these elements of mutual benefit, respondents on the whole professed little doubt as to who had the upper hand. According to Paul Lashmar:

> One of the things that the people around intelligence realise is that information is power and that if you give journalists information that no one else can get, you give them power. And then you nurture your own people and you have a relationship that isn't a straightforward relationship. It's about control.

Phillip Knightley went further: 'Those very few journalists who do have some sort of access or privilege are so jealous and guard it so closely that it's almost worthless. They're in the pocket of the person who's providing them with what information they can get.'

Part of the problem is an instinctive deference that one journalist alluded to in reflecting on his own experiences: 'You have to police yourself very carefully when you do come into contact with them. There is a bit of a thrill – we've all been brought up on James Bond. We were taken in to see "C" at MI6 and you have lunch and you chat away and you're in the heart of this building that nobody goes into and it's absolutely thrilling and fascinating.'

Reflecting on his own experiences as a journalist, Robin Ramsay suggested that 'friendly' contacts were not only used to plant stories, but also to prevent or modify others:

When I was working at *Channel 4 News* on the Colin Wallace story, there were several attempts by journalists on the ITN staff to disinform the investigation that we were doing because their friends, their allies in the secret state whispered in their ears and said 'these chaps are off on the wrong lines why don't you steer them towards X'.

Some respondents, including Norman Baker, went as far as to suggest that some of these contacts were not just 'friendly' but paid employees of the security services: 'If I had to guess I'd say there's probably someone in every paper and there's probably a retainer paid but that's my speculation.'

This raises the question of whether some journalists who actively opposed campaigners may have been doing the bidding of higher powers within the security state. It is certainly the case that the most vociferous views in defence of the suicide verdict were espoused not by official sources but by journalists themselves. Dr Margaret Bloom reflected on a phone interview with one such journalist:

He just phoned me up and started attacking me, which doesn't strike me as being particularly clever journalism because I don't think I said very much at all, because he was just so rude. He was the only one who said 'why are you doing this?' and 'poor Mrs Kelly', and 'why aren't you satisfied?' and 'how can you properly question it?' and 'who are you to question Lord Hutton's decision?' and 'he's interviewed all these people' and on he went like some kind of raving loon.

As noted in the previous chapter, Tom Mangold has appeared persistently on television news to endorse the suicide verdict and he was also the journalist who first 'explained' the lack of fingerprints found on the knife by referring to the alleged tape around the handle, a story subsequently adopted by Andrew Gilligan but discredited by a Freedom of Information (FOI) response from the Thames Valley Police. Miles Goslett reflected on this and his own encounters with Tom Mangold:

> I did ask Mangold once where he'd got it from and he said he thought he had read it somewhere in some official file or some sort of publicly accessible paper, and I said 'right and you're sure about that?' and then I explained that we just got this FOI back and it's just completely untrue according to the police. He ended the conversation pretty quickly.

Whether such anecdotes reflect intentional disinformation or accidental misinformation is unclear. But in any case, the key purpose here is to assess whether they were *effective* in directing stories in favour of official source frames. Despite the earlier discussion of agenda consensus, a strong case can be made that in a proliferated news landscape, sporadic misinformation or disinformation in particular news outlets cannot disrupt the overall direction of a story. Respondents drew attention to elements of dissensus and chaos that clearly permeate much of the mainstream media, particularly within print. Martyn Day highlighted the unpredictability of editorial decisions which would appear to make covert manipulation more difficult:

> I think in the end the media decides whether an item is interesting or not and you never quite know. So for example I was talking to David Leigh a few months ago now about our case that we've got in Peru and he said 'I don't think they'll be interested in that' and he's one of the most senior people in the *Guardian*. Two weeks later it was on the front page of the paper [...] A good story today may turn to dust and vice versa.

Even if disinformation was part of an official source strategy, it was unlikely to have been as powerful as another key aspect of official leverage: bureaucratic delay. One of the most powerful strategic tools at the disposal of official sources is the timing of announcements. In this case, a succession of delays in response to submissions by campaigners has had two significant effects. First, it has limited the amount of evidence available in respect of Dr Kelly's death. As Dr Bloom observed: 'I think that we might have been in a very different position had an inquest been held timely back when further investigations could have been made with a much closer time juxtaposition.'

Second, the lapse of time has fostered a degree of media exhaustion. In the words of Miles Goslett, 'there's no doubt that the longer they string it out the less sensational it's likely to be'. The potential for bureaucratic delay to devalue the news currency of stories was summed up by Phillip Knightley: '[T]he whole edge goes off it, the whole urgency disappears and vanishes into a bureaucratic entanglement that the story never gets out of.'

But the momentum sustained in 2010 nevertheless enabled the campaign to break through the barriers of television news substantially for the first time. A new coalition government had just taken the reins amidst the Prime Minister's call for 'greater transparency across government'.[4] A slew of high profile public inquiries followed including an inquest into the 7 July 2005 terrorist attacks in London. The prospect of an inquest into the death of David Kelly no longer seemed remote and the Attorney General made public utterances to this effect on more than one occasion. As we saw in the previous case study, the prospect of an official inquiry both fuelled and was in turn fuelled by the media coverage. The force of the latter was underlined by a former senior intelligence chief who remarked that 'in my experience public inquiries are almost entirely driven by the media'.

But in this case neither the media spotlight nor political will were sufficient to induce a re-opening of the inquest. What was achieved amounted to a limited form of disclosure, namely the release of the post mortem and toxicology reports. This, as we have seen, was trumped up by broadcasters as an act of unrestrained openness on behalf of the state. In this way, the coverage exhibited the hallmarks of the closure framing we saw in the BAe case. Once again, viewers were presented with an approved accountability outcome that was portrayed as a definitive resolution to the controversy. In this case, however, the campaign still had legal legs following the post mortem release in October 2010. Five months later, a formal submission was made to the Attorney General in light of the outstanding questions and lingering doubt expressed by campaigners.

The result was more or less a re-run of the kind of spectacle we observed in the release of the post mortem. The Attorney General decided not to re-open the inquest but crucially produced a detailed report attempting to justify this decision. This was covered in relatively brief reports, as we saw in the previous chapter, on the BBC and *Channel 4 News*. Here the framing emphasis was on delegitimising the campaign not by invoking conspiracy theory, but rather by associating it with the broader political context that surrounded Kelly's death. This reflected the closure discourse advanced by official sources themselves, namely the Attorney General. The emphasis on the inevitability of on-going controversy chimed with news values of closure: if an on-going campaign was inevitable and politicised, it was no longer news. Although both the Attorney General and the views of his detractors were featured, the brevity of the reports and the failure to draw attention to any of the detail in respective arguments underlined the sense of finality.

DRAWING THE LINES

Whether or not the forces outlined above are attributed to random chaos or conscious agency on the part of official sources, it seems clear that the coverage in relation to the inquest campaign was weighted heavily in their favour. This is perhaps most evident in the imbalance between attention to evidence that underpinned the official verdict, and evidence that undermined it. This manifest in an uncharacteristic benefit of doubt afforded to official sources both in accepting the verdict of suicide, and in rejecting a notion of cover-up. It was encapsulated in the following assertion by one journalist: 'there might be very good reason why Hutton decided against publishing medical reports. I don't know what they are.'

More broadly, it reflected a common underlying faith not in politicians or the powerful as such, but in the processes and procedures that legitimate their power, including the media itself. The obvious exception to this was the whitewash frame which poured scorn on the Hutton Report and heralded an unprecedented media critique of an accountability resolution. But this critique was short-lived, and unrelated to the more obvious failings of due process that were evident in the way Hutton reached his verdict of suicide.

Much of these failings concerned the investigation into the death of David Kelly. The subsequent marginalisation of the inquest controversy by television news was chiefly the product of cultural and intellectual blind spots that resulted in a misconception of the arguments underpinning the inquest campaign and a lack of awareness regarding their evidential basis. The result has been a collective 'don't go there' attitude which has severely restricted the capacity of campaigners to attract mainstream news attention. Although this problem may not be rooted in journalism, the news media stand as the last line of accountability and public interest defence. If there is a failure at the procedural level of justice we depend on journalists to uncover that failure, bring it to light, and either directly or indirectly ferment conditions for redress.

But the fact that this story has continued to recur in the mainstream media, however fleeting and sporadic, is an indication of its endurance and potential to overcome many of the containment forces outlined above. For Michael Powers, the failure of process and accountability may not make headline news, but it leaves 'a sore there all the time', to which the media might periodically return until that failure is redressed. In 2011, the government decided for the third time not to hold a formal inquest into the death and significantly, this decision appears to have closed off further legal action on the part of campaigners. Whether it has succeeded in finally bringing closure to the controversy as far as the mainstream news agenda is concerned, remains to be seen.

Part III

Covering the Leak

6
The Biggest Story on the Planet

BACKGROUND

Wikileaks emerged in 2006 as an internet-based project aimed at exposing state-corporate secrecy. From the outset, the project has been explicitly articulated as an engine of accountability, in both radical and reformist contexts (Fenster 2011). Although the precise workings and self-described objectives of the model have varied over time, the essential connection between unauthorised disclosure, scrutiny and accountability has been consistent:

> Publishing improves transparency, and this transparency creates a better society for all people. Better scrutiny leads to reduced corruption and stronger democracies in all society's institutions, including government, corporations and other organisations. A healthy, vibrant and inquisitive journalistic media plays a vital role in achieving these goals.[1]

According to this view, the scrutiny provided by unauthorised disclosure constitutes an accountability end in itself, irrespective of whether revealed abuses of power are subject to formal sanction. Underpinning this conception is a challenge to establishment power in two ways. The first lies in an implicit assumption that authoritative institutions cannot be relied upon to proactively disclose all information of public interest value, and especially not when information sheds light on illegitimate behaviour. Wikileaks therefore facilitates unauthorised disclosures in a bid to *enforce* public oversight of powerful institutions. The project's unique selling point has been its use of technology to provide a more effective, and crucially more secure mechanism for doing so than that offered by traditional media.

The second challenge is to traditional media themselves: 'In the years leading up to the founding of WikiLeaks, we observed the world's publishing media becoming less independent and far less willing to ask the hard questions of government, corporations and other institutions. We believed this needed to change.'[2]

Even when working in partnership with traditional media organisations, the publication of original source material by Wikileaks (often linked to or re-published by traditional media) is conceived as a check on the gatekeeping, agenda-setting, and framing power of established media. In short, by gaining access to non-mediated source material, publics no longer need to rely exclusively on the professional media to determine what *is* news, what is *important* news and what the news *means*.

Seen in another light, the model provides opportunities for journalists to resist and overcome many of the forces of containment identified in the preceding case studies. For instance, the provision of abundant original source material documenting crimes of the powerful can offset resource constraints on investigative journalists. In theory, media outlets no longer need to invest the same amount of time and resources that gaining access to whistleblowers and secret documents might ordinarily demand. The efficiency and security enabled by the technology might also provide a level of quantity and quality in source material simply not attainable through traditional means, regardless of resources. This in turn can offset cultural blind spots, according to which stories that challenge dominant narratives require a greater degree of authentication than those which endorse them (see previous chapter). Moreover, the publication of documents by Wikileaks itself provides a defence against legal injunctions on the basis that material is already available in the public domain (Lynch 2010). This, in theory at least, can mitigate the 'climate of caution' under which media organisations are increasingly wary of stories that carry significant legal (and hence financial) risk.

The potential of Wikileaks to have a radical impact on the structures of news production and delivery is therefore not contingent on a mass migration of audiences from television to the internet. It can play an integral role in shoring up journalist autonomy, helping the mainstream media to adequately expose, report on and contextualise crimes of the powerful. In essence, the Wikileaks promise is to uncover the cover-up, a notion at the heart of early musings by Julian Assange, its enigmatic founder (Assange 2006). Much of his writings since have chimed with those who have articulated a new pluralism wrought by the internet's decentralised infrastructure and resultant assault on information control (Poster 2001; McNair 2006; Shirky 2011).

In 2010, Wikileaks secured what has been regularly touted as the 'biggest leak in history' (Leigh and Harding 2011). Allegedly stemming from a single source within the US military, the trove contained close to a million documents consisting of military intelligence reports from the front lines, as well as diplomatic cables spanning more than two decades. The alleged source was Private Bradley Manning, a junior military intelligence analyst stationed in Baghdad who was arrested in May 2010, having been reported to the authorities by a fellow 'hacker'. He was to spend the next ten months in solitary confinement under conditions that have been the subject of a UN torture investigation.[3] But the arrest itself was to prove pivotal in ensuring that Wikileaks became etched into the fabric of global public consciousness. It was after reading about Manning's arrest and the rumoured leaks that Nick Davies of the *Guardian* approached Julian Assange in June 2010. Their subsequent negotiations formed the basis of a partnership between Wikileaks and the mainstream media dubbed a 'new model of journalism'. Whether the partnership lived up to such a triumphant moniker is a contested question. By the end of 2010, the relationship between the *Guardian* and Wikileaks had swiftly deteriorated into a bitter and acrimonious dispute. What seems certain however, is that the partnership succeeded at least in catapulting Wikileaks to the top of the global news agenda for the first time in its brief history.

No doubt the sheer size, range and origin of the leak were what prompted Davies to consider it, and subsequently make it 'the biggest story on the planet' (Leigh and Harding 2011). But the range and scale of the leak from the outset threatened to drown out serious public interest issues amidst a sea of global scandals. This problem was intensified by the co-ordinated release of the documents between the media partners – an effort to realise the goal of high impact exposure shared by all sides of the partnership.

In other words, there was from the outset a tension, and to some extent trade-off between maximising impact and promoting understanding of the leak's significance. It is a tension that the partners themselves appear to have been conscious of (Leigh and Harding 2011), and one that brings television's role sharply into focus. Though very much the junior partners within an ever expanding pact, television outlets became crucial arbiters of salience in their framing and selection of the leaks. This is partly down to the medium's ranking as the most credible and widely accessed news platform. But it is more importantly a function of the relatively constricted nature of the medium. A single television bulletin allows for considerably less breadth and depth of coverage than a daily newspaper edition. Consequently, television became a natural filter for the deluge of stories and leaked information unleashed by the press; a last line of defence against information overload.

It is for this reason that examining the relationship between Wikileaks and television can provide telling insight into the former's disruptive potential as well as shed further light on the forces of accountability and containment within the news media at large. Of the three sets of leaks co-ordinated over a period of six months in 2010, the focus here is on the third – a climactic release of secret and confidential communications between the US State Department and its embassies around the world. This followed leaks of military intelligence reports from the wars in Afghanistan and Iraq consecutively. But it was the diplomatic cable releases that marked the peak of coverage intensity and the architects of all three releases were in no doubt as to its ultimate significance. According to Alan Rusbridger, editor of the *Guardian*:

> You could say the World Trade Centre was a bigger story, or the Iraq War. But in terms of a newspaper, where by the act of publication you unleash one story that is then talked about in every single corner of the globe, and you are the only people who have got it, and you release it each day, this was unique. (Leigh and Harding 2011:199)

Such enthusiasm however was to prove far from universal. Amidst a torrent of stories centred on diplomatic 'tittle-tattle', television journalists quickly began to question the significance of the leaks both in terms of their content and consequences. Like the legitimacy debate, such questions were both inevitable and necessary. But how they were framed in television was to prove a critical indicator of the extent to which journalists either enhanced or undermined accountability potential. It is a core contention of this chapter that journalists were right to question both the legitimacy and significance of the leaks, but that a crucial missing dimension concerned the role of selection and prioritisation in marginalising stories of real public interest importance. Since measuring public interest value is a notoriously difficult task, I rely predominantly on the discourse of journalists themselves to identify leaks of key significance and then assess the relative prominence they received in the coverage. But the analysis also rests on the assumptions that 1) stories revealing or alluding to corruption are of greater public import than those which centred on personal pen portraits or high society gossip; and 2) stories revealing or alluding to corruption at home were of greater public interest value than those concerning corruption abroad.

The first stage of analysis – identifying evidence of accountability and containment – was therefore concerned with three questions:

1. How did television news frame the debate over legitimacy?
2. How did television news frame the debate over significance?
3. What was the relative prominence afforded to different leaks in the coverage?

The second stage of analysis addressed the issue of *why* television framed the debates in the way that it did, and why particular leaks (or types of leaks) were prioritised over others in the coverage.

The analysis is focused on the first week of cable releases, beginning 30 November 2010, since this was the moment in which Wikileaks became a household name with headline status persisting throughout the week. The case study culminates in a discussion of the accountability implications of Cablegate and unauthorised disclosure more broadly. It concludes that a spectacle of accountability consisted in a discursive emphasis by both official sources and Wikileaks supporters on 'the end of secrecy'. Though it was tempered somewhat by a narrative of hype that pervaded broadcasting reports in particular, this was to prove equally distracting. It was above all the distorted prioritisation of stories by broadcasters themselves which accounted for the apparent deficit in story gravitas.

UNAUTHORISED ACCOUNTABILITY

Perhaps the most vivid aspect of at least surface accountability consisted in the intensity of the media spotlight cast over the leaks during the first week of coverage. Whilst Assange moved to the centre of the story after his arrest on 7 December, the first week of coverage was, in fact, dominated by the leaks themselves. This demonstrates at least a surface element of accountability in so far as neither official source responses (which were overwhelmingly directed as an attack on the legitimacy of Wikileaks) nor the competitive dynamics of the partnership (which resulted in a deluge of stories) were able to marginalise the leaks' content. Although the dominant focus on the cables was observed across the board in the sample, there were notable differences between the bulletins and analysis programmes, as well as between early (before 7 p.m.) and late evening editions. This is in keeping with the findings in Part I which showed how the later evening and analysis programmes were both culturally and structurally better placed to cover complex controversies like Al Yamamah.

Yet even in the main bulletins, much of the language used by reporters seemed to emphasise the challenge Wikileaks posed to dominant narratives and policy discourses. For instance, a public statement condemning the leaks by US Secretary of State Hillary Clinton was preceded in one report by this somewhat cynical introduction: 'no wonder she judges that the only credible defence is a spirited attack'.[4] The cable in question was one which detailed the US State Department's instructions for diplomats to spy on UN representatives. The implication of the reporter's statement is clear: there was simply no defence against the allegations stemming from the leaks.

Over on the BBC, one bulletin featured an excerpt from an interview with Louis Susman – US ambassador to London – whose interviewer made no attempt to conceal her indignation:

> Just because everybody does it doesn't mean the public wouldn't be shocked when they found out. I mean what are we hearing about – Collecting passwords? Personal encryption keys? VIP networks used for official communication? That's snooping isn't it? It's illegal![5]

Perhaps the most damning critique was made by Lindsey Hilsum on *Channel 4 News*: 'The problem for [US President Obama] is not only that Wikileaks has made secrets public, but that the cables lay bare the hypocrisy and dissembling of diplomacy'.[6]

Nor did the selection of stories give priority to the sensational over substantial. The stories might not have radically altered our 'understanding' of world events or international relations, but they would be hard to dismiss as mere 'tittle-tattle'. Whilst a significant proportion of the leaked cables did consist of unflattering pen portraits of foreign leaders, in the television sample analysed these attracted only 3 per cent of the total airtime given over to the cables.

In a bid to further interrogate the question of story 'importance', the top ten cables that attracted the most television coverage were divided into four content categories: stories that focused on gossip, political controversy, corruption or criminality and security threats. The balance of coverage between them suggests that attention was focused predominantly on political controversy, corruption/criminality and security threats – all categories commonly associated with serious, rather than sensationalist news. In contrast, the more tabloid-oriented gossip stories occupied less than 10 per cent of the television spotlight (see Figure 6.1).

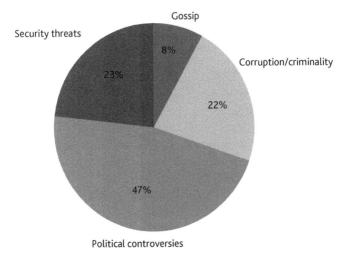

Figure 6.1 Balance of coverage between different types of cable stories (based on airtime)

Source: National film archives

This suggests that whilst the information contained within the cables might not have been especially revealing, they were certainly not limited to the 'indiscreet comments' of diplomats. It also suggests that television news prioritised stories of public interest value over mere sensationalism and scandal.

NARRATIVES OF CHANGE

Accompanying much of the coverage was a suggestion that Wikileaks had ushered in a new era of information chaos and was a transformative phenomenon in its own right. It is a narrative spawned from a wider discourse that posits the internet as a fundamentally disruptive technology, wreaking havoc on the social and economic structures of millennial capitalism (Castells 2001; Lessig 2004; Downes 2009). In more qualified terms, the narrative rests on an assumption not that Wikileaks has won the information war, but that it is *winning*. As Clay Shirky portends:

The state will fight back, of course. They will improve their controls on secrets, raise surveillance and punishment of possible leakers, try to negotiate multilateral media controls. But even then, the net change is likely to be advantageous to the leakers – less free than today, perhaps, but more free than prior to 2006. Assange has claimed, when the history of statecraft of the era is written, that it will be divided into pre- and post-WikiLeaks periods. This claim is grandiose and premature; it is not, however, obviously wrong.

In spite of this apparent modesty, the transformative nature of the Wikileaks project is conceived not in terms of potential but as having irrevocably shifted the balance of power between elites and publics (Fenster 2011). To some extent this is seen as evident simply in the extremity of responses to the leaks, particularly in the US. From the harsh treatment and alleged torture of Bradley Manning, to calls from senior political figures for the assassination of Julian Assange, Wikileaks has apparently rattled the world's only superpower and forced its establishment, if not to its knees, then certainly on to the back foot. What's more, the myriad responses did not succeed in even slowing the group's momentum, let alone stopping it. Although efforts to bring charges of espionage are on-going, it's possible that even ultimate success in the courts would only unleash a host of Wikileaks-inspired projects already waiting in the wings.[7]

Beyond the US, Wikileaks is credited with fermenting uprisings which have led to the overthrow of western-backed dictatorships. The so-called Arab Spring began in Tunisia after a cable released in December 2010 detailed the full scale of political corruption endemic to Ben Ali's regime. Though Tunisian activists hardly needed a reminder of the repression they faced, the timing of the leak – surfacing a matter of days before the uprising – was nevertheless striking.

In this light, it is not surprising that supporters of Wikileaks talk in feverish tones. Mikael Viborg is the owner of PRQ, a Swedish web hosting company that has provided refuge for Wikileaks under the shield of the country's unrivalled free speech protection laws:

I think they're losing. I think that it's too late to contain information. We have come to a point where whatever they do, whatever legislation they pass, information will still be free. In the end they lose. The technical competence and the majority of people believe in the freedom of information so they are fighting an enemy that has a million heads. A million, million heads.

A second crucial tenet of the change narrative is that the project's impact is exclusively a function of its innovative approach to protecting and maximising unauthorised disclosure. In other words, transformation is technology-enabled. As Phillip Knightley attested:

> I think Wikileaks has changed everything – a sea-change in the relationship between whistleblowers and the people they blow the whistle to and in the information that we can expect from the people who govern us. It really is a changing of the guard. Assange has found ways of protecting whistleblowers that journalists previously never even dreamed of. The technology is there now.

This is not just about secure methods of document encryption or the capacity to transfer and store eye-wateringly large caches of material in digital format. It is equally indebted to the de-territorialisation of the internet. With no national anchoring, both Julian Assange personally and the Wikileaks group as a whole have become elusive targets of prosecution. Even success in the courts can end up a net cost to plaintiffs. In 2008, the Swiss private bank Julius Baer managed to get a US court order for Wikileaks' domain hosts to de-list the site from the web. The move was in response to Wikileaks publishing documents which alleged the bank knew about and aided money laundering. But net activists were quick to respond by posting the IP address of Wikileaks, whose servers were unaffected by the domain de-listing. What's more, the case prompted reaction from civil liberties groups and brought more attention to Wikileaks than any of its previous leaks, prompting the court to reverse its decision and the bank to drop the case.[8]

The implication embedded in the narrative of change is that in 2010, Wikileaks became a major news story in its own right. In the mainstream media partnership that developed, it was the newspapers and broadcasters that needed Wikileaks more than the other way round. They were forced to respond to the game-changing events that Wikileaks had engendered and bestow the headline billing it was due.

An alternative narrative, however, posits the inverse: that it was Wikileaks who needed the mainstream media to achieve a game-changing level of impact. Not surprisingly, it is a view most strongly espoused by print and broadcast journalists themselves.

Kevin Marsh, former editor of BBC Radio 4's *Today*, made the point in no uncertain terms:

> I think even Assange was aware that if you've got half a million documents, what impact are they going to have if all you do is put them on a website where likeminded people make a few observations to other likeminded people? Even if the number of those likeminded people is a few hundred thousand, in global terms it ain't many. Get a headline in the national newspapers of three or four of the most important NATO members or whatever, then you've got real salience, you've got significance, you've got people's attention, it's much more clearly into the public discourse.

But even those close to Wikileaks acknowledged the resources and expertise that print and broadcasting journalists brought to bear in managing the cable releases. Vaughan Smith, founder of the Frontline Club in London, played host to Julian Assange's house arrest since December 2010, and to Wikileaks operations since the beginning of Cablegate:

> Fundamentally Wikileaks was not led with the right skills as an organisation – the right organisational management skills. Nor did it contain within it the people who have enough knowledge and experience of determining what is in the public interest in terms of individual stories. You have to have quite a lot of local knowledge about cultures to do that so it doesn't seem to me that it could have succeeded in the way it has without collaborating closely with organisations like the *Guardian* and the *New York Times*.

From Assange's point of view, the problem was not so much to do with Wikileaks – which had always been reliant on some form of external collaboration – but rather the failure of the project's original 'wiki' model. Initially, that model was designed to exploit the crowd-sourcing functionality of the web to authenticate, analyse and publicise its documents. The universally acknowledged failure of that model directly confronts conceptions of Wikileaks as harnessing the disruptive forces of the internet to create a sea-change in media power relations:

> Our initial idea was that, look at all those people editing Wikipedia. Look at all the junk that they're working on. Surely,

if you give them a fresh classified document about the human rights atrocities in Falluja[h], that the rest of the world has not seen before [...] surely *those* people will step forward, given fresh source material and do something. No. It's all bullshit. In fact, people write about things, in general, if it's not part of their career, because they want to display their values to their peers, who are already in the same group. Actually, they don't give a fuck about the material. That's the reality.[9]

Long before the big leak in 2010, Wikileaks had actively sought to court the mainstream press in a bid to offset the inevitable deficit of resources the organisation faced in handling the material it received. After regular press notices had largely fell on deaf ears, the group began to experiment in 2008 with new models to attract 'investment' from news organisations. These included an 'embargo pool' and an auction set up around specific releases, both of which failed to attract the attention, let alone time and resources of major news brands (Leigh and Harding 2011).

RESOURCE POOLS

The question we are left with is why did the mainstream media partnership succeed in sending Wikileaks to the top of the global news agenda? Notwithstanding the unprecedented size and nature of the leak, it is clear that the mainstream media partners invested a significant level of resources in dissecting the contents and then *producing* stories. Indeed, the entire back office machinery of some of the world's largest and most influential newspapers went into overdrive in the weeks preceding the cable releases. The task involved not only co-ordination between all the internal departments of the newspaper, but also between the international partners. Gill Phillips, a senior in-house lawyer at the *Guardian*, shed light on what was only one aspect of an extensive operation:

There was a co-ordinated effort so all of the papers were individually looking at the things they wanted to run [...] we would all do a redaction exercise of our own and then what we tried to do is co-ordinate the redaction exercise so it was effectively the highest common denominator – the most redactions [...] We had all of us plus extra people reading everything, trying to go through everything, making sure the packages all fitted together, to try to make sure we were as tight legally as we could be, and then we were having to liaise with production who were doing the physical redaction, we had to liaise with the journalists and the news desk.

The investment of resources was not, however, limited to the newspaper partners alone. Prior to Cablegate, the Bureau of Investigative Journalism – a non-profit organisation that produces current affairs documentaries – had put together a team of over 30 journalists to make a single documentary on the Iraq War Logs. And the BBC – though it had turned down an offer of partnership with Wikileaks – nevertheless devoted the full range of its extensive newsgathering operations in 'managing' the cable releases. According to Mary Hockaday, head of the BBC's newsroom, the added value of the BBC consisted in its unrivalled global expertise:

There were these deluges and so just the task of managing the assessment of, the sifting of, the reporting of any of these releases of information was a logistical challenge plus an editorial assessment challenge. So it was important for us depending on what the issue was, depending on which part of the world it was about or the nature of the topic, to be able to bring to bear our relevant specialist reporters. So in some cases that was security, in some cases it was diplomatic, in some cases it might be a particular bureau.

The important point here is that traditional news organisations were able to convert vast swathes of data into news *stories*. It was this functionality that gave Wikileaks documents the publicity they had been sorely missing. Obviously the nature and size of the leak prompted the mainstream media to 'invest' in the first place. But in publicity terms, the event had put Wikileaks on the map of public consciousness such that its releases might never again be treated with the kind of indifference and neglect that it had hitherto experienced.

The unparalleled mobilisation of resources by conventional media organisations in the build-up to Cablegate raises a question mark over more fatalistic portrayals of the professional news industry. Although undoubtedly affected by structural decline and the disruptive forces of new media, established 'serious' news brands are insulated to some degree from commercial pressures. Although Channel 4 is advertising funded, it is publicly owned and cross-subsidises its news operations. This allows what is effectively a loss-making news programme to occupy over 50 minutes of evening television each week night. It also invests significantly in investigative reporting, often 'pushing' its relatively small audience with in-depth stories outside of the mainstream news agenda. As a result, its journalists and presenters are regulars on the industry awards scene.[10]

The *Guardian* itself enjoys a commercial buffer which enables it to engage in reporting that carries relatively high financial risk. As *Vanity Fair* pointed out in the aftermath of Cablegate, the title's owners run 'profitmaking businesses that generate money to subsidize the paper, should it need the support'.[11] It is also this buffer which has enabled the newspaper to invest so heavily in its online presence, with little sign of a financial return. As a result, despite being only the tenth largest national newspaper in the country, it 'performs on a global stage in a way that most bigger British newspapers simply do not'.

Outside of the major news brands, alternative models of funding have emerged in recent years to support public interest journalism. Based on foundational support models pioneered in the US, the Bureau of Investigative Journalism was set up in April 2010 with a £2 million donation from the David and Elaine Potter Foundation, a family trust that aims to 'encourage a stronger, fairer civil society'.[12] The Iraq War Logs documentary was one of the Bureau's first major projects which it sold to 25 networks around the world, reaching an audience of more than 50 million. Yet despite this return, the project was a loss making enterprise according to its chief editor, Iain Overton: 'I lost loads of money. I put loads into making it. I threw 30 journalists at it. God, if it had been lucrative I would have hired three journalists to look at the stuff and then sold it.'

The film nevertheless attracted worldwide acclaim (except in the United States where all the major networks passed on it), winning a prestigious media award from Amnesty International.[13]

Clearly, there is an enduring and evolving public media infrastructure that was mobilised to capacity during the cable releases. This is not to denigrate the very real financial crisis affecting commercial newspapers and a long-term transfer of resources away from operational journalism in both broadcasting and print (see Chapter 1). Nor is it to downplay the fierce and relentless competition that exists within all sectors, fuelled in large part by the proliferation of digital and global news outlets. But it does suggest that the profit motive is not the exclusive engine for generating investment in news. What the BBC, *Channel 4 News,* the *Guardian,* and the Bureau of Investigation share in common is a competitive need to *justify* investment often in the absence of profit. That involves competition both for audiences, but also credibility as conferred by industry awards. There are clear signs that intensifying competitive pressures, coupled with an increasingly hostile legal climate, have led media organisations to steer resources away from the more high risk elements of public interest journalism – namely the sourcing of evidential material. That is the gap that Wikileaks appeared to fill with its seemingly endless supply of leaked documents covering a vast array of scandal and controversy.

But there was another important aspect of value that Wikileaks offered mainstream media organisations: security expertise. The phenomenon of digital surveillance has been a growing thorn in the side of investigative journalists. Although by its nature difficult to identify and verify, the threat of surveillance is for some journalists, omnipresent. There is certainly evidence to suggest that both private companies and state agencies have used illegal means to monitor the activities of campaigners in recent years (Lubbers 2009).[14] For Gavin MacFadyen, director of the Centre for Investigative Journalism and Wikileaks associate, the threat of digital surveillance to investigative journalists is almost self-evident: 'Corporations use private investigators and the government has its own security people whose sole job is to be interested in information and since journalism of the kind we're talking about is largely about information, they're very interested in it.'

Whilst in Britain, surveillance of journalists rarely if ever carries the threat of violence, it does carry the threat of the story being 'scooped' by competitors or sources being identified and turned away from journalists. Most importantly, it intensifies the risk factor associated with investigative journalism in two ways. First, surveillance threatens to *inform* investigative targets about an impending scandal, allowing crucial time prior to publication to develop a media counter-strategy. Often, this is not so much a defensive strategy against the allegations presented, as an offensive one aimed at the journalist or organisation behind them. According to Iain Overton:

> If you put out a report on something that implicates powerful individuals or institutions, their PR representatives have a very rapid response to ensure that story is either sunk or discredited [...] You don't attack the story, you don't even address the story – you attack the journalist.

The second way in which surveillance can contribute to the 'climate of caution' in major news organisations is by preparing the ground for legal assaults. Dorothy Byrne, head of *Channel 4 News*, suggested that in spite of the UK's relatively austere libel laws, legal threats against news organisations are often more about pre-emptive strategies to avoid damaging stories coming out:

> There have always been unpleasant organisations who would find ways of getting at your source, find out who your source is, and carry out illegal activity with a view to intimidating you [...] It is a fact that our lawyers are kept much busier than they used to be and although people don't win libel actions they do get their lawyers to send threatening letters [...] You feel with some of them they're almost just trying to put you off investigating them, to intimidate you out of making allegations. So you've got to have the stomach for it and you've got to have the time and the money for it.

In light of this, it is not surprising that journalists at the *Guardian* acknowledged the benefits of Wikileaks' superior technical expertise and broader understanding when it came to the issue of pre-publication security (Leigh and Harding 2011). That expertise, combined with their abundant supply of source material allowed major news organisations in turn to harness their scale of operations, established localised correspondents, and to invest heavily in relatively 'safe' forms of public interest journalism. These included authentication, redaction, analysis, and most crucially, publicity.

As we will see, it was the competitive tensions underlying the mainstream media partnership that were to prove its undoing in the aftermath of Cablegate – at least as far as the relationship between Wikileaks and the *Guardian* was concerned. But during its honeymoon period, the alliance was clearly based on some degree of mutual dependence: a resource pooling that allowed all sides to exploit value out of each other. In other words, the notion of Wikileaks as a 'game changer' is not necessarily at odds with a dependence on traditional news organisations. What the narrative of change and the new model of journalism share in common is a conviction that the cable releases *mattered* both in terms of what they exposed and their impact thereof.

DE-LEGITIMISING THE LEAKS

The broader picture suggests, as we have seen, that pockets of accountability discourse surfaced in coverage of the cable stories themselves. But what about the coverage which focused on Wikileaks as an organisation, and Julian Assange as a figurehead? Whilst not accounting for the dominant share of coverage, this nevertheless was a secondary focus; all the more significant if we consider the live two-ways between anchor and correspondents featured around the reports. As we have seen in previous case studies, it is here that journalists are most free to editorialise about the issues at stake.

Few would argue that Wikileaks and Julian Assange were not valid and important public interest news topics in their own right. According to Richard Watson of BBC's *Newsnight*:

> There was a tremendously big story behind the actual specific leak about who was Julian Assange, what was the organisation Wikileaks, what role were they playing? It was almost as significant as the leaks themselves – the fact that we had an organisation here that was riding a coach and horses through previous protocol.

The legitimacy issue had been seized upon by US officials following the first set of releases – the Afghan war logs – in which Wikileaks itself published more than 76,000 documents, with comparatively little redaction (Brooke 2011). With the cable stories, Wikileaks followed the *Guardian*'s lead both in terms of the cables published and in the redactions made. Nevertheless, questions of legitimacy remained pertinent particularly in respect of information that may have yielded little to no accountability value, but potentially damaged diplomatic progress towards peaceful resolution of conflict. Even information activists acknowledged that it was an issue which warranted public debate. According to Mikael Viborg: 'the judgement should lie with the public, after the fact. The public should decide whether this was justified or not.'

But the important question here is whether alternative frames were adequately represented. In this respect, television news overwhelmingly privileged official source definitions, perhaps most acutely revealed by the opening sentence of the BBC's first report on the cable leaks: 'reckless and irresponsible – the White House condemns the website Wikileaks'.[15]

Table 6.1 presents data showing the balance between critical and supportive sources featured in reports.

Once again, the findings reveal a similar pattern to that observed in Chapter 2, with analysis and late evening programmes exhibiting a greater propensity to challenge elite positions than the bulletins and earlier editions respectively. In Table 6.1 there is one significant outlier which accounts for the relatively extreme inverse proportions shown in the Analysis column. This was a special report by Mark Urban on BBC's *Newsnight* which featured excerpts from an extended interview with David Leigh of the *Guardian*. Not surprisingly, Leigh was supportive of the leaks given his instrumental role at the time in overseeing their release. If we were to exclude this outlier from the data, the overall proportion of supportive sources would be just 12 per cent.

Table 6.1 Comparing the prominence of sources critical and supportive of the leaks. (Based on the total seconds of airtime within reports featuring sources explicitly either defending or attacking Wikileaks. Sources providing impartial or ambiguous accounts were excluded.)

	Bulletins	Analysis programmes	Early programmes	Late programmes	All
	%	%	%	%	%
Supportive	12	79	14	35	27
Critical	78	11	86	65	73

Source: National film archives

Outside of reports, the absence of a 'right of reply' approach to relaying official source views was striking. Consider, for instance, the following two-way response:

> Downing Street and the Foreign Office have both in strong terms condemned the publication of these secret messages not necessarily because of their content but for the very fact that what started off as high level private communications has ended up being out there in public for all to see. They believe that governments do need to be able to communicate with each other in confidence and that governments internally should be able to have things that are private and keep them that way.

Though there is nothing intrinsically wrong with this statement on its own, the fact that it was not followed or preceded by any indication of a contrary view is clearly at odds with the BBC's commitment to impartiality. When reporters did on rare occasion reference alternative source views, they invariably did so in ways that subtly undermined them:

Some will say this shines a very bright light, important light, on the dark world of international diplomacy. But I just spoke to a former CIA director who says he believes that many lives will be lost as a consequence of the leaks. How damaging is it really I asked him? He said this is much worse for US national security than all of the espionage performed by the KGB during the cold war. That's how bad he said it was.

To understand the emphasis effect here, it is worth rearranging the extract to see what it would sound like if the two views were reversed:

I just spoke to a former CIA director who says he believes that many lives will be lost as a consequence of the leaks. How damaging is it really? I asked him. He said this is much worse for US national security than all of the espionage performed by the KGB during the Cold War. That's how bad he said it was. But some will say this shines a very bright light, important light, on the dark world of international diplomacy.

Even discounting the relative extremity of the official view (for which no basis is provided), the simple act of rearranging the order of references results in a markedly if subtly different tone.

Why did journalists so brazenly abandon impartiality discipline when it came to the legitimacy debate? One plausible explanation is that the legitimacy debate was instinctively seen as an effective right to reply for official sources in response to the leaks themselves. If the majority of the reportage was focused on the content of cables, the balance of live two-way exchanges was weighted significantly in favour of official source responses. But the problem with this is that officials by and large did not respond to the content of the leaks but simply attacked the legitimacy of the leak facilitator. In that sense, they effectively waived their right to reply. The attack on the legitimacy of Wikileaks should have been presented as a distinct narrative with appropriate right of reply afforded to Wikileaks and their supporters.

In the previous case study, we saw the explicit invocation of impartiality by broadcasters in respect of a debate between experts. Journalists appeared to consciously adopt a refereeing role, giving equal platform to sources both for and against the inquest campaign. In that case, the balance was found to be a distortion because it did not reflect the *actual* balance of expert views. In this case, impartiality became a mechanism of distortion in a different way. It allowed official sources to effectively attack the source of the leaks as a defence against what the leaks revealed. As a result, proponents in favour of Wikileaks were denied a platform. A recent poll found that 62 per cent of people in the UK either strongly or broadly supported Wikileaks' mission. But even the pull of journalist supporters with high profile media personalities – such as Jemima Khan, John Pilger and Vaughan Smith – was to prove an insufficient counter-weight to the dominance of official source frames.

NARRATIVES OF HYPE

As the week wore on, a different frame began to emerge in the coverage, positing that the cable releases were ultimately both unimportant and inconsequential, or at least nowhere near as important and consequential as the levels of coverage would suggest. This framing was particularly characteristic of discussion in the analysis programmes. It was in a sense vindicated by the time the dust had settled in early 2011 when the US government's own internal reviews suggested the cable releases had negligible effect on US interests abroad (Leigh and Harding 2011).

There were signs also that apparent triumphs elsewhere were proving to be temporary hiatuses. On 22 December, a US diplomatic cable revealed that a paramilitary force in Bangladesh was being trained by UK personnel. Reports by a human rights organisation suggest the group has been responsible for at least 700 extrajudicial killings since its inception in 2004.[16] The *Guardian*'s self-ascribed architects of Cablegate proudly announced in January 2011 that 'since the squad's exposure in the cables, no more deaths have been announced' (Leigh and Harding 2011:226). But no sooner had they done so, the *Guardian* itself reported that the killings had in fact resumed.[17] The fading of the mainstream media spotlight appeared to be heralding a return to business as usual for state-corporate malfeasance.

Clearly there was good reason to believe that the leaks had not delivered on their accountability promise. But the problem with the narrative of hype was that it was founded only secondarily on a belief about the leaks' consequences. First and foremost, it is a narrative about the leaks themselves which are conceived as lacking the kind of substance befitting of their headline status. During the first week of cable releases, television reporters in live two-ways repeatedly denigrated the very stories they had covered as revealing information that was more 'embarrassing' than 'damaging'. There was also reference to some leaks as not actually revealing anything new: 'awkward maybe but we guessed it already'. According to John Simpson, the BBC's most senior correspondent:

> An awful lot of it is really not much more than refined tittle-tattle and the only thing that I've really raised my eyebrows at is the suggestion – and you've got to put a question mark over it – that a Chinese diplomat said to a South Korean diplomat 'we don't really care if Korea is united under South Korean control [...]' If true, that is potentially important.[18]

Such a view was echoed by television journalists during case study interviews. In essence, the problem came down to a perceived lack of 'newness' – the essential ingredient of headline material. It was encapsulated by Lindsey Hilsum, international editor for *Channel 4 News*:

> There was little in the leaks that was particularly surprising. There was stuff in there which were indiscreet comments by diplomats and there was stuff which was extremely well written. But so far nothing has come to light which changes our understanding of anything.

The subtext to this narrative was a kind of conscious self-correction by journalists – a suggestion or acknowledgment that the leaks made headlines more because of where they came from and how they were sourced than what they actually contained. BBC News correspondent Allan Little articulated the problem as an over-attention to the value of secrecy:

> Because it's come in the form of a leak, because it's a confidential document that got into the public domain it immediately finds its way on to the front page where as if that analysis or information is obtained through more conventional means it might make it onto page 17 of the foreign pages you know, but because it has the added frisson of being leaked documents that the State Department wanted to keep secret, it makes an impact in the way that more conventionally obtained information hasn't.

The over-valuing of secrecy was exacerbated by the scale of the leak which obviated against closer attention to its contents. The essential premise underlying narratives of hype is that closer attention to contents might have otherwise resulted in more subdued coverage. For some respondents, the importance of the cables was diminished by the very fact that they were not the kind of original source material contained in the preceding sets of leaks. Rather than giving viewers a first-hand view of statistics and events covered up by the US military, the diplomatic cables merely provided a perspective through the eyes of ambassadors, complete with their own careerist agendas and personal motives.

The problem with this view is that it implicitly labels all the cable stories as rumour-oriented or lacking veracity by virtue of the primary source – US diplomats. There was a sense in which their natural bias undermined the informational value of the leaks. But although the cables may have universally expressed the views or impressions of individuals working within the state, such a feature is common to all inside source accounts, on or off record. There was certainly no intrinsic reason to consider the diplomats as less reliable sources of information than official sources who brief the media on a daily basis. If anything, the leaked cables were *more* reliable sources precisely because they were never intended for publication and were hence not 'part of the armoury of news management', in the words of one interview respondent.

UNTOLD STORIES

Even if we were to limit our attention to the television coverage itself, the assessment that selected cable stories were predominantly or universally rumour-oriented is invalid. As we have already seen, gossip-related stories attracted just 8 per cent of the airtime given over to the cable stories during the first week of coverage. More importantly, certain cables *did* emerge during the first week, which pointed to serious political corruption in the UK, particularly as regards military co-operation with the US. Two stories stand out in this respect. The first emerged on the third day of the cables and revealed that, according to the US ambassador in London, British officials had assured the US government that they had 'put measures in place' to protect US interests during the Iraq War Inquiry. The news value of this cable, both in terms of 'new information' and public interest weight was underlined by several journalists interviewed for this study. According to Carl Dinnen, reporter for *Channel 4 News*, 'if somebody's potentially saying that they're capable of influencing an independent public inquiry into something as important as the Iraq War, that's hugely significant'.

Television journalists were asked during interviews to rank selected stories based on their news value. Five out of the six respondents ranked the above story as of equal or greater news value than the story regarding criticism of the UK war effort in Afghanistan by US and Afghan officials. Four of the respondents considered it to be headline material warranting extended analysis and investigation. This contrasts sharply with the content sample analysed in which criticism of the UK war effort attracted more airtime than any other story during the first five days of coverage, despite only emerging on the penultimate day of the sample period. In stark contrast, the Iraqi Inquiry story was absent from all news reports and received only passing mention as a 'news in brief' piece on one edition within the sample.[19] This marginalisation was broadly reflective of the *Guardian* coverage which featured the story only as a relatively minor 300-word article on page twelve.[20]

The second story pointing to high-level corruption involving military co-operation with the US emerged on day four of the coverage. It was based on a secret account of a meeting between British foreign office officials and their US counterparts in 2009. In it, UK officials are said to have suggested that a planned loophole in forthcoming legislation banning cluster bombs should be kept from Parliament. Crucially, the loophole would allow US cluster bombs to be kept on British soil in the island territory of Diego Garcia. The cable paraphrases the Foreign Office official as saying:

> It would be better for the [US government] and [Her Majesty's Government] not to reach final agreement on this temporary agreement understanding until after the [cluster bomb bill] ratification process is completed in Parliament, so that they can tell Parliamentarians that they have requested the [US government] to remove its cluster munitions by 2013, without complicating/ muddying the debate by having to indicate that this request is open to exceptions.[21]

The striking implication of this communiqué is that the US and UK governments had effectively colluded in a bid to mislead Parliament and undermine a crucial piece of human rights legislation. Once again, however, the story was all but entirely absent from television news, mentioned only briefly during a live two-way at 11 p.m. on the BBC's second channel.[22] The topic was introduced by the anchor not as a story pointing to corruption, but rather 'confusion over what the former foreign secretary said about cluster bombs'.

Curiously, however, in this case marginalisation on television was not entirely reflective of the *Guardian*'s coverage which featured the story as a 900-word article on its front page.[23] The title also contrasted starkly from the anchor introduction on *Newsnight*: 'SECRET DEAL LET AMERICANS SIDESTEP CLUSTER BOMB BAN: Officials concealed from parliament how US is allowed to bring weapons on to British soil in defiance of treaty.'

Nevertheless, the edition as a whole was dominated by stories about Russian state corruption which dwarfed the cluster bombs story in both billing and word count. Following suit, television outlets devoted their scarce air time to the package of stories about corruption within the Russian state, marginalising and in most cases excluding the cluster bombs story.

We are left with a picture of public service news as seemingly more concerned with corruption in foreign governments than that within the British state. For all the resources and publicity that the mainstream media brought to bear on the cable releases, information arguably of the most acute British public interest remained confined to the side-lines.

Indeed, three quarters of television airtime was given over to stories about foreign governments, a proportion largely in line with the balance of coverage in the *Guardian*.[24] Whilst this might be an appropriate reflection of the globalised nature of the content, closer analysis revealed significant skews in favour of international over domestic coverage. For instance, when we consider the number of stories that emerged from the cables (based on articles that appeared in the *Guardian*), the television coverage was significantly weighted in favour of Russia compared to the UK, as shown in Table 6.2.

Table 6.2   Balance of coverage between UK and Russia-related cable stories

	Number of cables released	Number of articles	Word count of articles	Seconds of TV airtime
UK	72	29	14,684	1,380
Russia	48	17	6,804	4,102

Sources: Proquest database; BFI archives; Guardian.co.uk

The data shows that in the *Guardian* both the number of articles and relative word counts were more or less in proportion to the number of cables released, with the coverage weighted in favour of UK-related stories. The final column however, showing the relative airtime allocated in television news reports, is a dramatic inverse of the correlation.

There are several possible explanations for this skew. First, the cables concerning Russia mostly emerged on a single day within the five-day sample and were neatly packaged by the *Guardian* around the theme of a 'mafia state'. This story package itself was given significantly greater prominence in the newspaper than the individual UK-related stories. Indeed, if we consider it as a single news story, it was the most widely covered by the *Guardian* during the five-day sample period. In its inherent attraction towards the 'big story', it is not surprising that television would have overlooked a complex of smaller, differentiated stories related to the UK.

But whilst this might bring the balance of television coverage more in line with the *Guardian*, it does not explain why the skew in favour of foreign stories apparently existed in both outlets. There certainly did not seem to be a similar tendency to favour foreign over domestic stories in the coverage of other European partners – *Der Spiegel*, *El País* and *Le Monde* – although detailed analysis was beyond the scope of this research.[25]

DEFINING THE AGENDA

It is worth discussing in some depth the enduring dependence of television news on the agenda setting power of the press, a point increasingly overlooked amidst popular attention to the growing influence of digital media. Overall, television's coverage of Wikileaks was attributable almost entirely to the *Guardian*'s exclusive rather than anything Wikileaks could leverage on its own. This is evident in comparative levels of coverage of Wikileaks releases prior to and after the intervention of the *Guardian* in 2010. Wikileaks had initially 'gone it alone' with a handful of releases believed to be from the same source as the cables. Most significantly, they released in April 2010 video footage from an Apache helicopter gun sight over Baghdad. Dubbed 'Collateral Murder', the footage showed the helicopter firing repeatedly at a Reuters cameraman mistaken for an armed insurgent as well as surrounding civilians. Worse still, the secret report released along with the video revealed that victims tried to surrender on the ground prompting the air crew to radio back to base for advice. The stark message they received can be heard over the dramatic footage: 'Crazy horse 18 cleared to engage. Lawyer states they cannot surrender to aircraft and are still valid targets.'[26]

The leak appeared to demonstrate in a nutshell Wikileaks' essential raison d'être: Reuters themselves had previously attempted to acquire the secret incident report via the US Freedom of Information Act but had failed on grounds of national security. Unauthorised disclosure had now succeeded where authorised channels had failed in exposing what was at best a tragic mistake of high public-interest import, and at worst a war crime. More importantly, it had uncovered a cover-up. There was clearly no justification for suppression of the incident report other than to protect reputations and the public image of America's war effort. The drama of the footage and the simplicity of the story only added to its news value. But whilst the video attracted significantly more attention from mainstream media than previous Wikileaks releases, it clearly did not create the kind of firestorm that either Julian Assange or the *Guardian* believed it warranted (Leigh and Harding 2011).

Curiously, television journalists repeatedly cited the video in interviews, unprompted, as being by far the most significant release to date, eclipsing anything that came out of Cablegate. What's more, its dramatic and brief televisual footage was considered particularly well suited to the medium in ways that the cable documents were not.

Caroline Wyatt, defence correspondent, BBC News:

> I mean, to me, I thought, as someone who covers defence, the most remarkable thing that's come out of Wikileaks was actually the footage from the Apache helicopter gun sight. That I thought was one of the strongest things that came out through Wikileaks which I don't think would have come out another way. It was a very serious news story whereas I think an awful lot of the other leaks sort of resulted in stories that were mostly gossip.

Carl Dinnen, presenter and home affairs correspondent, *Channel 4 News*: 'The only thing I can really think of is the apache footage because that does indicate one of the features of TV news which is that it obviously over emphasises anything that has a picture.'

Yet for all the acknowledged gravitas and news value of the story, the BBC devoted only one relatively brief report on the *Ten O'Clock News* with a similar-length piece appearing on Channel 4. Although the release coincided with the commencement of general election campaigning in Britain, the coverage was eclipsed by a range of other stories, including that of a family which tried to smuggle a dead relative on to a plane.[27] The *Ten O'Clock News* and *Channel 4 News* reports ran on the day the video was released but the story was to receive no further mention until the co-ordinated release of Iraq War Logs in October. The comparatively marginal coverage was revealing to the extent that it demonstrates the enduring agenda-setting power of the press. Even though the collateral murder video release was better suited to the dynamics of television and more newsworthy, it did not attract comparable levels of coverage that the co-ordinated release of documents later did. Figure 6.2 illustrates the comparative coverage between Collateral Murder and key stories that emerged during the first week of Cablegate.

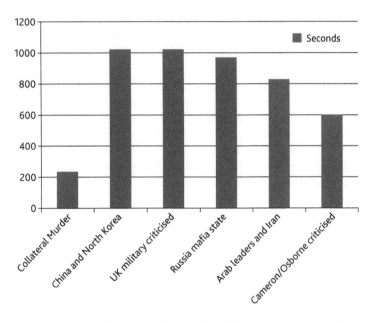

Figure 6.2   Collateral murder and the top five cable stories – comparative levels of coverage during the first week of release.*

*Explanation of stories:
  • The 'China and North Korea' story centred on the publication of an embassy cable suggesting China's apparent willingness to accept a united Korea with Seoul as its capital.
  • The 'UK military criticised' story concerned reported criticism of the British war effort in Afghanistan from both Afghan and US officials.
  • The 'Russia mafia state' story was based on a complex of cable releases suggesting endemic levels of criminality within the Russian establishment.
  • The 'Arab leaders and Iran' story focused on cables revealing Arab hostility to Iran and support for a US military attack.
  • The 'Cameron/Osborne criticised' story referred to a cable detailing criticism of the current Prime Minister and Chancellor of the Exchequer by the Bank of England governor in 2009.

7
Behind the Wall of Transparency

THE BIGGEST LEAK IN HISTORY

Having examined the contours of the coverage, it seems clear that the various limitations stemmed from a general perception of transparency overload. This is what underpinned official source frames which sought to de-legitimise Wikileaks, but it was also used to explain the lack of focus on particular 'nuggets' of public interest disclosure. For some interview respondents, even with the full weight of mainstream media resources, it was inevitable that important stories would get buried amidst the unimaginable scale of the leaks. According to Gavin MacFadyen:

> You've got to understand the sheer scale of it. It was like going into a main library somewhere and saying which books are interesting? Well you have to start reading the books to know and there's just a vast amount of material. So it's very difficult I think to make choices other than on subjects we already know about so that you can interrogate the data looking for some stories on the banking crisis say, or something else that you had already had in mind but there might be a lot of material in there on subjects that you don't even know about. So that's part of the problem [...] You can also go back over some of the documents and realise there are stories in it that you didn't see the first time reading them [...] It was just the most gigantic mass of material, the most daunting pile you could imagine.

Clearly, the unprecedented size of the leak meant that extracting newsworthy material from it in the first place was a significant logistical and technical challenge. But as we have seen, it was a challenge that journalists overcame in several respects. Above all, the *Guardian* succeeded in uncovering material from which a wide range of stories covering radically different contexts and locales was produced. Indeed, in some ways the effort to extract news stories from the cables was too successful to the extent that there were too many, and they were too wide ranging for any to leave a meaningful imprint on the public consciousness. One recurring theme that emerged in analysis of interviews was the preponderance of responses that invoked memory loss in respect of the cable stories. In one illuminating interview, Dorothy Byrne – director of *Channel 4 News* – reflected on the importance and legacy of the cables:

> Wikileaks revealed all sorts of very important information to the public across the world and anybody who says otherwise is just manifestly wrong. I find it bizarre that anybody would say that actually. Very strange. How could they think that it hadn't revealed anything? [...] Surely when we look back historically that will be what we will remember – we'll remember the important revelations.

But when asked to pinpoint any particular outstanding stories none could be recalled: 'Oh God, to be honest I can't answer that question. I can't remember that far back so I'm not going to be of use to you [...] I would have to get it all out and look at it again. So I'm afraid I've got no answer to that question.'

It seems that the real problem was not so much the scale of the data, but the way they were released. In particular, the huge 'dump' of stories that emerged during the first week of coverage was destined to deflect attention and limit memory recalls of particular issues.

THE VALUE OF EXCLUSIVITY

To understand why the stories were released in such a torrent requires attention to political economic factors and in particular, the value of exclusivity. According to David Leigh and Luke Harding of the *Guardian*, Assange was acutely conscious of the dangers presented by front-loading the releases, and made explicit requests to avoid it: 'He stressed that he wanted the cables to be released in an orderly way and not in a "big dump". Ideally, a "gradual release played out over two months"' (Leigh and Harding 2011:170).

In the event, the newspaper guaranteed only to publish 'in a staggered form' but the data available on its website reveal a somewhat different picture. A total of 392 articles on the cables appeared on the website between 29 November 2010 and 29 January 2011. Of these, almost half ran in the first week and over 90 per cent were condensed into the first month. What's more, a review of the full range of stories casts doubt over claims that selection was based purely on a public interest conception (Leigh and Harding 2011). As Gill Phillips of the *Guardian* acknowledged:

> A lot of the stuff that the *Guardian* put out on the cables was undoubtedly I think, story by story, in the public interest. But some of it – there was a bit about [former Libyan dictator] Gadaffi's mistress – and you sort of think, well if this was a story in isolation we probably wouldn't run it. But as part of this package, ok it may not pass the public interest test in that way but in terms of the whole it was considered ok to do it.

This suggests that the 'package' of cable stories created an opportunity for the paper to publish stories that might otherwise have been considered too downmarket. But the central problem with the way the release was packaged concerned the quantity of stories it contained. It was this above all which obviated against understanding of their significance and, more importantly, diluted attention to the critical public interest stories that emerged.

Several respondents drew a contrast with the gradual release a year earlier of secret files detailing expenses fraud by Members of Parliament. The newspaper that had the exclusive – the *Daily Telegraph* – allowed the story to move in and out of the headlines in a way that extended the longevity of their exclusive. According to Mary Hockaday, head of the BBC newsroom:

> The MPs' expenses was an interesting one because that was absolutely a *Telegraph* story and it was managed by them in a way to help sell newspapers but also get the story out, and they kind of drip fed it day after day after day. That had its own logistical challenges for us – it meant we had days where our bulletins were leading on the latest details in the *Telegraph*. We would sort of joke about how we were the *Telegraph's* horn blower – but you're going to do it because the story's there, the journalism's there and you've got to credit the fact that they've got it.

But one important difference between the two is the extent of exclusivity that each paper held over the leaked documents. The *Guardian*'s exclusivity was diluted at the outset when it was agreed to invite the *New York Times* and other international papers into the pact. To some extent, this added value for the *Guardian* in terms of being able to collaborate over the resource-intensive mining of the data. More crucially, it mitigated the legal risk as Gill Phillips explained:

> We had exclusivity in the UK and that was crucial. The partnership with the other papers was actually very important I think given that our law in terms of pre-publication risk is probably more repressive than any of the other European countries [...] There was a lot of comfort in the fact that there were other people there.

Much less welcome to the *Guardian*, however, was the subsequent extension of the partnership to include television. It was specifically a tie-up with *Channel 4 News* prior to the release of the Afghan war logs – the first batch in the series – which planted the seed of relationship breakdown:

> Nick Davies personally broke off relations in the summer, after Assange breached the original compact, as Davies saw it, by going behind his back to the *Guardian*'s TV rivals at Channel 4, taking with him all the knowledge acquired by the privileged visits to the *Guardian*'s research room [...] after the publication of the Afghan war logs, Assange proposed to change the terms of the deal once again, before the planned launch of the much bigger tranche of Iraq logs. He wanted more television, in order to provide 'emotional impact'. (Leigh and Harding:136)

The second addition to the partnership was the Bureau of Investigative Journalism, whose documentary film about the Iraq War Logs was broadcast by Channel 4's *Dispatches* series. The problem for the *Guardian* was not just that more partners were now involved, including competitors in the UK. The dynamics of news delivery are such that *multimedia* partnerships have a particular weakening effect on exclusivity, as Iain Overton pointed out:

> In order to really give stories impact you need multimedia collaborations and yet the inherent internal competition existing in the media means that multimedia collaborations are very hard to achieve [...] particularly when you're looking at multi-national collaborations. We're just lining up something at the moment with the *Financial Times* [FT] and a paper in Pakistan and one of the considerations is by going on Pakistan's time, then the rest of the world's media can pick up the story and the FT feels it may lose the exclusivity. And that certainly weighs up in people's minds.

I mean obviously the internet is useful to remedy that because you're not entirely dedicated to a print run but it's about other people being able to grab the story. One of the major concerns I think that happened with the Iraq War Logs is that Al Jazeera English ran early with the story by around 40 minutes.

There were also less overt linkages with, for instance, BBC's *Newsnight*. According to one respondent the programme had its 'own ways of getting hold of the leaks before they were going to come out'. Regardless of the extent of such connections, it is clear that the *Guardian* had what could be at most described as partial exclusivity. What's more, this was prone to dilution over time as media organisations around the world began to negotiate their own direct access to the secret archive. It stands to reason that in such a climate, the newspaper with initial exclusivity would seek to extract most value by front-loading its output as much as possible. That would at least make the most of the title's association with the stories, before others gained access to their source.

One of the great paradoxes of the Wikileaks story is that in order for the group to maximise ultimate exposure of its documents, it had to initially restrict supply. Herbert Snorrason was a former Wikileaks employee who put the paradox in these terms:

> It's a question of economics. The experience with Wikileaks is that when the information is out there, it gets overlooked because of the risk of being scooped. If there's an exclusivity period, you stand a much better chance of getting a media organisation to show interest in the material.

For Julian Assange, the ultimate goal is 'to increase perceived value to the point that journalists will invest time to produce quality stories'. The question then becomes 'which method should be employed to apportion material to those who are most likely to invest in it.'[1]

But as we have seen, the *Guardian* could not be described as a purely commercially-driven company. The value of exclusivity must therefore be seen in a broader context than the pursuit of profit which takes into account the less tangible value derived from credibility branding and peer recognition. Though these may well provide an indirect boost to profitability, they also provide important justification for financial *losses* and hence, for cross-subsidy support. For the individual journalists and editors who negotiated the basis of exclusivity and had their names attached to the stories that came out, credibility and peer recognition were ends in themselves. Several journalists reflected in interviews on the careerist competitiveness between individuals that often underpins competition between outlets. Individualism within the press is more extensive than in broadcasting 'because broadcast journalists have to work in a team'. There is also, as Vaughan Smith pointed out, a relatively higher and growing proportion of newspaper journalists who work on a freelance basis. This includes Nick Davies, the journalist who brokered the Wikileaks partnership for the *Guardian*.

But it was not just the *Guardian* and its journalists whose decisions were driven at least in part by a need for name association and recognition. According to Iain Overton, a branding battle developed between all multimedia partners:

> I remember that there was a real ding-dong about the number of times we mentioned Wikileaks on our web page and things like that. They wanted more mention and I was, like, fine we can mention you a few more times if you want [...] They just wanted branding. But you can understand – everyone wants branding. The challenge is of course – when you're doing a multimedia collaboration – to work it so that people don't feel that they somehow are going second fiddle. Everyone always wants it to be 'in an investigation with etc'.

THE COST OF IMPACT

The problem was not that the drive to exclusivity and branding restricted the supply of stories. On the contrary, the problem quickly became one of *over*-supply. The net effect of branding competition and partial exclusivity was that impact was maximised to the detriment of promoting understanding. But in some sense, this was still a measure of success for Wikileaks, as Vaughan Smith observed:

> Assange wanted to get the biggest impact [...] You can go to Kazakhstan and speak to a farmer and there's a chance, a reasonable chance, that they will know the name Assange and what he does. So there's that brand penetration that is frankly extraordinary and I think it's reached a point whereby this isn't really reversible. I think we will see what he's achieved built upon by other people. I think he's done something quite important.

It was a sentiment echoed by *Newsnight*'s Richard Watson: 'They certainly needed that initial kind of shock wave of leaks to actually grab people's attention, to actually demonstrate the significance, the true significance of the organisation and information that was being released.'

But the cost of going for impact was that the names – Wikileaks, Julian Assange, David Leigh etc. – became more memorable than the leaks themselves. It was a phenomenon fuelled by the news value of personality. Julian Assange quickly became a figurehead not only for Wikileaks, but for a globalised and generational cadre of information activists. He played both hero and villain – a champion of free speech values in one take, sexual predator and dangerous anarchist in the next. As Samira Shackle of the *New Statesman* put it, 'once someone has that kind of cult standing you know that it's going to sell papers'.

But television was equally up to the task of focusing on the character of Assange to dramatic and almost romantic effect, described in turns as 'elusive', 'unusual', 'a scarlet pimpernel' and 'the US government's undeclared enemy'. The point here is not that such ascriptions were an exaggeration or distortion (anecdotal evidence suggests Assange very much lived up to his on-news character). But the intensity of the media spotlight on Assange cannot be seen in isolation from the drive to exclusivity and branding, and in particular, the surge of stories it helped to foster. It was inevitable amidst such a surge that the spotlight would turn to 'the man behind the leaks', particularly one as enigmatic and forthcoming as Assange. As Gavin MacFadyen explained:

> The priorities of the news are personality, celebrity-driven. They're not particularly idea-driven [...] So suddenly they had this sort of curious character that was producing these enormous scoops and of course that in a sense was news itself because there was an unusual character involved in it directly and one who didn't fit any other traditional moulds. So I think it played right into the hands of the sensationalists who are the great majority in television. Suddenly they had a subject which was sexy for them and they went for it.

One incident recalled by Wikileaks insiders was particularly illuminating of the media's penchant for celebrity over substance. As Iain Overton observed:

It was very interesting, very telling on the day that we went live with the Iraq War Logs. The Bureau hosted the press conference for it and Julian [Assange] and Gavin [MacFadyen] and others were on stage talking for the first time. The point was they were going to talk about the background to it and then I was going to stand up and talk about what we'd found. The world's press were taking photos of Julian like never before and then he left the platform before I went up to talk. Then he left the room and everyone left after him and I was just stood there in front of an empty room. It was kind of like a really bad *Wedding Singer* moment. And I remember saying in exasperation, surely this is why you should all be here? This is what we've found, this is what the stuff contains! You call yourselves journalists – don't you want to know what we found? And nobody did.

Beyond the need for celebrity, casting the spotlight on Assange was also a useful deflector. With all the alleged threats to national security and 'lives on the ground' spewing from official sources, Assange the celebrity gave media outlets a way of diverting attention from their own complicity in publicising the leaks. For Vaughan Smith, this explained the particularly critical editorials that emerged in the *New York Times* shortly after the first cable releases:

It's increased their ability to do the stories he's delivered through Wikileaks, because they can take this position of 'oh, we support Wikileaks but we don't support Julian'. So someone's to blame and it's not them. It's a deflector – they are deflecting a lot of the pressure towards Julian.

But the problem wasn't solely about journalistic shortcomings. Shortly after the first cable releases, Assange was arrested in London on charges of sexual offences brought by a Swedish prosecutor. Whether or not it was engineered by a smear campaign (for which there is no evidence other than apparently perfect timing), the event had arguably the most significant effect in diverting coverage away from the leaks. Nor can we discount the role played by Assange himself who, even according to some of his closest associates, was a willing accomplice in his own rise to stardom. Long before the onset of Cablegate, Assange had assumed a role as public representative of Wikileaks in a manner at odds with the political identity of other so-called 'hacktivist' groups – notably Anonymous. As one faceless video representative attests: 'with Anonymous there is no authorship [...] there is no control, no leadership, only influence – the influence of thought.'[2]

Clearly, Wikileaks as an organisation had goals distinct from much of the hacker movement that spawned it. In particular, its overriding concern is with publicising its documents as widely as possible. It is self-evident that taking to the spotlight as an organisation, and as a figurehead in the case of Assange, could potentially both further and inhibit that aim.

A VERY BRITISH VIEW OF CORRUPTION

This still leaves us with the problem of why UK corruption stories were comprehensively marginalised, even from the analysis and late evening programmes. The problem is located not at the point of story extraction, but of selection and prioritisation. That the raw material for UK corruption stories was uncovered in the first week of coverage is evident simply and obviously in the fact that the stories did appear, albeit at the margins. The question is why they were confined as such.

The deluge of stories was always going to create anomalies in the balance of coverage. We might consider the marginalisation of the Iraq Inquiry cable to be one such anomaly. On a day in which the *Guardian* coverage was scheduled to give priority to cables emanating from Moscow, it is feasible that this cable was overlooked simply because eyeballs were focused elsewhere. This might explain why the controversy was buried on page twelve and why television news outlets, in deference to the *Guardian*'s agenda-leading role, paid it equally little attention.

But the marginalisation of the cluster bombs story is less easy to explain away as a random event simply because the *Guardian* did give it headline status. This suggests that television news outlets – elsewhere remaining faithful to the paper's priorities – actively overlooked the story in this case.

An alternative explanation concerns the issue of complexity and the relative constraints impinging on the broadcast medium. According to this view, complex stories involving detailed documents simply do not make good television. As Angus Fraser, China correspondent for ITV news, explained:

Newspapers lend themselves more easily to large amounts of printed material. Putting that into a TV piece is very tricky in terms of what it looks like and whether the viewer could be subjected to what would essentially be page after page of graphicised text. It doesn't really lend itself to television where we deal with moving pictures.

But whilst this may be true of the bulletins, it is not in keeping with the culture and practice of the news analysis programmes. As we have seen, these outlets are not only better adapted to cover complex controversies than the main bulletins, but often prioritise them in a bid to distinguish their output. It was a point emphasised by Richard Watson of *Newsnight*:

> We've got to be distinctive from other broadcasters, we've got to be distinctive from other newspapers where possible, and also the other news outlets like rolling news, *News at Ten* etc. and the way that *Newsnight* does that is either through in depth analysis and discussion of stories, or it's with genuine exclusives and revelatory journalism.

Other journalists were at pains to stress that it is the issue of *salience* which matters most. For Kevin Marsh, former editor of the *Today* programme, salience can and should transcend problems of both complexity and scale:

> The question you're always asking yourself when you're looking at anything is you know, 'where's the wow thing here?' And even in a very complex story like the cluster bombs story, which is fantastically complicated [...] but if I can see in a document like that, however complicated the story is, something that makes me go 'wow, right I can tell that story, I can make it mean something' and it makes my jaw drop then I would go for that.

This would suggest that the cluster bombs cable lacked the 'wow' factor which propels stories to the top of the news agenda. It is worth reiterating that although the *Guardian* featured the story on its front page, it was dwarfed by the package of stories about Russian state corruption, which dominated the edition as a whole. This suggests that there may have been simply insufficient news value in the actual detail of the controversy.

There was certainly a crucial distinction between the UK and Russian corruption stories in that the latter tended to focus on criminality whereas the former centred on subversion of accountability institutions. The cluster bombs story was in essence about an attempt to undermine Parliament and the Iraqi Inquiry story was about the government exercising surreptitious influence over a supposedly independent public inquiry. There was no money laundering or contract killing and the central figures of the story were unknown bureaucrats. In many ways, they were reflective of the fact that institutional corruption was not, in relative terms, a particularly 'sexy' story to tell either on television or in print.

But we are still left with the problem of why subsequent stories, such as the Bangladeshi death-squad headline in the *Guardian*, failed to gain traction on television news. In the previous two case studies, the spectacles of accountability identified both revolved around public figures (notably Tony Blair, Alastair Campbell and Greg Dyke). The marginalisation of the controversy surrounding the actual death of David Kelly was attributed in part to the absence of such high profile individuals from the narrative. We do not have to conduct an extensive analysis to see a similar vacuum of official response and comment in respect of the UK corruption cable stories. This presents a paradox: the intervention of high profile officials such as the Prime Minister is only warranted in controversies that have acquired a given level of profile on the news agenda. But media attention is often itself to some extent contingent on their responses. In the preceding two case studies, we saw how a confluence of factors caused the two forces to coincide.

A BREAKDOWN OF TRUST

One particular oddity of Cablegate is that television reporters were wholly in step with official sources in framing the legitimacy debate exclusively around Wikileaks. As we have seen, however, it was the newspapers that took the lead role in publishing cable stories, with Wikileaks (and television) following both their cable selections and redaction decisions. Yet at no point was the issue of legitimacy raised in respect of the *Guardian* which, as we have seen, made questionable decisions over both selection and prioritisation of stories deemed in the public interest. On the contrary, a recurrent theme during interviews with broadcasters for this book was a sense of ultimate trust placed in the decisions and journalism of their newspaper rivals. This was expressed primarily in the context of prioritisation, and as an explanation as to why television news largely used the press, and the *Guardian* in particular, as a benchmark for salience. According to Lindsey Hilsum of *Channel 4 News*: 'if it wasn't prioritised by the *Guardian* or the *New York*

Times, whose journalists I respect, I would think it's because it didn't tell us anything we didn't know before.'

This kind of solidarity was also expressed in the context of the relationship breakdown between Wikileaks and its Anglo-American partners (namely the *Guardian* and the *New York Times*). For Kevin Marsh, among others, the blame for the breakdown appeared to lay squarely with Julian Assange: 'you only have to read what the *New York Times* and what the *Guardian* say about working with him to realise that he's not a guy that has helped himself hugely.'

Certainly, some journalists had what could be considered legitimate grievances with the way that Assange presented the leaks. For Alex Thomson of *Channel 4 News,* this did not diminish the public service function of Wikileaks. Interviewed in the aftermath of the Iraq War Logs, he referenced the official lies that the logs exposed before offering a sustained critique of Assange's handling of the press:

> It exposes the lie – it was a lie – by the British and Americans that they weren't keeping a body count because we know they counted 109,000 people, 66,000 of whom were unarmed civilians. That is a body count. That was a lie. And we can go on from there. That was an incredibly important function to do [...] but I do think there are serious questions to be asked about Julian Assange and his own personal hypocrisy in terms of being on the one hand a champion – so-called – for truth and freedom of information and standing up in press conferences and simply refusing to answer any questions that get difficult. And I'm not referring to questions about his private life and allegations there.

The problem for BBC reporter Allan Little was not a refusal to answer difficult questions in press conferences as much as elusive behaviour when it came to interview requests:

> Julian Assange won't answer questions. I've asked him for an interview often – I say here are the questions I want to ask you. I don't want to ask you about the Swedish case. I won't ask you about the criminal charges... I'd like to do a proper audit of what we know now that we didn't know before as a result of Cablegate.

Such behaviour appears to conflict with accounts of Assange willingly taking to the limelight. But there is a broader context here which concerns a breakdown in trust between Wikileaks and

Anglo-American journalists. It began with a highly critical personal profile of Assange in the *New York Times* seen by some as a move to deflect pressure from the US government. We have also seen that even prior to the cable releases, tensions had been brewing as a result of Wikileaks' moves to bring television outlets into the partnership fold. What is most notable about the interview responses of broadcasters is that they universally absolved the *Guardian* and the *New York Times* from any responsibility in the breakdown of relations with Wikileaks. Assange was repeatedly described by some respondents as 'odd' or 'difficult' – often as an explicit or implicit explanation of why the partnership failed.

Other accounts pointed to a clash of values at the heart of the mainstream media partnership. According to these, there was always latent conflict between the somewhat anarchistic values of Wikileaks and those of the liberal media. For Steve Aftergood, a senior analyst at the Federation of American Scientists and free-speech campaigner, the problem comes down to the fact that Wikileaks is a fundamentally illiberal organisation:

> They do not respect individual rights, they do not respect personal privacy, they do not respect intellectual property, freedom of religion, freedom of association. They practice a form of coercive transparency against disfavoured groups and they're basically not a nice bunch of people. So in a world dominated by Wikileaks basic values, American constitutional government would not survive. My interest is in preserving those values not in undermining them. My approach basically is to take what is good from Wikileaks, to learn what can be learned from the materials they offer, but to be cognoscente of the fact that they are not allies of ours or of people who believe in liberal democratic values.

But the problem is that Wikileaks itself has not acted consistently in accordance with a stable set of values, either in the manner in which it operates or in its self-expressed identity. Even between the three sets of releases co-ordinated with the mainstream media in 2010, we have seen a marked evolution in Wikileaks' approach and rhetoric. This is partly reflective of the fact that a clash of values has permeated and ruptured Wikileaks itself. It has surfaced at times in the articulation of radically different, if not necessarily irreconcilable self-conceptions (Fenster 2011) and resulted in the high profile defection of senior figures from within the group. According to one of those, Herbert Snorrason, 'any compromise to any factor other than what [Assange] perceives as important at the time is a sign of weakness and a sign of someone betraying principles'.

But similar controlling instincts are attributed to mainstream media organisations by Wikileaks supporters, and with no less basis. Consciously or otherwise, professional news makers perceived Wikileaks as impinging on or threatening what they saw as their rightful domain – the right to define news. According to Vaughan Smith:

> They feel they own news and there is this idea that you're not really a journalist unless you work for one of these which is something I've come across in my career a great deal and I resent and reject that [...] Journalism isn't owned by organisations that purvey it and this is where they get it wrong and one of the reasons I found Assange appealing was because he was throwing a cat amongst the pigeons and he has upset the news industry in America and Britain.

Indeed, for Smith, the icing of relations between Wikileaks and their Anglo-American media rivals was not about a clash of values, but a clash of institutional cultures. What made it all the more intense were the *similarities* between Assange and his traditional media rivals. Ultimately all partners shared a common drive towards maximising the impact of the cable releases on the global news agenda. Part of that drive was no doubt a genuine desire to deliver on the whistleblower's intentions and to publicise the leaked material as widely as possible. Part of it was a genuine intention to affect some kind of accountability as a result of the leaks. But part of it, as we have seen, was also about institutional branding and competition between all members of the partnership.

That said, it is worth emphasising that the actual breakdown of relations has only manifested in the partnership between Wikileaks and the leading Anglo-American outlets: the *Guardian* and the *New York Times*. As we have seen, the triggers for these breakdowns were distinct but the fact that other international partners remain on amicable terms raises some potentially interesting comparative research questions (albeit ones beyond the scope of this book).

TELEVISION STRENGTHS AND VULNERABILITIES

The crucial point for the analysis here is that broadcasters demonstrated an instinctive camaraderie with their counterparts in the mainstream press, to the extent that even prior to the release of the first cable stories, Wikileaks was seen as something of a pariah organisation. It seems reasonable to infer that such perceptions fed into the legitimacy debate, resulting in the deference to official source frames. But the united front presented by the mainstream media was not a defence against a perceived existential threat posed by a new breed of journalism. It was reflective of a relationship between broadcasters and newspapers that has long been etched into the political economic fabric of the news industry.

There is nothing new for instance, in the relative dependence of broadcasters on the agenda setting functions of the press. It was exhibited in this case in the tendency of television news to follow the prioritisation of cable stories set by the *Guardian*. But clearly, given its relative time and space constraints, television news functions as a super layer of story selection and prioritisation. By virtue of its extended influence and universal audience reach, television confers salience on news stories and acts effectively as a bridge between the news agenda and the public agenda. This makes television news less dependent on exclusives and 'getting there first', as Iain Overton explained:

> There is a self-confidence in television that you can ride something a couple of days after the event. And there's some value to that anyway because I guess it gets traction and people's appetites are whetted. And to be honest when the *Guardian* does an 18-page special on something people only read the first two pages. I don't think anyone sits down and reads all 18 pages. Even I don't, and I think I'm fairly autistic on these matters [...] but a newspaper rarely will run with a lead story the day after television whereas TV's quite happy to put something on the top of its bulletins if it's been the lead story in the paper that morning. So I think therein lies the problem. TV is more influential because more people watch it but print is more determining often in keeping a story alive or not.

To say that broadcasters place no value on exclusives would be an overstatement. Certainly the analysis programmes – *Channel 4 News* and *Newsnight* – are structurally and culturally adapted to forge relatively independent agendas (see Chapter 3). We have seen that this relative independence is manifest not just in a greater degree of exclusives, but also in a greater propensity to challenge elite positions. But television news is dominated – both in terms of schedule and audience – by the bulletins and rolling news channels.

It is also more vulnerable as a whole to the climate of caution that we have seen manifest in different ways in the preceding case studies. The financial risk associated with in-depth and investigative journalism has had a particularly acute impact on television in view of the relative costs of filming over printing. In Part II, we saw how the Hutton Report has engendered a culture of compliance within the BBC that has spawned a new breed of public service journalism that is both 'less questioning' and 'more directed'. And both BBC and commercial broadcasters have become increasingly sensitive to perceived legal threats which, as we saw earlier in this case study, are related to a growing investment in legal posturing by the targets of investigative reports. One BBC journalist pointed to the chilling effect of a growing tendency to settle rather than fight cases in the court:

I think sometimes the BBC in recent years has been too quick to cave in actually and pay out on these cases and that is a real problem. I think – I can't go into details about this I'm afraid – but there is one case that I'm thinking about […] where the BBC settled in our view far too early and amongst the journalists I work with it raised big questions about really whether the BBC was prepared to be robust enough and fight and what it would mean to actually settle this case early. Because often settling cases early may be a way of limiting your ultimate losses in the libel courts, but it also has a chilling effect because if you settle cases early it means effectively that you can't go back and investigate those people again because you've already settled.

TRACES OF SMEAR

We have seen how the coverage offered a free hand for official sources to attack the source of the leaks rather than respond to allegations that emerged from them. This was in keeping with what several interview respondents referred to as the practice of 'smearing'. Broadcasters in particular appeared to be acutely conscious of it, as Allan Little observed: 'The impulse to character assassination – to try to decontaminate what somebody's said by destroying the character of the person that's saying it – is very strong and ruthless. You've got to be wary of that. I'm sure it happens.'

The question remains whether the official source response to Cablegate was tantamount to a smear campaign. There is certainly no evidence to substantiate allegations that such a campaign lay behind the sexual misconduct charges brought against Assange in the aftermath of the leak. But one senior civil servant press officer suggested that a 'smear' need not be consistent with an orchestrated campaign:

> If you look at how much Assange has been targeted and you look at whether or not that's purely on the facts of his [alleged sexual conduct] crime or on the basis of the leak of the American cables and you think – were the authorities around the world trying quite as hard before it leaked?

Assange himself pointed to evidence of an orchestrated smear campaign against Wikileaks in a 2008 special report on the organisation prepared by the US Army Counter-intelligence Unit. But closer analysis of the detail in the report shows that its recommendations were limited to 'identification, prosecution, termination of employment and exposure' of whistleblowers as a means to 'damage and potentially destroy' the site's 'centre of gravity'. Ominously for Bradley Manning, the report suggests that such actions would potentially 'deter others from taking similar actions'.[3] But it did not amount to what could reasonably be considered an orchestrated smear campaign.

More substantive evidence of a smear campaign did emerge *after* the cable releases following a retaliatory cyber-attack by the hacking group 'Anonymous'. The target of the attack was computer security firm HBGary and the result was a leaked report detailing the company's planned 'black arts' operations against Wikileaks. These included options to plant fake documents with Wikileaks in order to discredit them when published; launch cyber-attacks against the site's infrastructure; and 'to create concern over the security' of the site. The targets of the secret campaign included some of its high profile journalist supporters whom the report refers to as 'established professionals that have a liberal bent'. With an unmasked sinister undertone the report adds that 'ultimately most of them if pushed will choose professional preservation over cause'.

Other emails leaked by the Anonymous attack suggested that the initiative against Wikileaks was funded by the Bank of America – the subject of rumoured and as yet unreleased Wikileaks documents detailing corruption in the banking sector. They also contain evidence that the firm was hired on the recommendation of the US Justice Department, suggesting one way in which the state and private sector may covertly co-operate in attempting to destroy the reputations of offending journalists as well as leakers.

HBGary's chief executive, Aaron Barr, was forced to resign as a result of the leak but it nevertheless raised serious concern over other similar operations that remain undisclosed. For Vaughan Smith, the incident was reflective of a relatively new phenomenon of 'dark marketing' facilitated by digital media:

> You have companies that are set up to slander and smear online mainly, having millions of dollars a week to do so like HBGary Federal where they have actually had the money to smear people and had an impact on the story and that money has been given to them on the basis that they would use it to promote mistruths, propaganda. And it's been quite an interesting thing to see. For example there's been a lot of astroturfing – I'd given interviews mainly in December and the first comments on the online versions were clearly not by real people.

UNACCOUNTABLE POWER

It is worth emphasising, however, that whilst the evidence sheds light on an *intention* to smear, there is no evidence that it was carried out in practice. By its very nature, smears are covert and rarely if ever traceable to an identifiable source. What we do know is that the official source response to the cable releases – overtly at least – was concerned not with smearing Julian Assange but with attacking the legitimacy of his actions on the basis of purported threats to national security and 'lives on the ground'. In the BAe case, we saw that this was the most effective response by official sources in silencing their journalist critics. One broadcaster highlighted the particular aspect of national security discourse which imposes a pressure that is perennially difficult for journalists to resist. This concerns the transatlantic relationship and the threat to national security that could result from a chilling in military and security co-operation with the US. According to Angus Fraser:

> The way I think that most pressure comes is actually in anything that threatens the US–UK relationship. Certainly in intelligence aspects as well because that elicits a very strong response from government who may say things like 'you're putting that

relationship at risk' and then it's sort of hinted that this is national security and you could be damaging relationships that are relied on to protect people in the country from attack.

As we have seen, some of the most controversial cable stories involving the UK were centred on transatlantic military and security co-operation. But there were other aspects of unaccountable power which the leaks gave rise to. A prominent theme in the UK-related cable stories concerned the indiscretion and misdemeanours of royal figures. This was particularly focused on Prince Andrew, whose role as the UK's unofficial trade envoy places him in a position that bridges the establishment power centres of government, royalty and big business. The prince's candid comments regarding the 'lunacy' of the SFO inquiry into BAe were reported in one cable. But it was just one amongst a host of other scandalous allegations and rumours that emerged from the leak. En masse, they served to undermine support for his representation of British business interests abroad. But according to one respondent working within the Department of Trade and Industry, the episode precipitated the kind of pressure reminiscent of a royal prerogative:

> The Palace were on our backs – we had to just behave and not give any sense that we're working behind the scenes to push him out or anything like that. But the line to the general public just seems preposterous – that we can just doggedly stand by this man who hangs out with convicted paedophiles and God knows what [...] It's just bonkers but we just don't have a choice because of the Palace.

This unguarded acknowledgement was offered with a tone of exasperated derision that, during the interview, seemed to dilute the significance of its meaning or implication. On reflection however, it stands as a stark reminder of how confidentiality and secrecy can protect and maintain unaccountable power and how unauthorised disclosure can expose the fragility of constitutional checks and balances. Equally however, it serves as a profound reminder that even with the full force of 'vigilante' oversight made possible by digital media, very old conventions of power can still remain largely in the shadows.

Nevertheless, at the very least Wikileaks has demonstrated that unauthorised disclosure is a necessary accountability mechanism in advanced capitalist societies, for five ostensible reasons. First, it is inevitable that powerful institutions will seek to withhold information from publics often illegitimately – that is to say, when the public interest benefits of disclosure outweigh any costs – and sometimes to protect reputations or conceal illegal or criminal activity. Some whistleblowing accounts emanating from Wikileaks and other sources indicate that formal institutions of oversight designed to ensure the legitimacy of state-corporate secrecy are insufficient to the task. According to Steve Aftergood, unauthorised disclosure acts as a 'crucial safety valve when information is wrongly withheld'.

Second, Wikileaks and unauthorised disclosure generally acts as an important counterweight to increasingly sophisticated media management techniques by official sources. As Angus Fraser surmised:

All the media training and bland answers that politicians provide these days means it's harder for the public to really know what's going on when it comes to negotiations and when it comes to relationships between states. So I think Wikileaks has kicked a lot of people up the backside and it has also been a wake-up call for politicians. The gulf between what they say in public and what they say in private was exposed.

Third, Wikileaks to some extent redresses the *expansion* of official secrecy regimes in advanced capitalist societies, accelerated since the atrocities of 11 September 2001 in New York, and 7 July 2005 in London (Keeble 2010). As we saw in the previous chapter, formal political oversight and accountability of the security state remains wholly inadequate. This places the burden of oversight on journalists who themselves face inordinate obstacles, a point emphasised by Gary MacFadyen: 'How do you control something when you don't know what it does, when it won't tell you what it does, when you don't even know what its budget is, when you don't know who its members are and they can only speak to you from behind a screen?'

Fourth, Wikileaks to some extent redresses the increasing resource and time pressures acting on journalists who seek disclosure through authorised means. As a government press officer explained:

Often a journalist will come to us and say 'I want this information' and we'll say 'you can't have it', and they say 'fine, well I'll [make a Freedom of Information application]' and we'll go, 'all right, up to you, but, great, well we've now got at least 20 days to get back to you whereas if we don't we're supposed to try and get back to you for the next day'. And you know that nine times out of ten they'll drop it because they can't be assed to wait 20 days, because it's not the cycle that they work in. The cycle they work in is basically a news list goes up to the news editor at eleven o'clock to discuss at a conference and whatever's on that news list has to be delivered that day. If it can't be delivered that day forget about it.

Finally, Wikileaks and unauthorised disclosure play an integral role in fostering a culture of openness, in tandem with the mutually enhancing forces of proactive and enforced disclosure (such as that precipitated by applications under the Freedom of Information Act). Specifically, the ever-present threat of leaks can prompt institutions to disclose information voluntarily that they might not do otherwise. The link between these different types of disclosure was alluded to by another senior government press officer: 'Government is so leaky and the media is so ferocious and 24-hour that actually the presumption often is "shit this is going to come out, we better get it out before it's leaked because then we've got a chance of controlling it".'

Clearly, unauthorised disclosure alone cannot provide a level of accountability that ensures powerful institutions and individuals will be held responsible for exposed wrongdoing. But although Wikileaks may not carry the threat of enforcement or sanction, it does carry the threat of reputational damage. The fruits of this kind of surveillance in a 'public relations democracy' (Davis 2002) were highlighted by Martyn Day, head of the human rights law firm Leigh Day and Co:

> I think it is a very good thing that people have to be very cautious, big companies have to be cautious about how they treat their staff, how they treat people on the ground in the developing world where they're operating. I think that the fear for them that their name may become mud within wider society and the speed with which that can operate and bring you down is an entirely good thing.

Regardless of effects, there is an argument which holds that exposure is a public good in and of itself. Indeed, according to Vaughan Smith, 'it's hard to work out what can improve anything except for more of the truth'.

But whilst recognising the value of unauthorised disclosure for institutional accountability, it is equally important to recognise its limitations. This research identified at least five key obstacles that make disclosure in all its forms a necessary but insufficient tool of oversight. First, the threat of reputational damage might have effects that run counter the public good as expressed above. Several respondents referred to the likelihood of Wikileaks having already instituted *greater* levels of secrecy within state-corporate institutions. For one government press officer, the state's capacity to adapt was more than just speculation:

> If you look at something like the [Freedom of Information Act], the Civil Service knows the exemptions and knows how to work the exemptions and knows that when it's writing advice to ministers if you do it in a certain way it will be exempt. So it gets written in a certain way so it's exempt or potentially exempt in the future. And I think it will be the same with Wikileaks [...] I mean certainly there's a general rule that we have in pretty much every press office I've worked in which is if you don't want it to be somewhere, do it on the phone. If you look at things like Jo Moore [who infamously declared the 9/11 atrocities in New York 'a good day to bury bad news'], it wasn't necessarily what she said, it was the fact that she got found out and she wrote it down and that's only going to get more and more so now with something like Wikileaks. People are going to be more and more concerned about that.

Second, there is a need for analysis of disclosed information that grows in tandem with the capacity for digital data storage and publication. We have seen that the Wikileaks tranches of documents necessitated the pooled resources of some of the largest journalist organisations in the world in order to ensure that the leaked information was authenticated, appropriately redacted and transformed into coherent accounts, with still questionable results. But the need for analysis is just as pertinent in respect of authorised and enforced disclosures, often prohibitively large in scale, codified in highly technical language and requiring specialised navigation skills:

> The whole transparency agenda is fine in the sense that, yes, it is transparent – it is transparent in the sense that the information is there but in another sense it's completely opaque because who

knows how to look at the sort of spreadsheets that get put out about government spending and work them out [...] If it ever comes to it, you can say well the information's there, it's always been there, we publish this stuff regularly.

The third limitation is a need for narrative. This is the next layer up from making sense of the data and consists in the capacity of journalists to communicate their meaning. According to Kevin Marsh: 'the key thing about investigative journalism as opposed to just transparency is that there's a narrative there. Transparency is fantastic but there tends not to be a narrative in transparency alone.'

Fourth, there is, as we have seen, an inherent need for publicity in order for the public interest value of disclosed information to be actually accrued. This demands a distinction, along the lines drawn recently by judges, between what is in the public domain and what can be considered to be in the 'public consciousness'.

Finally, there is a risk not only that key data of potential public interest value will be buried amidst information abundance, but also that abundance can provide a smoke screen for enduring secrecy. A government press officer cautiously hinted at how proactive disclosure can be used in such a way:

If you think that it's inevitable it will get out in the public domain then you think 'right we get out there first and we present the information in the best way' and that will inevitably mean usually that there is some bit of it that you just can't – I mean it's just too bad.

CONTAINMENT

It is clear that Wikileaks can neither on its own, nor in partnership with mainstream media organisations, fulfil the promise of 'an intelligence agency for the people' (Fenster 2011). Whether it will advance or hinder the cause of open information remains to be seen. The analysis here has shown that television news – in providing an essential filter for the eruption of leaks in late 2010 – succeeded to the extent that it drew attention to the leaks during the first week of coverage, rather than focusing on the 'star power' of Julian Assange.

But it was ultimately contained in favour of official sources by the failure of broadcasters to adequately challenge their responses and in particular, their lack of engagement with allegations stemming from the leaks. This opened the door to a vociferous and largely unquestioned attack on the legitimacy of Wikileaks and unauthorised disclosure itself. It precipitated at least in one sense a spectacle of accountability, to the extent that it fed into a broader narrative of change amongst Wikileaks supporters. The very aggression of official source responses was seen on one level as evidence of a game-change in the balance of informational power between citizens and elites. But the hollowness of official source concerns began to surface in early 2011. According to one Reuters source, the US administration had publicly exaggerated the Wikileaks threat in order to buttress its legal efforts against the group.[4]

Nevertheless, this spectacle did not go unchecked. It was instead tempered by a narrative of hype surrounding the leaks, according to which broadcasters in particular poured scorn on the significance and public interest weight of the information disclosed. But this narrative was equally distracting in its neglect of both the press and broadcasters' own role in prioritising the *wrong* stories in public interest terms, at least as defined by journalists themselves. Instead, broadcasters both in interviews for this book and in live two-ways with their news anchors, firmly placed the responsibility for 'hype' with Wikileaks and in particular, Julian Assange. Yet in spite of the latter's long-cultivated media presence, it was (according to the agreed terms) exclusively the domain of mainstream media partners to select, prioritise and publicise the stories.

Distortions in the coverage were partly a function of political economic and organisational factors and in particular, the peculiar dynamics of exclusivity which led to an initial surge of stories. Television's relative dependence on a press-led agenda inhibited its natural role as an arbiter of salience amidst the deluge of controversies. There was also a tendency to select 'easier' stories from the point of view of both 'cultural congruence' (Entman 2004) and complexity. And finally, a degree of inevitable randomness must be taken into account which may have played a part in coverage distortions.

Behind all these forces, there were signs that pointed to some degree of ideological filtering at the point of selection and prioritisation of stories. What is certain is that even in the first week of releases, at least two key public interest stories emanating from Cablegate were left squarely in the shadows of the television spotlight.

8
Conclusion

This book started from an assumption that news stories centring on suppression of accountability forces by powerful interests – obstructions, whitewashes, cover-ups – tend to attract acute attention from public service media. They offer a dramatic news narrative that conforms to the values of serious news and we might reasonably consider that uncovering, investigating and exposing such transgressions is at the heart of journalism's social purpose. In other words, where formal mechanisms of accountability fail, journalists step into the front line of public defence.

Not all journalists identify with this ideal type of 'activist' reporting. But it captures the liberal narrative which dominates the discourse of serious news. This narrative places special emphasis on journalist autonomy as a foundation of professional credibility and a pillar of democracy (Curran 1991). It gives rise to three distinct stages in the performance of journalism's watchdog role. Driven by an instinctive drive to uncover abuses of power, journalists select and pursue cases free from any corrupting influence of powerful interests. In doing so, they source and collate all information relevant to the case and condense it into an accessible and comprehensible narrative. The second stage is then a bi-product of the first: by selecting, constructing and publishing a particular story, journalists both expose previously hidden information and signify its accountability significance.

The final stage of the watchdog role is then to mobilise for redress. Through editorials accompanying reports, and through persistent attention to the on-going developments of a particular story, journalists build pressure on authorities for an accountability resolution. Advocates of popular democracy have tended to conceive of this pressure as the product of public opinion which has been mobilised behind a particular cause or issue. Pluralist political scientists, on the other hand, place emphasis on journalism's capacity to mobilise interest group stakeholders who act on behalf of the general public. More recently, a third conception has been advanced which suggests that pressure for reform is often the result of pre-publication transactions between journalists and policymakers (Protess, Lomax Cook et al. 1991).

But however they emerge, watchdog journalism is intimately associated with accountability *outcomes*. These outcomes are a legitimising force both for journalists and the centres of power that they scrutinise. Accountability outcomes promote the idea that no one is above the law, and that concentrated power is ultimately and always checked by the free flow of contesting voices, views and ideas. It is not surprising, therefore, that news organisations are drawn to the spectacle of accountability on the various stages in which it is set – public inquiries, select committee hearings, judicial reviews etc.

But the notion of accountability spectacle in this sense does not by itself tell us anything about whether or not journalists live up to this role. The research underpinning this book was designed to investigate this core question – how far do the news media deliver on the accountability promise of watchdog journalism? In each of the cases examined, this promise went unfulfilled in various ways and for various reasons. Overall, the coverage painted a picture of transparency or restorative justice that was ultimately in tune with elite sources, to the exclusion or marginalisation of alternative frames. In each case the coverage intensity faded against a backdrop of resolution that suggested justice had either been done, or had been proved unnecessary, even though events and available evidence pointed to the contrary. This is not to suggest that the news was wrong in implying resolution, but rather that it persistently marginalised frames that implied otherwise. In this sense, journalism failed because it did not adequately consider failure of accountability at large.

The questions we are left with, and ones which take us back to the discussion in the opening chapter, concern the extent to which this failure is in some sense functional. In other words, do accountability spectacles serve an ideological purpose? To tackle this, we need to first show that failure is more or less systematic; that it is not the result of purely random factors. Second, we need to consider how far the cases are representative of broader discourses (it stands to reason that a meaningful ideological function would not be restricted to individual and exceptional cases). Finally, we are compelled to ask what, if any, are the common ideological properties of the failures observed; what kind of essential worldview, or what aspects of an essential worldview are being promoted?

Before reflecting on this, let us first summarise the patterns and causes of failure across all three case studies.

NARRATIVE BOUNDARIES 1: ABSTRACTION

Coverage of controversy in the news is often criticised for failing to provide adequate context to stories, linking them with broader themes that promote rather than require understanding of a given issue (e.g. Lewis et al. 2005). Whilst this problem was certainly observed in particular instances during this research, a much more significant limitation appeared to be the opposite. There was a notable and persistent tendency in the coverage towards abstraction – focusing on the historical context – which submerged concrete evidence of corruption occurring contemporaneously to the coverage. This time dimensional effect was perhaps most obvious in the first case study, involving alleged corruption in state-sanctioned arms sales to Saudi Arabia. The big picture of the story was a decades-long controversy and the murky world of the international arms trade at large. But attention to historical and international contexts underplayed the assertions of campaigners that corruption was *on-going* and that there was an urgent need to call individuals, the government and BAe to account. The problem, according to alternative frames, was not that corruption had been rife and long-standing, but that it was persisting and not a lot was being done about it.

In the second case study, we saw how the Hutton Report became intimately linked with the broader and well-established controversy surrounding the failure to find weapons of mass destruction (WMD) in Iraq. This precipitated an unprecedented conflict between the government and the BBC which reached its zenith in the aftermath of David Kelly's death. Whilst this story undeniably carried strong public-interest weight, journalistic attention was diverted from the questions left unanswered regarding Kelly's death itself. This is not to say that journalists were wrong to give due attention to the whitewash frame. But in doing so, they did not adequately scrutinise official definitions relating to the death and the views of alternative sources went unacknowledged.

As a result of this neglect, the focus of coverage was drawn inexorably to events in the past dating back to the decision to go to war with Iraq. The overriding criticism of Hutton featured in the coverage was not that the scope of his report submerged the investigation into Kelly's death, but rather that it was not wide enough, failing to adequately resolve the broader WMD controversy.

In the third case, abstraction shifted the narrative focus not to historical contexts, but to the unprecedented scale of the leaks. This opened the door to questions of legitimacy and the debate over whether transparency had gone too far. The editorial slant at points lent towards frames that opposed official source assertions that the leaks were dangerous. But this was only on the basis that they were insignificant; a view encapsulated by the phrase 'embarrassing, but not damaging'. In this way, the coverage appeared to sidestep the question of legitimacy in favour of a frame that devalued the leaks in public interest terms. Rarely were they seriously considered as cause-worthy – that is, exposing corruption that warranted some kind of redress and reform.

NARRATIVE BOUNDARIES 2: LIMITS WITHIN THE SCHEDULE

On deeper analysis it became clear that limits to contestability were circumscribed to some extent within the news schedule. In the BAe case, we saw that the news analysis programmes on Channel 4 and BBC Two were consistently more likely to cover the controversy, and with a greater degree of prominence compared to the main bulletins. And amongst the bulletins, coverage was relatively concentrated in the late evening editions. More crucially perhaps, coverage in the news analysis programmes was more favourable to alternative sources and frames. A similar pattern was observed in the Wikileaks case study where the favourable balance afforded to official sources across the sample was actually inverted in the news analysis programmes.

Thus, patterns emerged according to which late evening and news analysis programmes were more likely to adopt frames commensurate with alternative sources than the main bulletins.

But this trend was not observed in the second case study and if anything, was reversed. Coverage of the controversy surrounding the death of David Kelly was covered in a total of 16 editions which included only one edition of BBC Two's *Newsnight* and one edition of *Channel 4 News*. This suggests that where boundaries are drawn within the schedule depends to some extent on the nature of the controversy at hand. The notion of 'conspiracy theory' invoked associations with tabloid news and internet gossip, prompting 'serious' journalists to steer clear of the story and dismiss its significance. In any case, boundaries within the schedule were ultimately transcended in all three cases by a more compelling narrative force – one which demanded and engineered an 'end' to the story.

NARRATIVE BOUNDARIES 3: CLOSURE

The emphasis on scale that characterised much of the Wikileaks coverage was also evident at key points within the BAe case, most notably in the coverage surrounding the joint penalty and plea bargain settlements announced in February 2010. Virtually all headlines were constructed around the total figure which this amounted to, providing a dramatic backdrop to frames that promoted a sense of accountability triumph. BAe sources were afforded a virtually unchallenged platform to emphasise the narratives of reform and redress – 'we are a changed company' – cementing historical boundaries constructed around the controversy. All of this contributed to a dominant discourse of resolution centring on restorative justice, but it was one which eclipsed compelling frames of accountability failure.

To be clear, alternative sources were to some extent complicit in this framing as their initial responses sought to highlight BAe's culpability rather than the limits of accountability. But adversarial journalism in the terms considered here is not dependent on sources – official or alternative – in the frame building procedure. As we saw in early responses to the Hutton Report, even under impartiality constraints broadcast journalists are capable of playing a leading role in both constructing and advancing critical positions. But this demonstration of journalist autonomy did not last long. On the third day after the report was published, the BBC issued a public apology to the government and officials in turn began to talk of 'drawing a line' on the conflict. This was followed by an abrupt end to the coverage intensity.

Nevertheless, the controversy surrounding the report was to re-emerge intermittently for years to come. This time the issue was not the conflict between the government and BBC, but the question marks that continued to surround David Kelly's death. Here we saw much more explicit attempts by journalists to bring closure to the story. In particular, the release of the post-mortem document in 2010 was portrayed as 'lifting the lid' on official secrecy surrounding the case. The government had seemingly relented to the demands of campaigners in publishing the document, ensuring that transparency prevailed and the matter could be laid to rest, even if it would not stop the 'conspiracy theories'. Alternative views – pointing to the on-going *suppression* of key documents surrounding the case – were not excluded from reports. But introductory and concluding remarks by broadcasters betrayed an editorial slant that favoured an 'end of secrecy' polemic. The overriding sense that transparency had revealed nothing intrinsically newsworthy or controversial was observed even more emphatically in the final case study. Although much of the broader coverage relating to Wikileaks centred on the implicit dangers of excessive transparency, the end of coverage intensity was precipitated by a dominant frame which dismissed the significance of the leaks. As in the previous case, closure was manifest in a dilution of the transparency spectacle: official sources, after all, did not appear to have much to hide in what was exposed. In this way, the spectacle of transparency exhibited distinct but also comparable characteristics to that observed in the first case study. Where the BAe penalty and plea bargain settlement had seemingly heralded a restoration of justice, the closure framing in the other cases appeared to absolve the *need* for justice. Underlying all three cases was a sense of accountability resolution, detracting from key aspects of the controversy which remained unresolved.

NARRATIVE BOUNDARIES 4: SOURCE TREATMENT

In keeping with much of the literature on journalist-source relations, we have seen that treatment of both alternative and elite sources in news reports was dynamically differentiated over time and across the news schedule. In the BAe case, journalists widely scrutinised and critiqued the government's justifications for terminating the official investigation. This was not dissimilar in tone or vernacular to the outrage expressed in early responses to the Hutton Report. Even in the Wikileaks case there were at least isolated moments of outrage, such as when the US ambassador to London was pulled up on allegations of diplomatic espionage.

This kind of challenge contrasted sharply with the deference afforded to BAe following the plea bargain settlement. In particular, the claim by the company's chairman that 'we are a changed company' appeared to be accepted without question. Sources that endorsed the official verdict of David Kelly's death were given an equally unchallenged platform throughout the duration of the controversy; as were elites who attacked the legitimacy of Wikileaks during the first week of Cablegate.

With regard to alternative sources, the picture was equally complex. In the BAe case, we saw how the legal battle between campaigners and the government leant itself to a David and Goliath narrative. But when the case went against campaigners, the coverage fell silent. In the second case study, we saw how campaigners, at times repeatedly dismissed as conspiracy theorists, were eventually elevated to the status of protagonists in a debate among experts. And in the third case, prominent Wikileaks supporters were virtually excluded altogether from the pseudo-debate over the leaks' legitimacy.

Overall, alternative sources were at turns ignored, devalued, delegitimised and villainised. But they were also on occasion championed or admitted as equal participants in the debate. This suggests that whilst the odds are stacked against alternative sources, a degree of openness and contestability pertains in the television newscape. But amidst this complexity one relatively constant theme emerged from the analysis. Rarely were alternative sources acknowledged as legitimate, cause-worthy and *unsuccessful* in their attempts to bring about meaningful accountability, even when available evidence and outcomes strongly supported such a view. In other words, alternative sources were only admitted into the contest when it appeared to be in some way sanctioned by official process. The forces that sustained coverage in the BAe case were the official pronouncements and procedures that picked up where the SFO left off – via the High Court, the OECD and the US Department of Justice. When these actions drew to a close or ran out of steam, the media appeared to follow suit. In the controversy over David Kelly's death, the coverage only surfaced along with the prospect of an inquest. For more than six years the noise made by campaigners fell largely on deaf ears in television news, even when a front bench MP released a book about the controversy. But the incoming government in 2010 promised a new era of transparency and the engagement of a leading human rights law firm by campaigners put an inquest on the horizon of possibilities. When that inquest was formally denied in June 2011, the coverage appeared to go silent once again.

In the Wikileaks case, we can only speculate as to whether the absence of any official investigations arising from the leaks confined alternative sources to relative obscurity. It is perhaps interesting to note that the on-going coverage of Wikileaks after Cablegate *did* focus on an official investigation. But it stemmed from the charges of sexual misconduct made against Julian Assange, rather than anything to do with the leaks.

CAUSES OF FAILURE 1: INDEXING

The momentum of official investigations was no doubt also carried to some extent by the intensity of the media spotlight, a point that was substantiated in interviews with lawyers and government press officers. In any case it seems clear that both official investigations and the media spotlight were sustained, and in some cases triggered by authoritative endorsement of alternative frames; be it from experts, lawyers, or politicians. The whitewash frame adopted in response to the Hutton Report was one notable exception to this trend, and an exception to the general finding in respect of source treatment highlighted above. Here was an official resolution to a long-running controversy that was broadly rejected by journalists. What's more, they appeared to take the lead ahead of their sources in questioning and challenging the report's conclusions. It was the politicians in the chamber who responded to whispers in the press gallery, rather than the other way round. This leaves the question of why journalists were so keen to adopt contesting frames in this case compared to others.

Three distinctions are worth highlighting here. First, in its castigation of the BBC, the Hutton Report was widely perceived as an attack on journalism – and broadcast journalism in particular – provoking a characteristic self-defensive response from the media. Second, and perhaps more crucially, the controversy was exceptional among the cases here inasmuch as it hinged to some extent on party political conflict. Though the Conservative opposition focused its attack on the government rather than Hutton, the kind of political consensus apparent in the BAe and Wikileaks cases, as well as the controversy surrounding Kelly's death, was notably absent. Indeed, the whitewash frame was consistent with a broader and mainstream political line of argument adopted by both major opposition parties. It traced its roots to the controversy surrounding the government's decision to go to war in 2003 which created unprecedented fissures across the British establishment. By the time the Hutton Report was released, the government's public credibility was all but in tatters. The implications of 'whitewash' can therefore be understood partly in political terms not dissimilar from dominant media frames such as 'Labour spin' or 'Tory sleaze'. In other words, the problem was not systemic corruption so much as a government that had overstepped the mark and outstayed its welcome.

The view that media contestability hinges on elite dissensus has found a strong voice in the literature dating back to studies looking at coverage of the Vietnam War (Hallin 1986). As discussed in the opening chapter, this has been articulated more recently in terms of indexing theory, according to which frames gain prominence in the media only when they receive endorsement from elites. Importantly, this endorsement need not stem from political actors alone (Entman 2004). We saw that coverage in the BAe case was sustained in the medium term not by the force of political dissent, but rather the outrage of lawyers who were willing to offer pro bono services to campaigners and thereby provide a suitable focus for the media spotlight. Similarly, the controversy surrounding the death of David Kelly resurfaced in the news in response to legal action brought by senior medical experts whose opinion was difficult to dismiss entirely and routinely as conspiracy fodder. And television news outlets were induced to prioritise Cablegate at least partly because highly reputable journalists at the *Guardian* had promoted it as 'the biggest story on the planet'.

But whilst some kind of elite endorsement may be a necessary condition for alternative frames to surface in television news, it is not always a sufficient one. As we have seen, the expert seniority of campaigners in the controversy over David Kelly's death did not help their cause until a change in the political climate suggested their demands may be met. Celebrity support for Wikileaks was not enough to redress the dominance of official source definitions over its legitimacy. And we have seen that the closure frame in the BAe case overwhelmingly favoured the Prime Minister, Attorney General, and chairman of BAe, in spite of detraction from senior Liberal Democrat MPs and, off the record, even members of the cabinet.

One essential problem with indexing theory traces its roots back to the earlier literature on power concerning the boundaries of an elite stratum. Radical accounts have tended to conceive of elites in narrower and more confined terms than their pluralist critics. For Mills (1959), the 'power elite' did not operate through the formal structures of politics where partisan conflict is rife. It was more akin to a super layer of decision-making power that operated at the nexus between the military, industry and government and largely in the shadows of the media spotlight. That the chairman of BAe was said to have had 'the key to the garden door of Number 10' is perhaps illustrative of an elite vanguard in this sense.

The fact that controversies involving partisan political conflict are likely to attract more media contestability than those involving consensus is not, by itself, particularly enlightening. We might speculate as to whether the kinds of controversies that engender political conflict are really just the stuff of low or mid-level power tussles as Mills suggested, or the politics that really *matters* as Daniel Bell argued (1993). But in any event, we should not overestimate the role of indexing in setting the boundaries of contestability. The case studies uncovered key points where relative elite cohesion was insufficient to stem the outpouring of journalist outrage, just as elite dissent was at times insufficient to prise open the gates of containment.

CAUSES OF FAILURE 2: POLITICAL ECONOMY

Another set of variables associated with containment in the media may be broadly categorised as political economic. As we saw in our earlier discussion of the propaganda model, these factors span a range that includes the influence of advertisers, media owners and official sources (both in offering journalists a carrot of subsidised news, and wielding a stick of flak). With regard to advertisers, our case studies found no evidence that they wield influence over the news agenda; a finding that is not surprising given our focus on public service television. Those outlets within the sample that do carry advertising – ITV and Channel 4 – operate their news services in accordance with their license mandates and on the basis of cross-subsidies from more profitable genres. Equally, there was no evidence that channel proprietorship had any sort of influential role in news output, directly or otherwise. Again, this is perhaps not surprising in view of the fact that ITV is the only channel within the sample that is not publicly owned.

But not even the BBC is shielded entirely from market pressures and the question of whether these may be exploited by official sources warrants further attention. Journalists in interviews did talk openly about a 'climate of caution' that pervades television newsrooms and in the case of the BBC, this was linked directly to the legacy of the Hutton Report. The incident led to the foundation of the BBC College of Journalism along with an expanded editorial standards department, both of which drew money away from operational journalism (along with a huge investment in online services). The new compliance regime also added a substantial administrative burden to journalists that, combined with broader resource pressures affecting the profession as a whole, resulted in a journalism that is said to be more 'directed' and less 'risky'. A similar sentiment was expressed by ITN journalists in respect of the libel threat which has instituted a round-the-clock legal presence in newsrooms.

But most BBC and ITN respondents insisted that this did not have a chilling effect on output to the extent that it deterred newsrooms from pursuing particular stories or particular angles within stories. Nor did case study evidence suggest that journalists had at any point succumbed to either tacit or explicit threats from editors, executives or official sources. And with regard to financial pressures at large, it is worth re-emphasising that much of the serious news sector – even beyond public service broadcasting – is supported by cross-subsidies. Newsrooms may compete fiercely for audiences and market shares but they are not an economic lifeline. What's more, their flagship status guarantees a degree of access to official sources, regardless of how far they deviate from the official script. We might speculate that the threat of flak in political economic terms can still impose a subconscious weight on journalists in an increasingly precarious professional environment. But the evidence supports journalists' assertions that they do not shy away from stories that put official sources on the back foot. Far from it, the fact that each of the cases examined here *were* covered by television news suggests that the 'Watergate effect' still has some resonance in newsrooms. If we want to understand why the coverage was ultimately contained, we have to look to other indicators that have more to do with journalism as a cultural practice, as well as the broader cultural blind spots which shape and filter journalistic worldviews.

CAUSES OF FAILURE 3: COLLECTIVE LEGITIMATION

In her book examining media coverage of the John F. Kennedy assassination over several decades, Barbie Zelizer argued that sociological studies of journalism had paid too much attention to the field as a profession with linear effects on audiences. This came at the expense of looking at journalism as a cultural and interpretive community engaged in collective self-legitimisation in the construction of news narratives (Zelizer 1992). One common theme that emerged in the analysis of each case study here was an implicit challenge to journalistic authority. This is not to be confused with the perceived challenge to journalistic *autonomy* that prompted a self-defensive response to the Hutton Report. The challenge to journalistic authority was most evident in the third case study where conventional newsrooms were on one level confronting a discourse emerging from the growing culture of hacktivism, of which Julian Assange had long been an exponent. This discourse had positioned itself in confrontation with conventional journalism, employing rhetorical terms like 'the mainstream media' with characteristic disdain. The 'new model of journalism' – touted by journalists at the *Guardian* among others – was presented in a way that reasserted and reaffirmed the value, role, legitimacy and necessity of conventional journalism in the digital age. When that partnership began to falter and descend into acrimony, it is perhaps not surprising that the coverage increasingly lent towards frames that delegitimised Wikileaks as an organisation (irrespective of the personal scandals embroiling its figurehead).

In the second case study, we saw how the campaign for an inquest into David Kelly's death was based principally on the failures of the initial investigation and the subsequent measures that had been taken to suppress information. But it is not hard to see how this carried an implicit attack on the credibility of journalism that had all but entirely accepted the official explanation of death from the outset. In case study interviews, it became clear that most journalists were simply unaware of the growing expert testimony and evidence that suggested the official verdict was unsafe. In other words, it had not entered the radar of shared knowledge amongst journalists, even those who had covered the Hutton Report in depth. This compels us to ask whether collective self-legitimisation served as an *a priori* filter – restricting the perspectival horizon of journalists themselves.

But a more fundamental cultural blind spot led journalists to instinctively and persistently draw conspiracy theory associations with the inquest campaign. Whilst the notion of cover-up certainly invoked the spectre that David Kelly *may* have been murdered with the complicity of the state, or elements within it, the principle concern of the inquest campaign was failures in the official investigation. Nevertheless, the implication of possibility was sufficient to preserve journalists' faith in the official verdict on the basis that the alternative seemed simply too far-fetched to be credible.

Interestingly, the lack of journalistic attention to the controversy was itself invoked in interviews with journalists who dismissed the news value of the Kelly controversy. In referring to the paucity of coverage in various reputable news outlets, respondents legitimised their own inattention to the case. It was a view reaffirmed by the fact that the only outlet pursuing the controversy in any depth was the *Daily Mail*, a newspaper widely perceived within serious news circles as harbouring a penchant for tabloid hysteria and appealing to a right-wing and nationalistic audience.

The reference to what other outlets were doing in respect of the controversy underlines Zelizer's thesis regarding the collective legitimisation of journalism's cultural authority. But what about the BAe case study in this respect? In contrast to the cases discussed above, here we saw journalists align themselves *with* campaigners throughout the duration of the controversy. But in doing so, they overplayed their hand, preparing the narrative for a climactic resolution that was to deliver substantive accountability. When this failed to emerge in respect of the legal case waged by campaigners against the government, the coverage fell silent. And when the various official investigations into BAe reached a conjoined conclusion, the coverage was both muted and exaggerated in its portrayal of redress and reform. In this way, the closure frame vindicated the campaigning stance adopted by journalists and diverted attention from errors in their own predictions over likely outcomes.

CAUSES OF FAILURE 4: ORGANISATIONAL CONSTRAINTS

This fourth set of influences spanned the various limitations imposed by the day-to-day rigours of professional journalism. They include the demands of the news cycle, exclusivity, television confines, and differential newsroom cultures.

The News Cycle

The pressures of the news cycle created an almost desperate need on the part of editors for closure in respect of the Al Yamamah scandal. One inescapable reality of the newscape is that all controversies have limited shelf lives – albeit to varying degrees – including those which involve crimes of the powerful. Coverage cannot be sustained indefinitely, regardless of whether a 'satisfactory' accountability outcome is attained. Eventually, a perceived dearth of new 'facts' or events in relation to the story, combined with a sensitivity towards audience tolerance and expectations, means that cases like the ones examined here will inevitably cease to qualify as 'news'. There is nothing intrinsically wrong with this premise. If the job of news is first and foremost to 'inform', then it makes no sense to repeat information that has already been relayed to an audience. A problem arises when the inescapable dynamics and boundaries inscribed by the news cycle mesh with the broader cultural forces that shape and contain news narratives.

Thus, the fact that the intensity of news coverage subsided following the culmination of official investigations is by itself relatively unproblematic in the context of this study. What matters is that it was not enough simply for the coverage to fade away – it had to be circumscribed in such a way that *justified* closure and this was manifest in the exaggerated portrayals of transparency, redress and reform. In the controversy over David Kelly's death, closure was justified by the release of the post-mortem and later, a detailed exposition of arguments by the Attorney General against the reopening of an inquest. Rather than critically evaluating these arguments, the coverage overwhelmingly endorsed them to the neglect of alternative frames. And in the Wikileaks case, the fading of the media spotlight was implicitly justified by editorials which claimed that there was not much, after all, of public interest value in the leaks. Such aspersions were made without reference to those leaks exposing corruption in the British state.

The extent to which the news cycle contained the coverage was also related to the strength of spectacle in each case. It is notable in this respect that in those controversies which achieved headline prominence over successive days – in the aftermath of the Hutton Report and the Wikileaks cable releases – the duration of coverage proved particularly short-lived. In contrast, the BAe case and the controversy surrounding David Kelly's death never attained such prominence but laboured at the margins of the schedule for substantially longer periods. Story fatigue therefore appears to be intimately associated with the intensity of the media spotlight cast on the story during its embryonic stages.

Exclusivity

The condensation of stories that emerged following the Wikileaks cable releases was a product of the way in which the overall story was managed by the mainstream media partnership. In particular, it was a function of the *Guardian*'s attempt to exploit exclusivity as far as possible. This in turn was partly related to the immediate economic rewards associated with exclusivity. But it was also about broader competitive advantages in the arenas of branding, prestige and credibility – all of which are acutely relevant to serious news organisations of all types.

It was inevitable that increasing numbers of competitors would gain access to the treasure trove of leaks as time wore on. In order for the *Guardian* to maximise the value of its limited exclusivity, stories therefore had to be front-loaded rather than drip-fed. This resulted in a degree of overload both in terms of the sheer quantity of information that was coming out, as well as its saturation of the headlines. In this way, the force of exclusivity both triggered and contained the coverage. Without this force, it is unlikely that any of the leaks would have seen the light of television. But its effect was that the gradual drip feed of stories initially envisaged by Wikileaks and the story's chief architects at the *Guardian* was to prove impossible.

Television Confines

As a result of this overload, imbalances and anomalies in the coverage were perhaps inevitable, as was the fact that some stories of public interest import would be overlooked. But when we examined coverage outside the week of Cablegate, it became clear that without the force of the avalanche, individual leaks struggled to break through the barriers of television news. Even the infamous 'collateral murder video', which Wikileaks released as a prelude to its tranche of secret military communications from the Iraq War, failed to match the coverage intensity of individual leaks during the week of Cablegate. This was in spite of the dramatic, public interest and television-friendly nature of the video which was highlighted by journalists during interviews for this book. A cursory look at cables released after the first week of coverage suggested that these barriers were quickly resurrected. For instance, a cable released in the third week contained evidence that British forces had helped train a Bangladeshi special operations unit. This unit had been repeatedly labelled by one human rights group as a 'death squad' responsible for the murder of hundreds of political activists (Human Rights Watch 2011). Subsequent coverage in the *Guardian* revealed that activities of the unit had resumed after a pause for several months following release of the cable (Cobain 2011).

This suggests that exposure accountability depended on the publicity power of news organisations, and terrestrial television in particular. Whilst Wikileaks provided the source material for stories, it was ultimately a newspaper that determined which leaks were newsworthy, and television that determined which of those leaks really mattered. The overwhelming publicity power of television, combined with the relatively narrow range of output that can be covered in any given edition, made it a natural arbiter of salience in this sense.

Newsroom Cultures

As we saw earlier in the discussion, the coverage was contained not just in terms of framing and duration, but also by boundaries within the news schedule. This was strongly related to the identification of distinct newsroom cultures. Both news analysis programmes and the late-evening bulletins were generally perceived as more suited to the coverage of in-depth and complex stories. This is partly because their position within the schedule invoked consideration of an audience that was relatively more attentive and news-conscious compared to the earlier bulletins. Related to this was the flagship status that these programmes enjoyed, attracting more senior editors with a view to producing original and exclusive content.

In the case of the news analysis programmes – *Newsnight* and *Channel 4 News* – the additional time allocated in the schedule compared to the bulletins allowed a more in-depth focus and this in turn helped shape their remit to 'go beyond' the bulletins, to examine news behind the headlines and to be more provocative and interpretive in its coverage. The elite status of these newsrooms is underlined by their editorial and newsgathering autonomy and relative shielding from resource pressures affecting broadcast news divisions as a whole.

Not surprisingly, analysis news programmes proved to be more in tune with alternative frames in the BAe and Wikileaks cases, but also relatively unconcerned with the tabloid-stigmatised controversy over David Kelly's death. This kind of differentiation within the schedule meant that certain key frames either never reached the critical mass audience of the bulletins, or the so-called 'opinion-leading' elite audiences of the analysis programmes. The latter's flagship status ensures that elite sources are more likely to both appear – and be *challenged* – on these editions. Nevertheless, the existence of alternative frames in the schedule in all three cases meant that the coverage as a whole exuded diversity whilst being contained in subtle but important ways; a point that makes differential coverage a potentially illuminating aspect of ideological functionalism (Bourdieu 1998).

CAUSES OF FAILURE 5: OFFICIAL SOURCE STRATEGIES

Into this mix we must also factor in the role of official source strategies. Interviews with press officers from both campaigning organisations and the government suggested that strategic errors on the part of official sources could have a significant bearing on the direction of coverage. The way in which the government announced its decision to terminate the official investigation into BAe was cited as one such example. According to respondents, this resulted in considerably more publicity than would have been the case if the announcement was more carefully planned, with greater attention to the timing and circumstances. But we have already seen how the timing and circumstances of the plea bargain announcement produced considerably more favourable coverage, suggesting that strategic successes can be as significant as errors. And in the final case study, we saw how official sources managed to shift the focus of coverage to the legitimacy of the leaks, away from their content, without provoking significant journalistic challenge.

In the time extended analyses of the first two case studies, official source strategies appeared to move in a more or less linear fashion from information suppression and silence, to the promotion of counter-frames and eventually, a closure strategy. Information suppression consisted in the termination of the official investigation into BAe and the classification of documents in relation to Kelly's death. The strategy of silence was observed in the apparent refusal of official sources to appear in the news and in the extended delays that accompanied their responses to journalists and campaigners alike. In the Kelly case, the delay in responses to formal submissions by campaigners made it difficult for them to sustain any kind of momentum in the fleeting and intermittent coverage.

The promotion of counter-frames involved amplification of threats – to the economy or the emotional well-being of the Kelly family – but most effectively to national security, where rhetorical constructs like 'blood on our streets' gained repeated traction in news reports. Finally, successful closure framing revolved around apparently staged resolutions – most notably the fine and plea bargain settlements in the BAe case, and the release of the post-mortem report in the Kelly case.

BROADER DISCOURSES

We can now turn our attention to the bigger question of whether the accountability failures observed in the coverage amount to an ideological force. At the outset of this chapter it was argued that in order to establish this, we need to consider the extent to which the observed containment was systematic, representative and promoted common properties of an essential worldview. The analysis has satisfied the first condition to the extent that containment was clearly not the product of purely random anomalies, as we have seen. With regard to the second condition, it is worth speculating over alternative cases that might have been selected and how findings might have differed accordingly.

One such example is a long-running scandal led by a *Daily Telegraph* exclusive, which culminated in the conviction and imprisonment of two members of parliament for expenses fraud in 2011. On the surface, this case might challenge our findings since it involved corruption at the heart of the British establishment and its exposure triggered progression through an accountability process, resulting in a resolution that was both substantive and widely accepted. Yet at the same time, the stakes were clearly not comparable to the cases examined here. Exposing corruption in the British arms trade threatened to expose a legacy of government sponsored bribery that had spanned several decades and risked the collapse of a deal worth several billions in export revenue. Reopening an inquest into the death of David Kelly threatened to put the spotlight back on an issue that, for whatever reason, is still protected by high levels of official secrecy. And attention to the ethics of transatlantic military cooperation that might have been invoked by the leaking of US diplomatic cables negotiates the invisible boundary between the interests of public disclosure and national security.

Several related controversies have, however, succeeded in calling attention to the latter in ways that eluded Cablegate. In particular, a complex of stories in recent years has shone a light on alleged UK complicity in the secret rendition and torture of terror suspects abroad. This bears similar hallmarks to the BAe and Wikileaks cases to the extent that it revolves around highly sensitive issues concerning international security co-operation. As with those cases, critical coverage of stories relating to secret rendition and torture complicity appeared to be concentrated in the news analysis and late evening parts of the schedule. More crucially, this coverage was followed by a public inquiry which, in the shadows of a fading media spotlight, quickly descended into farce as campaigners and lawyers boycotted proceedings over the withholding of documents by the government. Just when no prospect of an acceptable resolution seemed possible, the inquiry was called off altogether.

An alternative case with a very different outcome is the Bloody Sunday Inquiry and the Saville report which followed it. In response to a decades-long campaign for a second inquiry led by the family of victims killed by UK security forces during the height of ethno-political violence in Ireland, the British government finally relented in 1998. The final report published in 2010 condemned the initial inquiry and offered an accountability resolution that was broadly accepted by core participants. But it came nearly 40 years after the event rendering the force of accountability somewhat muted. More acutely, it suggests that the media had failed to adequately scrutinise the initial inquiry or give a sufficient platform for victims and campaigners that might have hastened the course of justice and provided a more timely and meaningful resolution. It underlines the importance of timing in relation to accountability observed in the case studies here and, in particular, the need for the media to expose inadequacies or obstructions of due process while they are *happening*.

Finally, it is worth reflecting on the on-going scandal sparked by the discovery of widespread illegal activity in newspapers owned by News International. There can be no doubt that exposure and investigation by the *Guardian* among others – which broke through headline news barriers in 2011 – has already had tangible outcomes in curtailing the ambitions of Rupert Murdoch's empire. In particular, a planned and approved take-over of BskyB was withdrawn amidst the height of the scandal. But the coverage has also brought attention to wider and endemic corruption in relations between journalists and the police, as well as politicians, and at the time of writing, it remains to be seen what kind of resolution will emerge in this respect. What seems clear is that, like the backdrop to the Hutton Report, the hacking scandal hit the headlines just as deep fractures within establishment power began to surface – namely between the government, News International and the police. The case certainly provides a well of opportunities for further research related to the core concerns of this book.

IDEOLOGY RECONSIDERED

It remains for us to return to our case studies and consider the common ideological properties of the discourse. In the opening chapter it was argued that 1) an essential function of the media in liberal democracies is to legitimate power by holding it to account and 2) providing an arena in which dominant narratives can be contested is a foundation of media accountability. We might conceive of this as a four-step process in which contestability underpins accountability; accountability underpins legitimation of power; and legitimation of power is foundational to the consensual ties that bind societies together in liberal democracies. The essence of the liberal pluralist model is that such consensus need only ensure general acceptance of legal and accountability procedures – elections, law and order etc. Concentrated power is legitimate so long as it is kept beneath the law and within the bounds of scrutiny.

This book has strongly suggested that the powerful, in this sense, are not a ruling class but rather an elite core of decision-makers – a network that transcends party politics and operates at the nexus between government, industry and military. It operates largely informally and 'off the record' and, in line with the professional values of watchdog journalism, carries special significance and interest for the serious news media. It is this important characteristic which translates into widespread demonstrations of adversarial journalism, and which radical accounts of the media have not managed to capture.

But this does not mean that the media are immune to ideological forces. The above analysis underlined a crucial frame that was systematically undermined in the coverage; one which conferred both legitimacy and significance on alternative sources, whilst at the same time acknowledging their ultimate failure to achieve their accountability goals. This was the one frame which directly challenged conclusions based on restorative justice and its exclusion ultimately promoted the credibility of accountability institutions at large, on false pretences. At the same time, the credibility of journalism was underlined to some extent by the existence of broader counter-hegemonic frames. But these tended to be circumscribed by limits within the news schedule which meant their reach was restricted to particular audiences.

There have been several related strands to this thesis in the media studies literature. The idea that the media function to project social stability in the aftermath of crises and moral panics has found voice in various studies (Tuchman 1978; Hall 1982; Ericson, Baranek et al. 1991) and invokes a similar preservation of faith in the established order. But the notion of restorative order does not quite capture the hegemonic force of restorative *justice*. This is because the latter does more than just discourage deviance or dissent. It creates a false or distorted *impression* of transparency, contest and accountability. The guiding principle underpinning this book is that if the media have any hegemonic or ideological function in liberal democracies, it must be two-fold in the sense of 1) promoting ideas consonant with a particular dominant group and 2) creating the impression that no such ideas are being promoted. This is an essential paradox that has long obstructed critical media inquiry.

There have certainly been plenty of other studies, including liberal pluralist accounts, which have acknowledged instances in which the media align with official sources and present corruption as essentially isolated and containable (Schlesinger and Tumber 1994; Bennett 2009). But these accounts do not acknowledge the systematic and ideological nature of containment. According to the findings here, the systematic element comprises the routine undermining or exclusion of frames that point to accountability failure. The ideological quality of this is the promotion of a worldview which sees power as effectively contained by the institutions set up to monitor and control it – including the media themselves.

Liberal pluralist accounts also place undue emphasis on the causes and effects of containment in dismissing claims of ideological functionalism. They argue that the causes of containment in the media are most often to do with market dynamics, random anomalies or organisational constraints which do not bear the hallmarks of a dominant ideological force (Schudson 1995; Bennett 2009). With regard to effects, it is commonly asserted that the notion of ideological dominance carries an unavoidable implication about its impact on audiences which has not been substantiated by the empirical literature. Much of the source relations sub-strand of this literature has also emphasised the fluid and dynamic nature of media systems in liberal democracies which means that containment is never wholly predictable based on static models of radical functionalism. But these arguments overlook the fact that there are three distinct stages in which ideological forces can intervene in the media, corresponding to Hall's critical media 'moments' of production, output and reception (Hall 1973). As such, we might consider the news to be ideologically *driven*, ideologically *functional* and/or ideologically *effective*.

To be clear, this research did not engage substantively with the question of media effects, partly because of resource limitations, and partly because ideological containment in news output is a concern irrespective of how audiences decode and interpret media messages. At the same time, examining the production side of news through interviews with various news personnel and sources produced no evidence suggesting output is ideologically driven. In other words, at no point in the mix did we observe frame building or narrative construction on the part of journalists or sources according to an ideological agenda, consciously or otherwise. Clearly, source strategies were driven by a degree of self-interest, but this did not translate easily into interests identifiable with a dominant group or class. The degrees and character of elite dissent observed in all three cases is testament to the nuanced variances which preclude an overly-reductionist picture of ideological control. But this is not the same as saying that the output served no ideological *function* and, as we have seen, this notion is fully commensurate with the research findings.

Liberal pluralists are right, on the other hand, to criticise radical functionalists for being overly fixated on political economic forces. What radical accounts have tended to neglect is the complex and dynamic interplay of forces that shape media output. Importantly, the limits on dissent and openness are not always traceable to the pursuit of profits. The news organisations which constituted the focus of this book are engaged more in competition for prestige and credibility than market share, and the resource pressures that have afflicted operational journalism are not the principal cause of ideological containment in news output. As we have seen, the major commercial outlets in the serious news sector are financially cushioned by cross-subsidies and, along with the BBC, continue to make substantive investments in long-form journalism. This research has attempted to show that the forces of containment have more to do with the culture of journalism rather than the economics of journalism. But overall, they are best conceived as a confluence of instrumental and structural factors. Specifically – official source strategies, organisational constraints, and economic pressures interacted with the cultural values of journalism as an interpretive community in various ways and with various degrees of consequence.

IMPLICATIONS AND LIMITATIONS

The conception of ideology as outlined here has implications for the study of civil society and democracy in late capitalist societies. In his empirical account of democracy promotion by successive US administrations, William Robinson concludes that 'the intent behind promoting polyarchy is to relieve domestic pressure on the state from sub-ordinate classes for more fundamental change in emergent global society'. This co-option necessitated a shift 'from political to civil society, as the site of social control' (Robinson 1996:66–67). The notion of accountability spectacle in the news media may be said to function in a similar way to democracy promotion in this context. Our analysis has shown that offering gestures of concessions in response to journalist outrage or scrutiny is a more effective means for elite sources to curtail controversial stories in the news, and close off journalist demands for fundamental or radical change.

But whilst our research has uncovered evidence of framing effects on journalists themselves, the notion of spectacle adopted here makes no implicit inference regarding *audience* effects. It is entirely plausible that audience readings are in conflict with the preferred meanings of dominant frames; that BAe for instance, is not widely perceived by news audiences to have paid a penalty proportionate to its crimes, or that it is now a genuinely reformed company as a result; or that there was no case after all for an inquest into the death of David Kelly; or that the Wikileaks cables revealed nothing untoward about UK–US diplomatic relations. But it stands to reason that if television news had done more to highlight the limits of accountability in each case, there would have been greater public awareness and greater pressure on policymakers for reform and redress. The ideological 'function' of news in this sense is to mute (rather than eradicate) pressure for fundamental change.

At the same time, we have no basis on which to dismiss the possibility that the coverage might have led to genuine reform within BAe, or may yet provide a fruitful backdrop for accountability measures in future cases involving corruption in the arms trade; just as we can't be certain that the inquest into David Kelly's death might not someday be reopened or that the Iraq War Inquiry might, after all, produce an accountability resolution that is substantive and broadly accepted.

What the findings do point to is best described as a significant *tendency* towards ultimate containment in news controversies that threaten to unsettle the discourses that legitimise state-corporate power. Amidst this tendency there are clearly examples of reporters genuinely fulfilling the role of adversarial journalism, championing the disempowered and challenging elites without fear or favour. But this is not the whole picture which is precisely what we have to consider if we want to understand the ideological function of news. The paradox of hegemonic power is that ideology is likely to be most effective when it is *not* total, absolute or consistent. It is likely to depend on the very demonstrations of antagonism that give rise to pluralist notions of contest. The fact that, in the cases examined here, such demonstrations proved to be ephemeral and ultimately inconsequential in accountability terms, suggests that ideological influence is the rule rather than exception.

Notes

CHAPTER 2

1. *Channel 4 News*, 15 March 2007.
2. See Government News, 'Ministers launch anti corruption DVD at the start of Responsible Business month', *Gov-news.org* (November 2006). Available at www.gov-news.org/gov/uk/news/ministers_launch_anti_corruption_dvd_start/64671.html (last accessed 26 June 2012).
3. See article 5, Organisation for Economic Co-operation and Development. Available at www.oecd.org/dataoecd/4/18/38028044.pdf (last accessed 24 June 2012).
4. In 2003 David Leigh and Rob Evans began investigating the case uncovering documents that became central to the various investigations and judicial hearings that followed. Their stories led the wider press campaign and routinely provided both the impetus and content for mainstream television news reports.
5. *Channel 4 News*, 6 February 2010.
6. BBC *Ten O'Clock News*, 10 April 2008.
7. BBC *Newsnight*, 15 February 2008.
8. ITV *Early Evening News*, 7 June 2007.
9. *Channel 4 News*, 7 June 2007.
10. BBC *Six O'Clock News* and *Ten O'Clock News*, 7 June 2007.
11. BBC *Newsnight*, 15 February 2008.
12. Bea Edwards – Government Accountability Project (US). *Channel 4 News*, 20 June 2007.
13. BBC *News at Ten*, 10 April 2008.
14. ITV *Late Evening News*, 9 November 2007.
15. Ibid.
16. *Channel 4 News*, 14 December 2006.
17. BBC *Newsnight*, 14 February 2007.
18. *Channel 4 News*, 15 March 2007.
19. *Channel 4 News*, 20 June 2007.
20. Faisal Islam, *Channel 4 News*, 14 March 2007.
21. *Channel 4 News*, 10 April 2008.
22. BBC *Newsnight*, 9 January 2007.
23. ITV *Late Evening News*, 9 November 2007.
24. BBC *One O'Clock News*, 18 August 2006.
25. Mark Allen (trade union leader).
26. Andrew Brookes (aerospace analyst).
27. Tony Blair, BBC *Ten O'Clock News*, 7 June 2007.
28. Faisal Islam, *Channel 4 News*, 15 March 2007.
29. *Channel 4 News*, 20 June 2007.
30. *Channel 4 News*, 26 June 2007.
31. Peter Marshall, *Newsnight*, 8 February 2007.
32. Pierre Sprey – former Pentagon official, *Channel 4 News*, 20 June 2007.

33. BBC *Newsnight*, 15 February 2008.
34. Baroness Williams MP, *Channel 4 News*, 1 February 2007.
35. Faisal Islam, *Channel 4 News*, 14 March 2007.
36. *Channel 4 News*, 15 March 2007.
37. Ibid.
38. BBC *Newsnight*, 29 May 2008.
39. BBC *Ten O'Clock News*, 14 February 2006.
40. *News at Ten*, 10 April 2008.
41. BBC *Ten O'Clock News*, 10 April 2008.
42. BBC *Newsnight*, 12 March 2007.
43. ITV *Late Evening News*, 14 December 2006.
44. Symon Hill (Campaign Against the Arms Trade), *Channel 4 News*, 10 April 2008.
45. *Channel 4 News* actually recorded an interview with Richard Alderman, head of the SFO, immediately following the Lords ruling but this was never broadcast.
46. *News at Ten*, 14 February 2010.
47. *Channel 4 News*, 1 October 2009.
48. Peter Marshall, *Newsnight*, 29 May 2008.
49. *Channel 4 News*, 5 January 2010.
50. Loren Thompson (CEO and defence specialist, Lexington Trust), *Channel 4 News*, 20 June 2007.
51. BBC *Newsnight*, 15 February 2008.
52. Mark Miller (US investigations lawyer), *Channel 4 News*, 26 June 2007.
53. Dick Olver (BAe Chairman), *Newsnight*, 8 February 2010.
54. BBC *Newsnight*, 8 February 2010.
55. BAe Systems annual report, 2009.
56. *Channel 4 News*, 6 February 2010.
57. ITV *Early Evening News*, 7 June 2007.
58. BBC *Ten O'Clock News*, 26 June 2007.
59. BBC *Newsnight*, 14 February 2007.
60. BBC *Newsnight*, 15 February 2008.

CHAPTER 4

1. BBC *Newsnight*, 28 January 2004.
2. BBC *Six O'Clock News*, 28 January 2004.
3. *The Hutton Inquiry: Transcripts* (2003), http://webarchive.nationalarchives. gov.uk/20090128221550/http://www.the-hutton-inquiry.org.uk/ (last accessed on 14 March 2011).
4. Ibid.
5. N. Hunt, 'Statement of Witness', 25 July 2003. Available at www.guardian. co.uk/politics/interactive/2010/oct/22/david-kelly-iraq1 (last accessed 6 June 2012).
6. D. Grieve, 'Annex to written statement on Dr David Kelly', 9 June 2011. Available at www.attorneygeneral.gov.uk/Publications/Documents/Annex%20 TVP%206.pdf (last accessed 30 June 2012).
7. Thames Valley Police, 'Disclosure log item: Investigation into the death of Dr David Kelly reference RFI2011000301', 13 May 2011. Available at www.thamesvalley. police.uk/aboutus/aboutus-depts/aboutus-depts-infman/aboutus-depts-foi/ aboutus-depts-foi-disclosure-log/aboutus-depts-foi-disclosure-log-investigate/

aboutus-depts-foi-disclosure-log-item.htm?id=175657 (last accessed 6 June 2012).

8. M. Goslett, 'David Kelly post mortem to be kept secret for 70 years as doctors accuse Lord Hutton of concealing vital information', *Daily Mail* (25 January 2010). Available at www.dailymail.co.uk/news/article-1245599/David-Kelly-post-mortem-kept-secret-70-years-doctors-accuse-Lord-Hutton-concealing-vital-information.html#ixzz1x630FQ9t (last accessed 6 June 2012).

9. BBC News Online, 'New Call for Dr David Kelly inquest', www.bbc.co.uk (13 August 2010). Available at www.bbc.co.uk/news/uk-10961016 (last accessed 6 June 2012).

10. BBC News Online, 'Pathologist says David Kelly's death "textbook suicide"', www.bbc.co.uk (22 August 2010). Available at www.bbc.co.uk/news/uk-11050587 (last accessed 6 June 2012).

11. T. Mangold, 'David Kelly murdered? Yes, and I bet you believe in the tooth fairy too', www.independent.co.uk (4 July 2010). Available at www.independent.co.uk/news/uk/politics/david-kelly-murdered-yes-and-i-bet-you-believe-in-the-tooth-fairy-too-2017805.html#comment-60548168 (last accessed 6 June 2012).

12. A. Gilligan, 'David Kelly was not murdered', www.telegraph.co.uk (16 August 2010). Available at www.telegraph.co.uk/news/politics/7947544/David-Kelly-was-not-murdered.html (last accessed 6 June 2012).

13. Thames Valley Police, 'Disclosure log item: Investigation into the death of Dr David Kelly reference RFI2010000841', 8 March 2011. Available at www.thamesvalley.police.uk/aboutus/aboutus-depts/aboutus-depts-infman/aboutus-depts-foi/aboutus-depts-foi-disclosure-log/aboutus-depts-foi-disclosure-log-investigate/aboutus-depts-foi-disclosure-log-item.htm?id=168251 (last accessed 6 June 2012).

14. ITV *Lunchtime News*, 28 January 2004.

15. ITV *Early Evening News*, 28 January 2004.

16. Nick Robinson, ITV *Early Evening News*, 28 January 2004.

17. ITV *Late Evening News*, 28 January 2004.

18. Tom Bradby, ITV *Lunchtime News*, 29 January 2004.

19. Nick Robinson, ITV *Evening News*, 28 January 2004.

20. *Channel 4 News*, 28 January 2004.

21. Ibid.

22. Ibid.

23. ITV *Lunchtime News*, 29 January 2004.

24. ITV *Early Evening News*, 29 January 2004.

25. ITV *Late Evening News*, 4 February 2004.

26. ITV *Early Evening News*, 28 January 2004.

27. ITV *Early Evening News*, 29 January 2004.

28. *Channel 4 News*, 30 January 2004.

29. ITV *Early Evening News*, 4 February 2004.

30. Ibid.

31. *Channel 4 News*, 28 January 2004.

32. *The Hutton Inquiry: Transcripts* (2003).

33. *Channel 4 News*, 30 January 2004.

34. Within the analysis sample, the word 'whitewash' appeared only three times within BBC news transcripts, compared to twelve for ITN.

35. BBC *One O'Clock News*, 29 January 2004.

36. Ibid.

37. BBC *Newsnight*, 28 January 2004.
38. BBC *Six O'Clock News*, 28 January 2004.
39. BBC *One O'Clock News*, 28 January 2004.
40. BBC *Six O'Clock News*, 28 January 2004.
41. Anchor introduction, BBC *One O'Clock News*, 4 February 2004.
42. BBC *One O'Clock News*, 29 January 2004.
43. Ibid.
44. BBC *Six O'Clock News*, 28 January 2004.
45. *The Hutton Inquiry: Transcripts* (2003).
46. ITV *Evening News*, 28 January 2004.
47. Ibid.
48. *Channel 4 News*, 9 March 2003.
49. ITV *Evening News*, 19 August 2010.
50. ITV *News at Ten*, 19 August 2010.
51. BBC *Newsnight*, 13 August 2010.
52. *The Times*, 13 August 2010.
53. Dr Michael Powers QC, *Channel 4 News*, 22 October 2010.
54. *Channel 4 News*, 22 October 2010.
55. ITV *News at Ten*, 22 October 2010.
56. The original inquest was suspended following announcement of the Hutton Inquiry. The first decision not to re-open the inquest was announced in March 2004 in response to initial calls from campaigners.
57. Matt Prodger, BBC *One O'Clock News*, 9 June 2011.

CHAPTER 5

1. J. Dean, 'Dyke played his cards right', *Guardian* (13 February 2002). Available at www.guardian.co.uk/media/2002/feb/13/broadcasting.bbc 2?INTCMP=SRCH (last accessed 26 June 2012).
2. D. Rose, 'I feel shame and regret for having supported the Iraq War ... So why can't Blair?', *DailyMail* (1 February 2010). Available at www.dailymail.co.uk/debate/article-1247424/I-feel-shame-regret-having-supported-Iraq-war---Blair.html (last accessed 26 February 2011).
3. Less than 15 pages of the 328-page report. See Lord Hutton, *Report of the Inquiry into the circumstances surrounding the death of Dr David Kelly CMG*, London: House of Commons, 2004. Available at: www.the-hutton-inquiry.org.uk/content/report/huttonreport.pdf (last accessed 27 February 2011).
4. David Cameron, 'Letter to government departments on opening up data', 31 May 2010. Available at www.number10.gov.uk/news/letter-to-government-departments-on-opening-up-data/ (last accessed 9 June 2012).

CHAPTER 6

1. See Wikileaks.org, *About*, http://wikileaks.org/About.html (last accessed 30 June 2012).
2. Ibid.
3. E. Pilkington, 'Bradley Manning's treatment was cruel and inhuman, UN torture chief rules', *Guardian* (24 May 2012). Available at www.guardian.co.uk/world/2012/mar/12/bradley-manning-cruel-inhuman-treatment-un (last accessed 30 June 2012).

4. Robert Moore, ITV *News at Ten*, 29 November 2010.
5. Bridget Kendall, BBC *Six O'Clock News*, 30 November 2010.
6. *Channel 4 News*, 29 November 2010.
7. See for instance www.openleaks.org (last accessed 30 June 2012).
8. R. Singel, 'Immune to critics, secret-spilling Wikileaks plans to save journalism ... and the world', Wired.com (7 March 2008). Available at www.wired.com/politics/onlinerights/news/2008/07/wikileaks?currentPage=2 (last accessed 30 June 2012).
9. Speaking to students of journalism at UC Berkeley, 18 April 2010 – see http://zunguzungu.wordpress.com/2010/12/12/julian-assange-in-berkeley/ (last accessed 30 June 2012).
10. See for instance www.channel4.com/news/channel-4-news-does-the-double-at-fpa-awards (last accessed 30 June 2012).
11. S. Ellison, 'The man who spilled the secrets', *Vanity Fair* (February 2011). Available at www.vanityfair.com/politics/features/2011/02/the-guardian-201102 (last accessed 30 June 2012).
12. See www.potterfoundation.com (last accessed 30 June 2012).
13. See www.amnesty.org.uk/content.asp?CategoryID=10058 (last accessed 30 June 2012).
14. See also R. Evans and P. Lewis, 'Undercover officer spied on green activists', *Guardian* (9 January 2011). Available at www.guardian.co.uk/uk/2011/jan/09/undercover-office-green-activists (last accessed 30 June 2012).
15. Bridget Kendall, BBC *One O'Clock News*, 29 November 2010.
16. See Human Rights Watch (2011), 'Bangladesh: Broken promises from government to halt RAB killings'. Available at www.hrw.org/news/2011/05/10/bangladesh-broken-promises-government-halt-rab-killings (last accessed 24 June 2012).
17. I. Cobain (2011), 'Bangladeshi 'death squad' trained by UK police resumes extrajudicial killings', *Guardian*. Available at www.guardian.co.uk/world/2011/jan/26/bangladesh-death-squad-killings-britain (last accessed 24 June 2012).
18. BBC *Newsnight*, 3 December 2010.
19. ITV *News at Ten*, 30 November 2010.
20. For the online version of the article see R. Booth, 'Wikileaks cable reveals secret pledge to protect US at Iraq Inquiry', *Guardian* (30 November 2010). Available at www.guardian.co.uk/world/2010/nov/30/wikileaks-chilcot-iraq-war-inquiry?DCMP=EMC-thewrap08 (last accessed 30 June 2012).
21. See www.guardian.co.uk/world/us-embassy-cables-documents/208206 (last accessed 30 June 2012).
22. BBC *Newsnight*, 1 December 2010.
23. For the online version see R. Evans and D. Leigh, 'Wikileaks cables: Secret deal let Americans sidestep cluster bombs ban', *Guardian* (1 December 2010). Available at www.guardian.co.uk/world/2010/dec/01/wikileaks-cables-cluster-bombs-britain?DCMP=EMC-thewrap08 (last accessed 30 June 2012).
24. 78 per cent of coverage during the first five days of cable releases (based on the word count of articles).
25. See www.guardian.co.uk/world/2010/nov/29/wikileaks-embassy-cables-key-points (last accessed 30 June 2012).
26. *BBC Newsnight*, 22 October 2010.
27. BBC *Six O'Clock News*, 6 April 2010.

CHAPTER 7

1. See R. Singel, 'Latest Wikileaks prize for sale to the highest bidder', *Wired.com* (27 August 2008). Available at www.wired.com/threatlevel/2008/08/wikileaks-aucti/ (last accessed 30 June 2012).
2. 'Who is Anonymous?', www.youtube.com/watch?v=x0WCLKzDFpI (last accessed 30 June 2012).
3. R. Quigley, 'Wikileaks leaks 2008 government plan to "destroy Wikileaks": Read it here', *Geekosystem.com* (15 March 2010). Available at www.geekosystem.com/wikileaks-government-takedown-plan/ (last accessed 30 June 2012).
4. M. Hosenball, 'US officials privately say Wikileaks damage limited', *Reuters.com* (18 January 2011). Available at www.reuters.com/article/2011/01/18/wikileaks-damage-idUSN1816319120110118 (last accessed 30 June 2012).

Bibliography

Alexander, J. C. (2006). *The Civil Sphere*. Oxford, Oxford University Press.

Althaus, S. (2003). 'When News Norms Collide, Follow the Lead: New evidence for press independence.' *Political Communication* 20: 33.

Althusser, L. (2008). *On Ideology*. London, Verso.

Assange, J. (2006). 'Conspiracy as Governance.' Cryptome.org. Availabe at http://cryptome.org/0002/ja-conspiracies.pdf (last accessed 24 July 2012).

Bachrach, P. A. B. and M. S. Baratz (1970). *Power and Poverty: Theory and Practice*. London: Oxford University Press.

Bagdikian, B. H. (2004). *The New Media Monopoly*. Boston, Beacon Press.

Baker, N. (2007). *The Strange Death of David Kelly*. London, Methuen.

Bale, J. M. (1995). 'Conspiracy Theories and Clandestine Politics.' *Lobster* (29).

Barnett, S. and Gaber, I. (2001). *Westminster Tales: The twenty-first century crisis in British political journalism*. London, Continuum.

Barthes, R. (1970). *Mythologies*. Paris, Editions du Seuil.

Bell, A. and Garrett, P. (1998). *Approaches to Media Discourse*. Oxford, Blackwell.

Bell, D. (1993). Is there a Ruling Class in America? In Olsen, M. E. and Marger, M. (eds). *Power in Modern Societies*. Boulder, Westview Press.

Bennett, W. L. (2009). *News: The politics of illusion*. White Plains, N.Y., Longman.

Bennett, W. L., Lawrence, R. et al. (2006). 'None Dare Call it Torture: Indexing and the limits of press independence in the Abu Ghraib scandal.' *Journal of Communication* 56(3):18.

Berg, B. L. (2009). *Qualitative Research Methods for the Social Sciences*. Boston, MA, Allyn & Bacon.

Berry, J. M. (1984). *The Interest Group Society*. Boston, Little Brown.

Blumler, J. G. and Gurevitch, M. (1995). *The Crisis of Public Communication*. London, Routledge.

Boczkowski, P. J. and de Santos, M. (2007). 'When More Media Equals Less News: Patterns of content homogenization in Argentina's leading print and online newspapers'. *Political Communication* 24(2): 14.

Born, G. (2005). *Uncertain Vision: Birt, Dyke and the reinvention of the BBC*. London, Vintage.

Bourdieu, P. (1998). *On Television and Journalism*. London, Pluto.

Brooke, H. (2011). *The Revolution will be Digitised: Dispatches from the information war*. London, William Heinemann.

Castells, M. (2001). *The Internet Galaxy: Reflections on internet, business, and society*. Oxford, Oxford University Press.

Chadwick, A. (2011). 'Britain's First Live Televised Party Leaders' Debate: From the news cycle to the political information cycle.' *Parliamentary Affairs* 64(1): 24–44.

Chibnall, S. J. (1980). *Crime Reporting in the British Press: A sociological examination of its historical development and current practice*. PhD thesis, University of Essex.

Cobain, I. (2011). 'Bangladeshi 'Death Squad' Trained by UK Police Resumes Extrajudicial Killings'. *Guardian*. Available at http://www.guardian.co.uk/

world/2011/jan/26/bangladesh-death-squad-killings-britain (last accessed 24 June 2012).

Cohen, B. C. (1965). *The Press and Foreign Policy*. Princeton, Princeton University Press.

Couldry, N. (2000). *The Place of Media Power: Pilgrims and witnesses of the media age*. London, Routledge.

Couldry, N. (2010). New Online News Sources and Writer Gatherers. In Fenton, N. (ed). *New Media Old News: Journalism and democracy in the digital age*. London, Sage.

Crenson, M. A. (1971). *The Un-politics of Air Pollution: A study of non-decisionmaking in the cities*. London, Johns Hopkins Press.

Curran, J. (1991). Rethinking the Media as a Public Sphere. In Dahlgren, P. and Sparks, C. (eds) *Communication and Citizenship*. London, Routledge.

Curran, J. (2002). *Media and Power*. London, Routledge.

Curran, J. (2010). *Media and Democracy*. London, Routledge.

Curran, J. and Seaton, J. (2009). *Power without Responsibility: The press and broadcasting in Britain*. London, Routledge.

Dahl, R. A. (1961). *Who Governs? Democracy and power in an American city*. New Haven, Yale University Press.

Dahlgren, P. (1991). Introduction. In Dahlgren, P. and Sparks, C. *Communication and Citizenship*. London, Routledge.

Dahlgren, P. (1995). *Television and the Public Sphere: Citizenship, democracy and the media*. London, Sage.

Dahlgren, P. (2005). 'The Internet, Public Spheres, and Political Communication: Dispersion and deliberation.' *Political Communication* 22(2): 147–62.

Davies, N. (2008). *Flat Earth News: An award-winning reporter exposes falsehood, distortion and propaganda in the global media*. London, Windus.

Davis, A. (2002). *Public Relations Democracy: Public relations, politics and the mass media in Britain*. Manchester, Manchester University Press.

Davis, A. (2003). 'Whither Mass Media and Power? Evidence for an elite theory critical alternative.' *Media, Culture and Society* 25(5): 21.

Davis, A. (2007). *The Mediation of Power: A critical introduction*. London, Routledge.

Deacon, D. and Golding, P. (1994). *Taxation and Representation: The media, political communication and the poll tax*. London, J. Libbey.

Deacon, D., Pickering, M. et al. (2007). *Researching Communications: A practical guide to methods in media and cultural analysis*. London, Hodder Arnold.

Dingwall, R. (1997). Accounts, Interviews and Observations. In Miller, G. and Dingwall, R. (eds) *Context and Method in Qualitative Research*. London, Sage.

Downes, L. (2009). *The Laws of Disruption: Harnessing the new forces that govern life and business in the digital age*. New York, Basic Books.

Downing, J. (1980). *The media machine*. London, Pluto Press.

Doyle, G. (2002). *Media Ownership: Concentration, convergence and public policy*. London, Sage.

El-Nawawy, M. and Farag, A. I. (2002). *Al-Jazeera: How the free Arab news network scooped the world and changed the Middle East*. Boulder, Westview.

Eldridge, J. (1993). News, Truth and Power. In Glasgow University Media Group and Eldridge, J. *Getting the Message: News, truth and power*. London, Routledge.

Entman, R. M. (2004). *Projections of Power: Framing news, public opinion, and U.S. foreign policy.* Chicago, University of Chicago Press.

Ericson, R. V., Baranek, P. M. et al. (1989). *Negotiating Control: A study of news sources.* Milton Keynes, Open University Press.

Ericson, R. V., Baranek, P. M. et al. (1991). *Representing Order: Crime, law and justice in the news media.* Milton Keynes, Open University Press.

Fenster, M. (2011). 'Disclosure's Effects: Wikileaks and transparency.' *Iowa Law Review* (97).

Fenton, N. (2010). *New media, Old news: Journalism and democracy in the digital age.* London, Sage.

Fishman, M. (1980). *Manufacturing the news.* Austin, Texas University Press.

Fiske, J. (1989). *Introduction to Communication Studies.* London, Routledge.

Fordham, A. (2011) 'Up next on Al Jazeera: Donald Rumsfeld'. *WashingtonPost.com.* September 2011. Available at http://washingtonpost.com/blogs/checkpoint-washington/post/up-next-on-al-jazeera-donald-rumsfeld/2011/09/29/gIQA1dOO8K_blog.html (last accessed 24 June 2012).

Foucault, M. and Sheridan, A. (1977). *Discipline and Punish: The birth of the prison.* London, Allen Lane.

Fowler, R., Hodge, B. et al. (1979). *Language and Control.* London, Routledge and Kegan Paul.

Franklin, B. (1997). *Newszak and News Media.* London, Arnold.

Freedman, D. (2008). *The Politics of Media Policy.* Cambridge, Polity Press.

Freedman, D. (2009). '"Smooth Operator?" The propaganda model and moments of crisis.' *Westminster Papers in Communication and Culture* 6(2): 14.

Galtung, J. and Ruge, M. H. (1965). 'The Structure of Foreign News.' *Journal of Peace Research* 2(1): 17.

Gans, H. J. (1979). *Deciding what's News: A study of CBS evening news, NBC nightly news, Newsweek, and Time.* New York, Pantheon Books.

Gans, H. J. (2004). *Democracy and the News.* Oxford, Oxford University Press.

Garnham, N. (1986). The Media and the Public Sphere. In Golding, P., Murdock, G. and Schlesinger, P. *Communicating Politics: Mass communications and the political process.* Leicester, Leicester University Press.

Garnham, N. (2000). *Emancipation, the Media, and Modernity: Arguments about the media and social theory.* Oxford, Oxford University Press.

Gitlin, T. (1980). *Whole World is Watching: Mass media in the making and unmaking of the new left.* Berkeley, University of California Press.

Glasgow University Media Group and Beharrell, P. (1976). *Bad News.* London, Routledge.

Golding, P. and Elliott, P. (1979). *Making the News.* London, Longman.

Graber, D. A., D. McQuail, et al. (1998). *The Politics of News: The news of politics.* Washington DC, CQ Press.

Gramsci, A., Hoare, Q., et al. (1971). *Selections from the Prison Notebooks of Antonio Gramsci.* New York, International Publishers.

Habermas, J. (1989 [1962]). *The Structural Transformation of the Public Sphere: An inquiry into a category of bourgeois society.* Cambridge, Polity.

Hall, S. (1973). 'Encoding and Decoding in the Television Discourse.' *Media Series* (17).

Hall, S., Critcher, T., et al. (1978). *Policing the Crisis: Mugging, the State, and Law and Order.* Basingstoke: Macmillan.

Hall, S. (1982). The Rediscovery of Ideology: Return of the repressed in media studies. In Bennett, T., Curran, J., et al. (eds). *Culture, Media and Society*. London, Routledge.

Hall, S. (1986). Media Power and Class Power. In Curran, J., Ecclestone, G. et al. *Bending Reality: The state of the media*. London, Pluto.

Hallin, D. C. (1986). *The Uncensored War: The media and Vietnam*. London, London University of California Press.

Hallin, D. C. (1994). *We keep America on top of the World: Journalism and the public sphere*. London, Routledge.

Hartley, J. (1982). *Understanding News*. London, Methuen.

Hebdige, D. (1979). *Subculture: The meaning of style*. London, Methuen.

Herman, E. (2000). 'The Propaganda Model: A retrospective.' *Journalism Studies* 1(1): 12.

Herman, E. S. and Chomsky, N. (2002). *Manufacturing Consent: The political economy of the mass media*. New York, Pantheon Books.

Hetherington, A. (1985). *News, Newspapers and Television*. London, Macmillan.

Hindman, M. S. (2009). *The Myth of Digital Democracy*. Princeton, Princeton University Press.

Holland, P. (2006). *The Angry Buzz: This week and current affairs television*. New York, I. B. Tauris.

Human Rights Watch (2011). 'Bangladesh: Broken promises from government to halt RAB killings'. hrw.org. Available at http://www.hrw.org/news/2011/05/10/bangladesh-broken-promises-government-halt-rab-killings (last accessed 24 June 2012).

Keeble, R. (2004). Information Warfare in an Age of Hyper-Militarism. In Stuart, A. and Zelizer, B. *Reporting War*. London, Routledge.

Keeble, R. (2010). Hacks and Spooks – Close Encounters of a Strange Kind: A critical history of the links between mainstream journalists and the intelligence services in the UK. In Klaen, J. *The Political Economy of Media and Power*. New York, Peter Lang.

Kepplinger, H. M. (2007). 'Reciprocal Effects: Toward a theory of mass media effects on decision makers.' *The Harvard International Journal of Press/Politics* 12(2): 20.

Kvale, S. (1996). *Interviews: An introduction to qualitative research interviewing*. London, Sage.

Lashmar, P. (2008). From Shadow Boxing to Ghost Plane: English journalism and the war on terror. In de Burgh, H. *Investigative Journalism*. Abingdon, Routledge.

Leigh, D. and Harding, L. (2011). *Wikileaks: Inside Julian Assange's war on secrecy*. London, Guardian Books.

Lessig, L. (2004). *Free Culture: How big media uses technology and the law to lock down culture and control creativity*. New York, Penguin Press.

Lewis, J. (2006). *Shoot First and Ask Questions Later: Media coverage of the 2003 Iraq War*. New York, Peter Lang.

Lewis, J., Cushion, S. et al. (2005). 'Immediacy, Convenience or Engagement? An analysis of 24-hour news channels in the UK.' *Journalism Studies* 6(4): 461–77.

Lindblom, C. E. (1977). *Politics and Markets: The world's political-economic systems*. New York, Basic Books.

Lippmann, W. (2009 [1927]). *The Phantom Public*. New Brunswick, Transaction Publishers.

Livingston, S. and Bennett, W. L. (2003). 'Gatekeeping, Indexing, and Live-Event News: Is technology altering the construction of news?' *Political Communication* 20: 17.

Lubbers, E. (2009). Public, Private, and Secret Activist Intelligence and Covert Corporate Strategies. *PSA Conference*. Manchester, UK.

Lukes, S. (1997). Three Distinctive Views of Power Compared. In Hill, M. (ed.) *The Policy Process: A reader*. Harlow, Pearson Education Limited.

Lukes, S. (2005). *Power: A radical view*. Basingstoke, Palgrave Macmillan.

Lynch, L. (2010). '"We're going to crack the world open".' *Journalism Practice* 4(3): 10.

Machin, D. and Mayr, A. (2012). *How to do Critical Discourse Analysis: A multimodal approach*. Thousand Oaks, CA, Sage.

Mancini, P. (1991). The Public Sphere and the Use of News in a 'Coalition' System of Government. In Dahlgren, P. and Sparks, C. (eds) *Communication and Citizenship: Journalism and the public sphere*. London, Routledge.

Manning, P. (2001). *News and News Sources: A critical introduction*. London, Sage.

Mansell, R. and Jarvery, M. (2004). New Media and the Forces of Capitalism. In Calbrese, A. and Sparks, C. (eds) *Toward a Political Economy of Culture: Capitalism and communication in the twenty-first century*. Oxford, Rowman and Littlefield.

Marx, K. and Engels, F. (1974). *The German Ideology*. London, Lawrence and Wishart.

McCarthy, C. (2011) 'Egypt, Twitter and the rise of the Watchdog Crowd'. *CNet. com*. February 2011. Available at http://news.cnet.com/8301-13577_3-20031600-36.html (last accessed 24 June 2012).

McChesney, R. W. (1999). *Rich Media, Poor Democracy: Communication politics in dubious times*. Urbana, University of Illinois Press.

McCombs, M. E. (2004). *Setting the Agenda: the mass media and public opinion*. Oxford, Polity.

McNair, B. (1988). *Images of the Enemy: Reporting the new Cold War*. London, Routledge.

McNair, B. (2003). 'From Control to Chaos: Towards a new sociology of journalism.' *Media, Culture & Society* 25(4): 547–55.

McNair, B. (2006). *Cultural Chaos: Journalism, news and power in a globalised world*. London, Routledge.

McQuail, D. (1986). Diversity in Political Communications: Its sources, forms and future. In Golding, P., Murdock, G. and Schlesinger, P. (eds) *Communicating Politics: Mass communications and the political process*. Leicester, Leicester University Press.

Melia, K. (1997). Producing 'Plausible Stories': Interviewing student nurses. In Miller, G. and Dinwall, R. (eds) *Context and Method in Qualitative Research*. London, Sage.

Meyer, D. S. and Tarrow, S.G. (1998). *The Social Movement Society: Contentious politics for a new century*. Oxford, Rowman & Littlefield.

Meyer, T. and Hinchman, L P. (2002). *Media Democracy: How the media colonize politics*. Cambridge, Polity.

Miliband, R. (1973). *The state in Capitalist Society*. London, Quartet Books.

Miller, D. (1994). *Don't Mention the War: Northern Ireland, propaganda and the media*. London, Pluto.

Mills, C. W. (1959). *The Power Elite*. New York, Oxford University Press.

Morley, D. (1980). *The Nationwide Audience: Structure and decoding*. London, British Film Institute.

Morley, D. (1997). Theoretical Orthodoxies: Textualism, constructivism and the 'new ethnography' in cultural studies. In Ferguson, M. and Golding, P. (eds) *Cultural Studies in Question*. London, Sage.

Morozov, E. (2011). *The Net Delusion: How not to liberate the world*. London, Allen Lane.

Mosco, V. (2004). Capitalism's Chernobyl? From ground zero to cyberspace and back again. In Calabrese, A. and Sparks, C. (eds) *Toward a Political Economy of Culture – Capitalism and Communication in the Twenty-First Century*. Oxford, Rowman and Littlefield.

Mouffe, C. (1999). 'Deliberative Democracy or Agonistic Pluralism?' *Social Research* 66(3): 745–59.

Murdock, G. (1982). Large Corporations and the Control of the Communications Industries. In Bennett, T., Curran, J. et al. (eds) *Culture, Media and Society*. London, Routledge.

Negroponte, N. (1995). *Being Digital*. London, Hodder & Stoughton.

Newman, N. (2010). '#UKelection2010, Mainstream Media and the Role of the Internet: How social and digital media affected the business of politics and journalism.' *Reuters Institute for the Study of Journalism.*

Norris, P. (2000). *A Virtuous Circle: Political communications in postindustrial societies*. Cambridge, Cambridge University Press.

Ofcom (2011). Communications Market Report. London, Ofcom.

Ofcom (2012). Adult Media Use and Attitudes Report, Ofcom.

Parsons, T. (1986). Power and the Social System. In Lukes, S. (ed.) *Power*. Oxford, Basil Blackwell.

Pew Research Center (2012). 'The State of the News Media in 2012'. *Project for Excellence in Journalism*. Available at http://stateofthemedia.org (last accessed 30 June 2012).

Pimlott, B. (2004). 'Accountability and the Media: A tale of two cultures.' *The Political Quarterly* 75(2).

Pintak, L. (2011) 'The Al Jazeera Revolution'. *ForeignPolicy.com*. February 2011. Available at http://www.foreignpolicy.com/articles/2011/02/02/the_al_jazeera_ revolution (last accessed 24 June 2012).

Poster, M. (2001). *What's the Matter with the Internet?* Minneapolis, University of Minnesota Press.

Poulantzas, N. (1978). *Political Power and Social Classes*. London, Verso Editions.

Price, V., Tewsbury, D. et al. (1997). 'Switching Trains of Thought.' *Communication Research* 24(5): 481–506.

Protess, D. L., Lomax Cook, F., Doppelt, J. C., Ettema, J. S., Gordon, M. T., Leff, D. R. and Miller, P. (1991). *The Journalism of Outrage: Investigative reporting and agenda building in America*. New York, Guilford Press.

Rawls, J. (1972). *A Theory of Justice*. Oxford, Clarendon Press.

Richardson, J. E. (2007). *Analysing Newspapers: An approach from critical discourse analysis*. Basingstoke, Palgrave Macmillan.

Robinson, W. I. (1996). *Promoting Polyarchy: Globalization, US intervention, and hegemony*. Cambridge, Cambridge University Press.

Rucht, D. (2004). The Quadruple 'A': Media strategies of protest movements since the 1960s. In Van de Donk, W., Loader, B., et al. (eds) *Cyberprotest: New media, citizens and social movements*. London, Routledge.

Schedler, A. (1999). Conceptualizing Accountability. In Schedler, A., Diamond, L. and Plattner, M. (eds) *The Self-restraining State: Power and accountability in new democracies*. Colorado, Lynne Rienner.

Scheufele, D. A. and Tewksbury D. (2007). 'Framing, Agenda Setting, and Priming: The evolution of three media effects models.' *Journal of Communication* 57: 9–20.

Schiller, H. I. (1996). *Information Inequality: The deepening social crisis in America*. London, Routledge.

Schlesinger, P., Murdock, G. et al. (1983). *Televising 'Terrorism': Political violence in popular culture*. London, Comedia.

Schlesinger, P. and Tumber, H. (1994). *Reporting Crime: The media politics of criminal justice*. Oxford, Clarendon Press.

Schudson, M. (1995). *The Power of News*. Cambridge, Mass., Harvard University Press.

Schumpeter, J. A. (1987). *Capitalism, Socialism and Democracy*. London, Unwin Paperbacks.

Shirky, C. (2011). Wikileaks has Created a New Media Landscape. *Guardian*. London.

Sigal, L. V. (1973). *Reporters and Officials: The organization and politics of newsmaking*. Lexington, Mass., D. C. Heath & Co.

Sparks, C. (1986). 'The Media and the State.' In Curran, J., Ecclestone, G., et al. (eds) *Bending Reality: The state of the media*. London, Pluto.

Sparks, C. (1995). 'The Future of Public Service Broadcasting in Britain.' *Critical Studies in Media Communication* 12(3): 16.

Sparks, C. (2009). 'Extending and Refining the Propaganda Model.' *Westminster Papers in Communication and Culture* 4(2): 68–84.

Sunstein, C. R. (2001). *Republic.com*. Princeton, N.J., Princeton University Press.

Thompson, J. B. (1990). *Ideology and Modern Culture: Critical social theory in the era of mass communication*. Cambridge, Polity.

Thussu, D. K. (2007). *News as Entertainment: The rise of global infotainment*. London, Sage.

Truman, D. B. (1951). *The Governmental Process: Political interests and public opinion*, New York, Knopf.

Tuchman, G. (1978). *Making News: A study in the construction of reality*. New York, Free Press.

Tunstall, J. (1971). *Journalists at Work: Specialist correspondents*. London, Constable.

Tunstall, J. (1993). *Television Producers*. London, Routledge.

van de Donk, W., Loader, B. et al. (eds) (2004). *Cyberprotest: New media, citizens, and social movements*. London, Routledge.

Van Dijk, T. A. (1998). Opinions and Ideologies in the Press. In Bell, A. and Garrett, P. (eds) *Approaches to Media Discourse*. Oxford, Blackwell.

Verschueren, J. (1985). *International News Reporting: Metapragmatic metaphors and the U-2*. Philadelphia, Benjamins Publishing.

Weber, M. (1993). Types of Authority and Imperative Coordination. In Olsen, M. E. and Marger, M. (eds) *Power in Modern Societies*. Boulder, Westview Press.

White, D. (1997 [1957]). The 'Gatekeeper': A case study in the selection of news. In Berkowitz, D. (ed.). *The Social Meaning of News*. London, Sage.

Widdowson, H. G., Cook, G. and Seidlhofer, B. (1995). *Principle & Practice in Applied Linguistics: Studies in honour of H. G. Widdowson*. Oxford, Oxford University Press.

Willis, P. (1990). *Common Culture: Symbolic work at play in the everyday culture of the young*. Milton Keynes, Open University Press.

Yin, R. K. (2003). *Case Study Research: Design and methods*. London, Sage.

Zelizer, B. (1992). *Covering the Body: The Kennedy assassination, the media, and the shaping of collective memory*. Chicago, University of Chicago Press.

Index